BRIAN **AZZARELLO**
writer

LEE **BERMEJO**
artist

MICK **GRAY**
KARL **STORY**
JASON **MARTIN**
additional inks

DAVE **STEWART**
colorist

PHIL **BALSMAN**
PAT **BROSSEAU**
ROB **LEIGH**
NICK **NAPOLITANO**
letterers

LexLuthor
MAN OF STEEL

SUPERMAN created by
JERRY **SIEGEL** & JOE **SHUSTER**

LEX LUTHOR: MAN OF STEEL

Published by DC Comics. Cover and compilation copyright © 2005 DC Comics. All Rights Reserved. Originally published in single magazine form in LEX LUTHOR: MAN OF STEEL #1-5. Copyright © 2005 DC Comics. All Rights Reserved. All characters, their distinctive likenesses and related elements featured in this publication are trademarks of DC Comics. The stories, characters and incidents featured in this publication are entirely fictional. DC Comics does not read or accept unsolicited submissions of ideas, stories or artwork.

DC Comics
1700 Broadway, New York, NY 10019.
A Warner Bros. Entertainment Company.

Printed in Canada. First Printing.
ISBN: 1-4012-0454-6
Cover art by Lee Bermejo
Publication design by John J. Hill

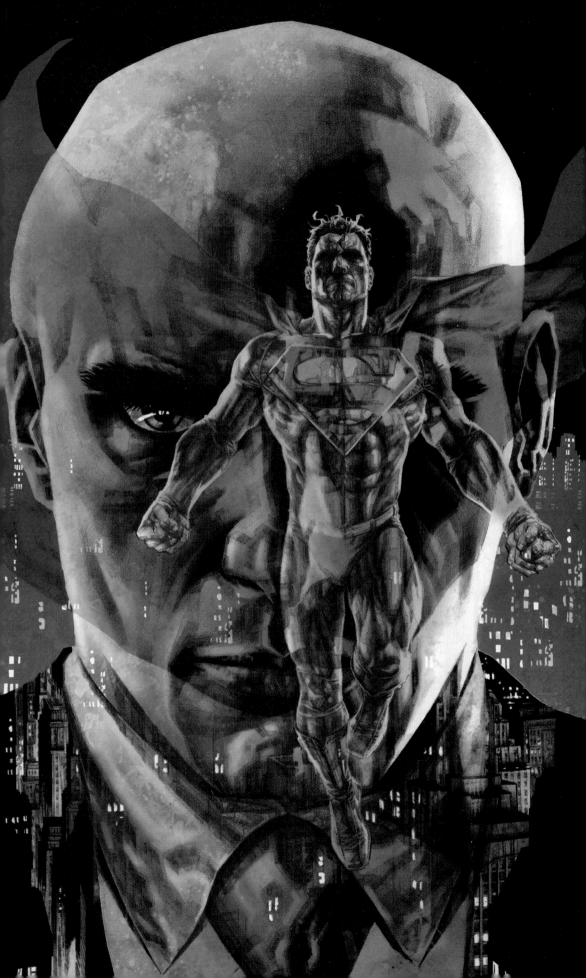

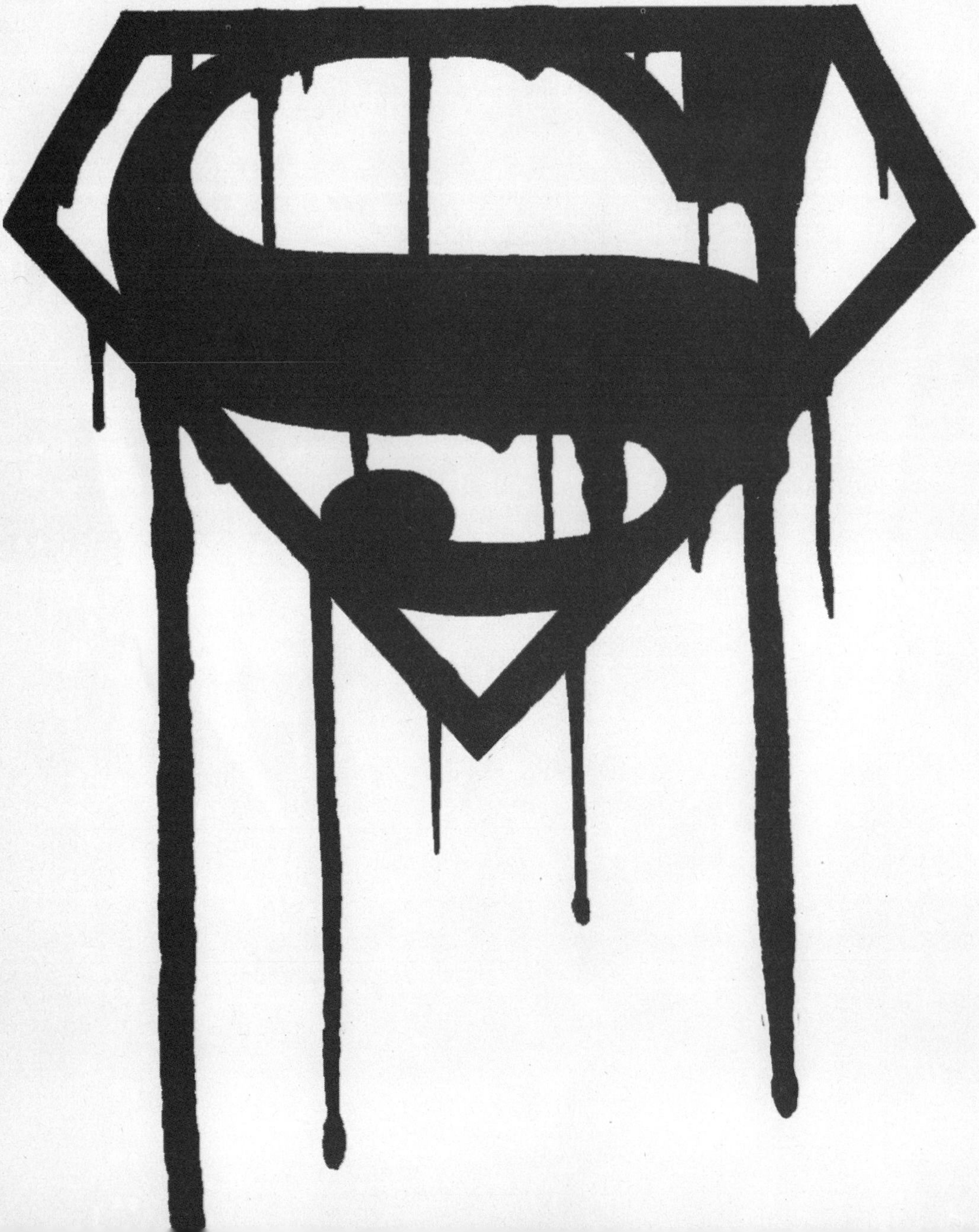

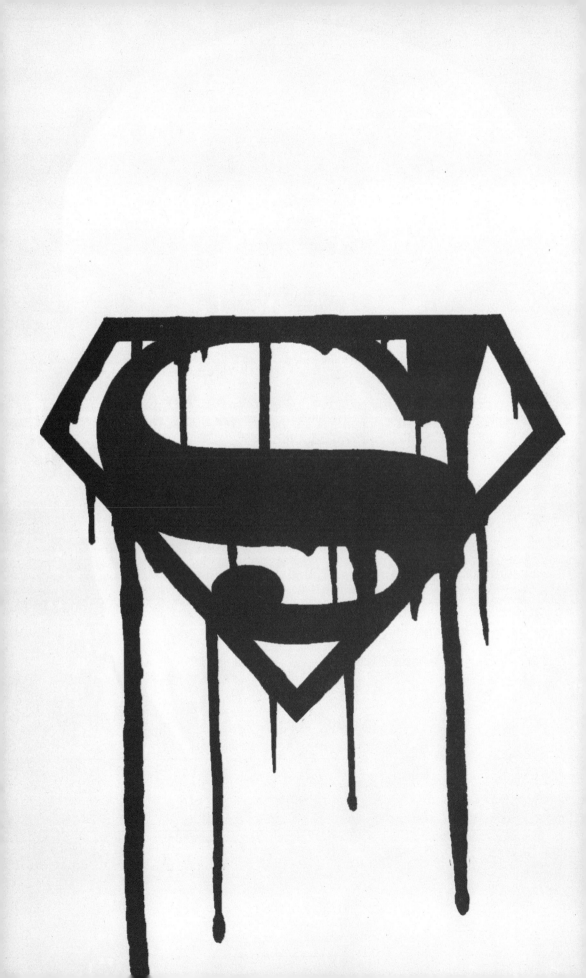

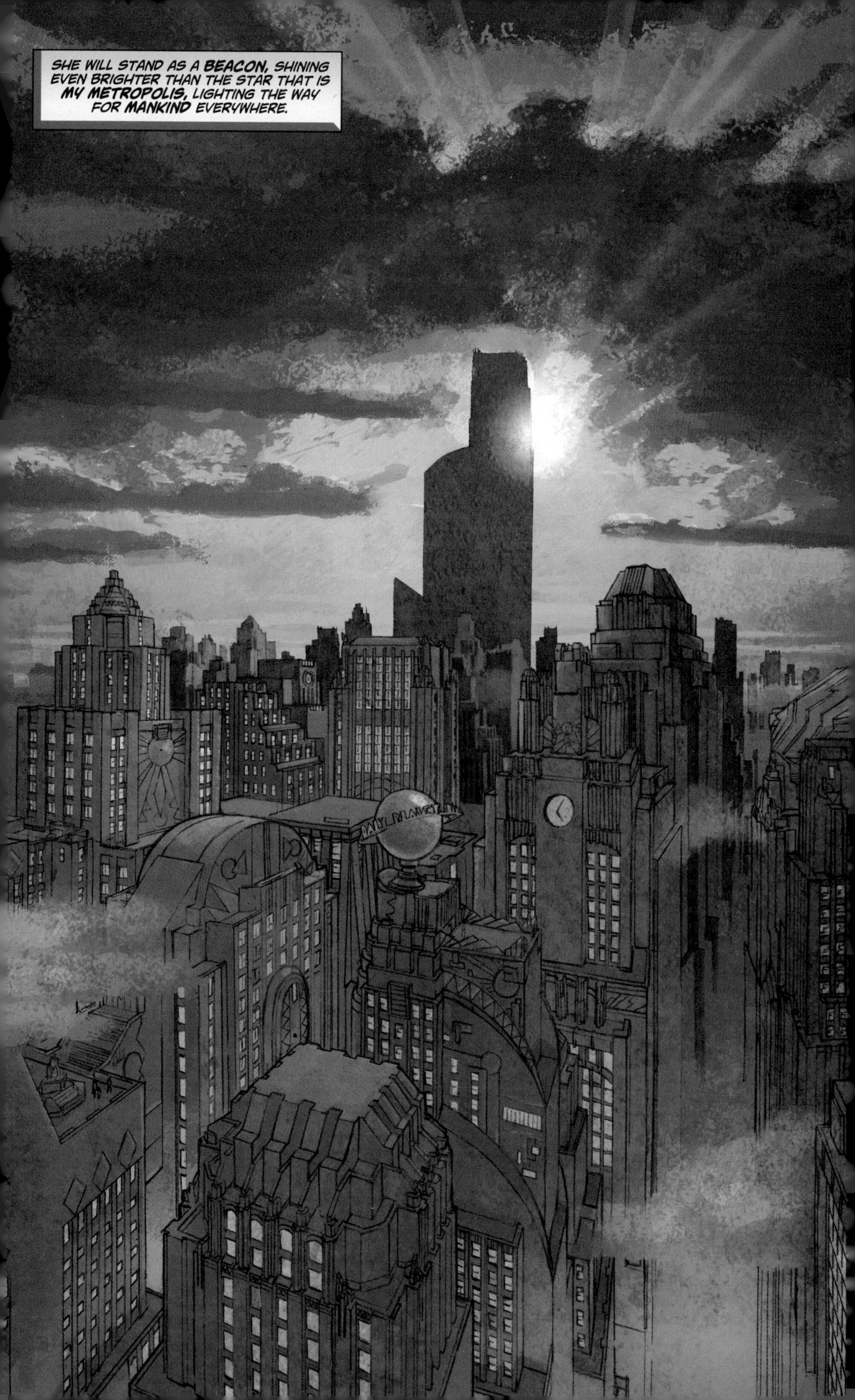
SHE WILL STAND AS A BEACON, SHINING EVEN BRIGHTER THAN THE STAR THAT IS MY METROPOLIS, LIGHTING THE WAY FOR MANKIND EVERYWHERE.

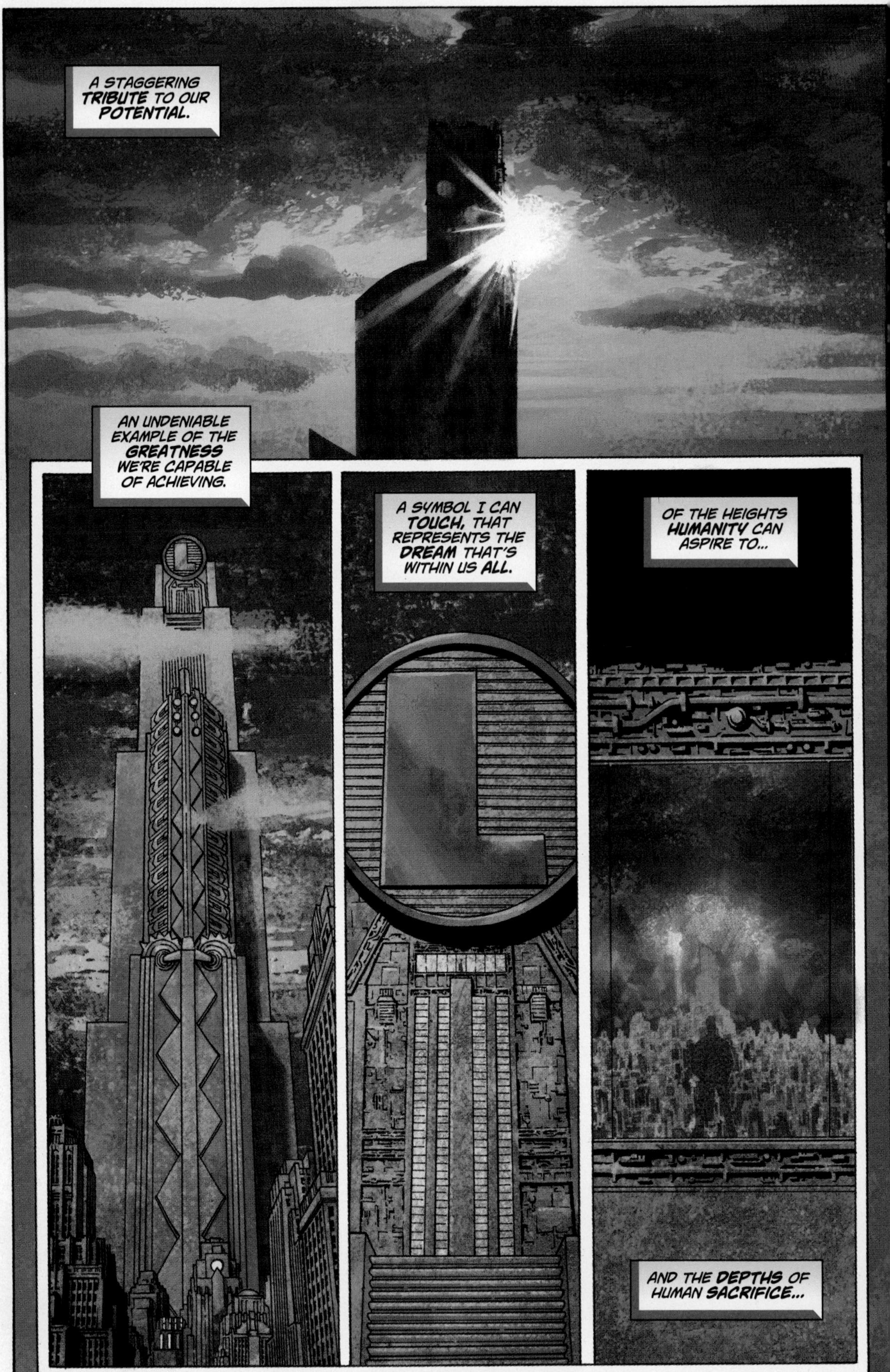
A STAGGERING TRIBUTE TO OUR POTENTIAL.
AN UNDENIABLE EXAMPLE OF THE GREATNESS WE'RE CAPABLE OF ACHIEVING.
A SYMBOL I CAN TOUCH, THAT REPRESENTS THE DREAM THAT'S WITHIN US ALL.
OF THE HEIGHTS HUMANITY CAN ASPIRE TO...
AND THE DEPTHS OF HUMAN SACRIFICE...

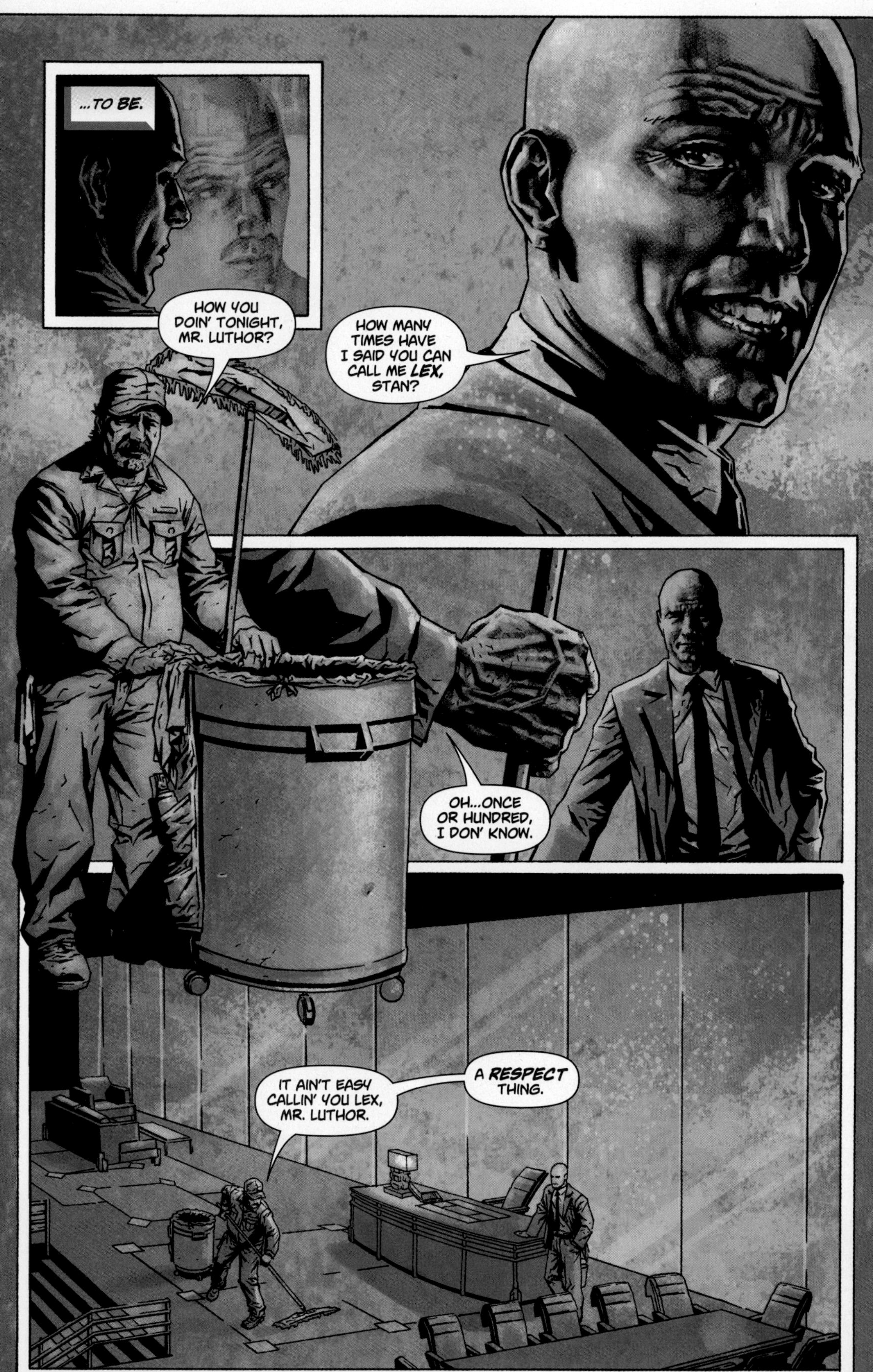

...TO BE.
HOW YOU DOIN' TONIGHT, MR. LUTHOR?
HOW MANY TIMES HAVE I SAID YOU CAN CALL ME LEX, STAN?
OH...ONCE OR HUNDRED, I DON' KNOW.
IT AIN'T EASY CALLIN' YOU LEX, MR. LUTHOR.
A RESPECT THING.

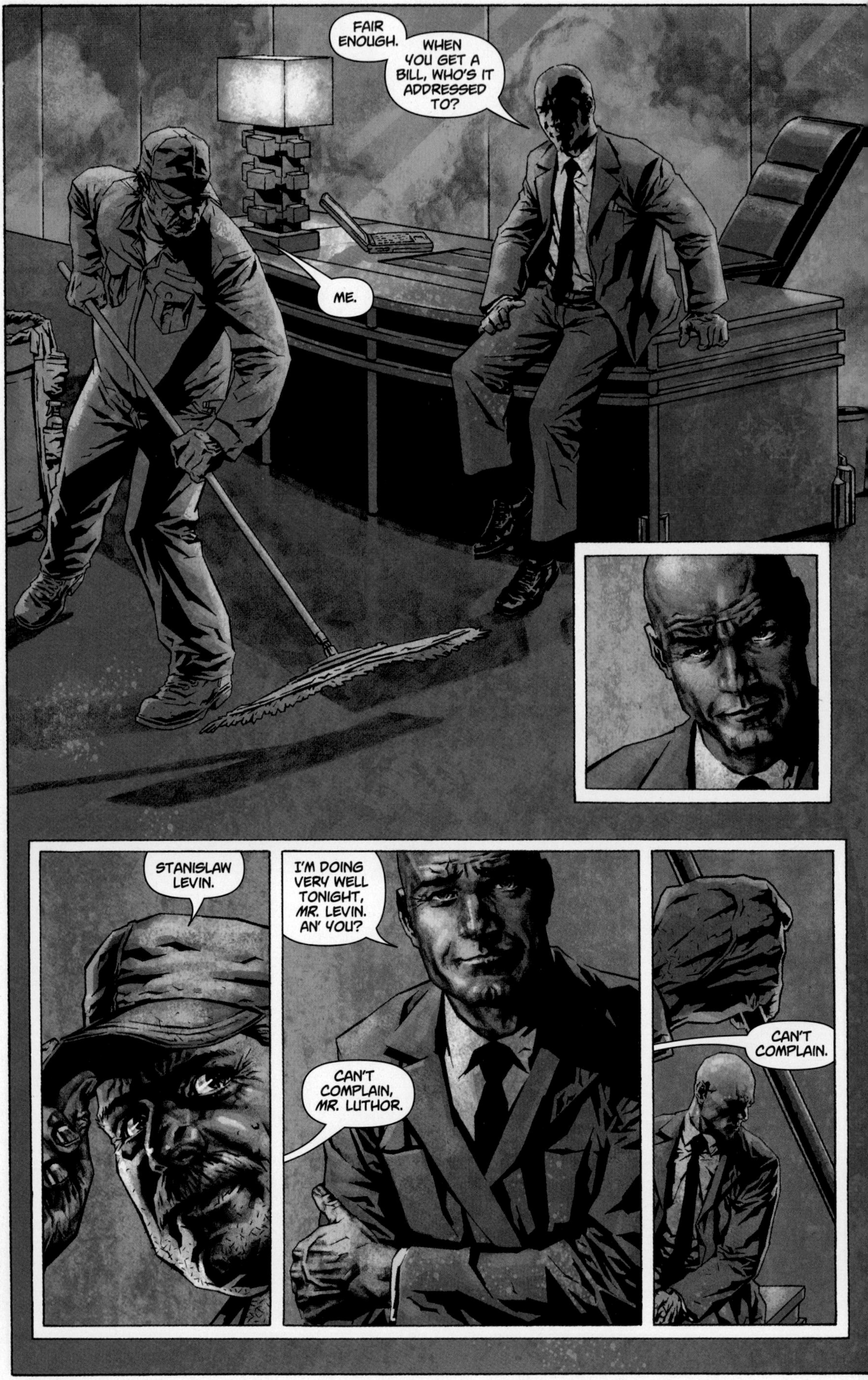
FAIR ENOUGH.
WHEN YOU GET A BILL, WHO'S IT ADDRESSED TO?
ME.
STANISLAW LEVIN.
I'M DOING VERY WELL TONIGHT, MR. LEVIN. AN' YOU?
CAN'T COMPLAIN, MR. LUTHOR.
CAN'T COMPLAIN.

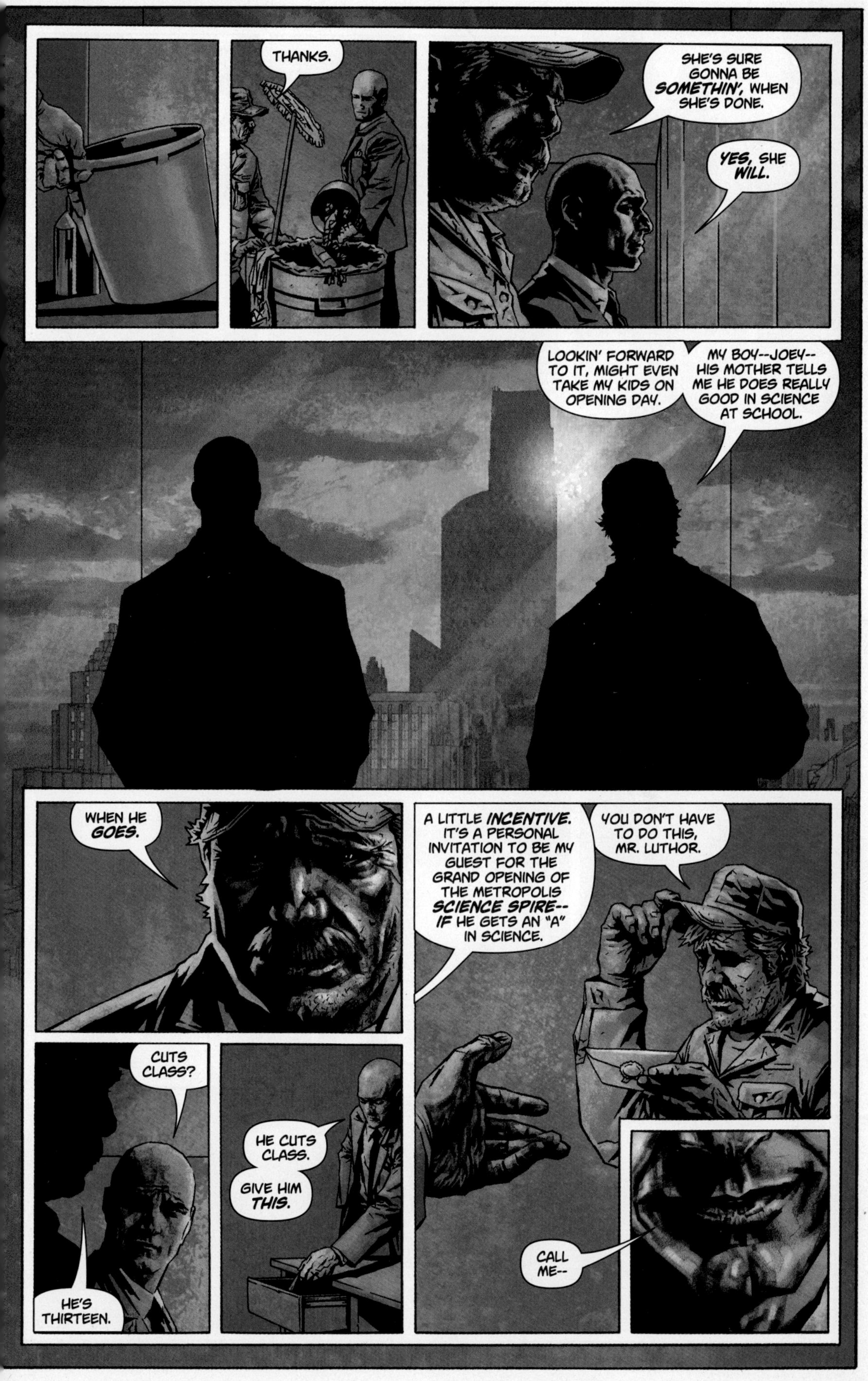
THANKS.
SHE'S SURE GONNA BE SOMETHIN', WHEN SHE'S DONE.
YES, SHE WILL.
LOOKIN' FORWARD TO IT, MIGHT EVEN TAKE MY KIDS ON OPENING DAY.
MY BOY--JOEY--HIS MOTHER TELLS ME HE DOES REALLY GOOD IN SCIENCE AT SCHOOL.
WHEN HE GOES.
CUTS CLASS?
HE'S THIRTEEN.
HE CUTS CLASS.
GIVE HIM THIS.
A LITTLE INCENTIVE. IT'S A PERSONAL INVITATION TO BE MY GUEST FOR THE GRAND OPENING OF THE METROPOLIS SCIENCE SPIRE--IF HE GETS AN "A" IN SCIENCE.
YOU DON'T HAVE TO DO THIS, MR. LUTHOR.
CALL ME--

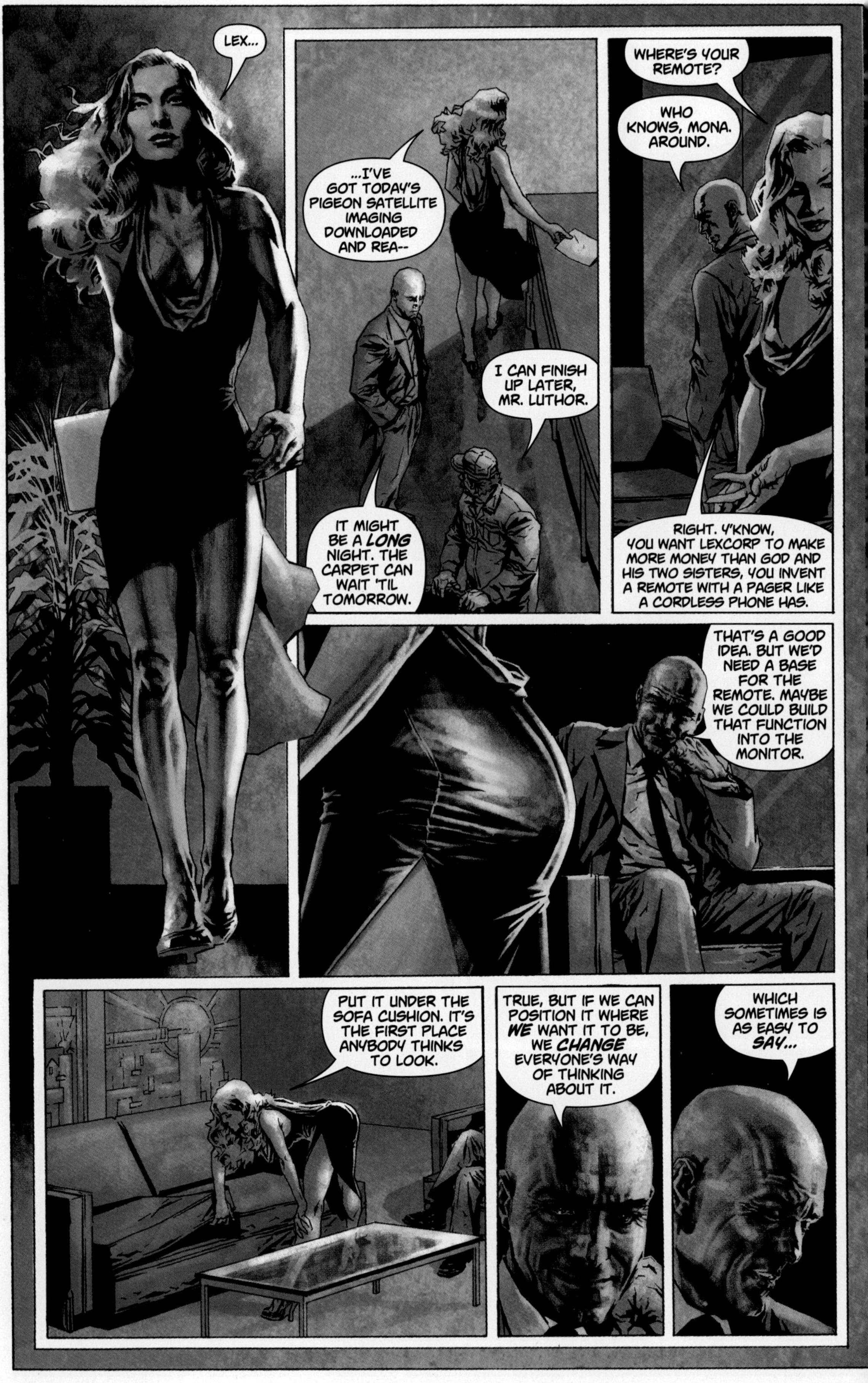
LEX...
...I'VE GOT TODAY'S PIGEON SATELLITE IMAGING DOWNLOADED AND REA--
I CAN FINISH UP LATER, MR. LUTHOR.
IT MIGHT BE A LONG NIGHT. THE CARPET CAN WAIT 'TIL TOMORROW.
WHERE'S YOUR REMOTE?
WHO KNOWS, MONA. AROUND.
RIGHT. Y'KNOW, YOU WANT LEXCORP TO MAKE MORE MONEY THAN GOD AND HIS TWO SISTERS, YOU INVENT A REMOTE WITH A PAGER LIKE A CORDLESS PHONE HAS.
THAT'S A GOOD IDEA. BUT WE'D NEED A BASE FOR THE REMOTE. MAYBE WE COULD BUILD THAT FUNCTION INTO THE MONITOR.
PUT IT UNDER THE SOFA CUSHION. IT'S THE FIRST PLACE ANYBODY THINKS TO LOOK.
TRUE, BUT IF WE CAN POSITION IT WHERE WE WANT IT TO BE, WE CHANGE EVERYONE'S WAY OF THINKING ABOUT IT.
WHICH SOMETIMES IS AS EASY TO SAY...

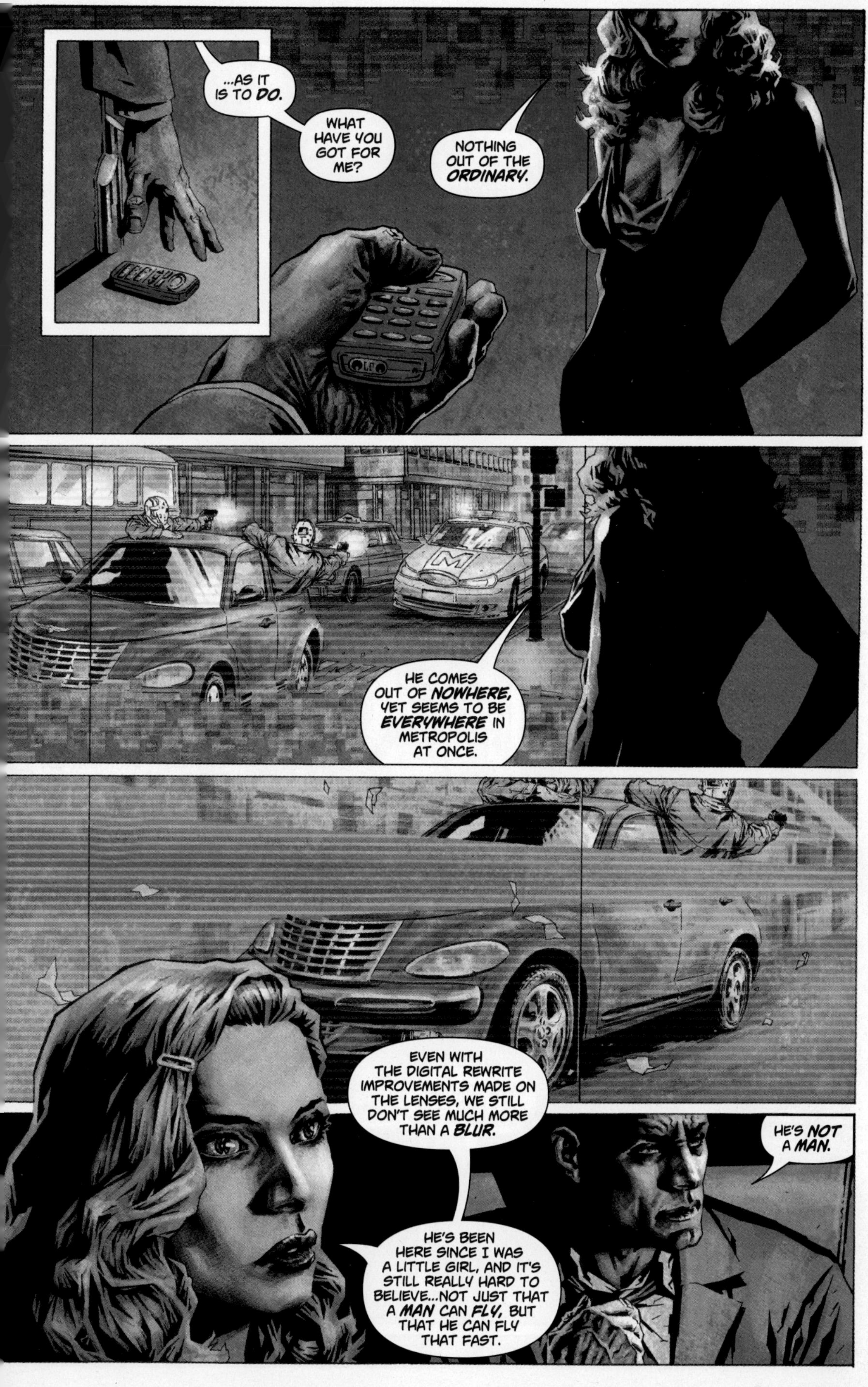
...AS IT IS TO DO.
WHAT HAVE YOU GOT FOR ME?
NOTHING OUT OF THE ORDINARY.
HE COMES OUT OF NOWHERE, YET SEEMS TO BE EVERYWHERE IN METROPOLIS AT ONCE.
EVEN WITH THE DIGITAL REWRITE IMPROVEMENTS MADE ON THE LENSES, WE STILL DON'T SEE MUCH MORE THAN A BLUR.
HE'S BEEN HERE SINCE I WAS A LITTLE GIRL, AND IT'S STILL REALLY HARD TO BELIEVE...NOT JUST THAT A MAN CAN FLY, BUT THAT HE CAN FLY THAT FAST.
HE'S NOT A MAN.

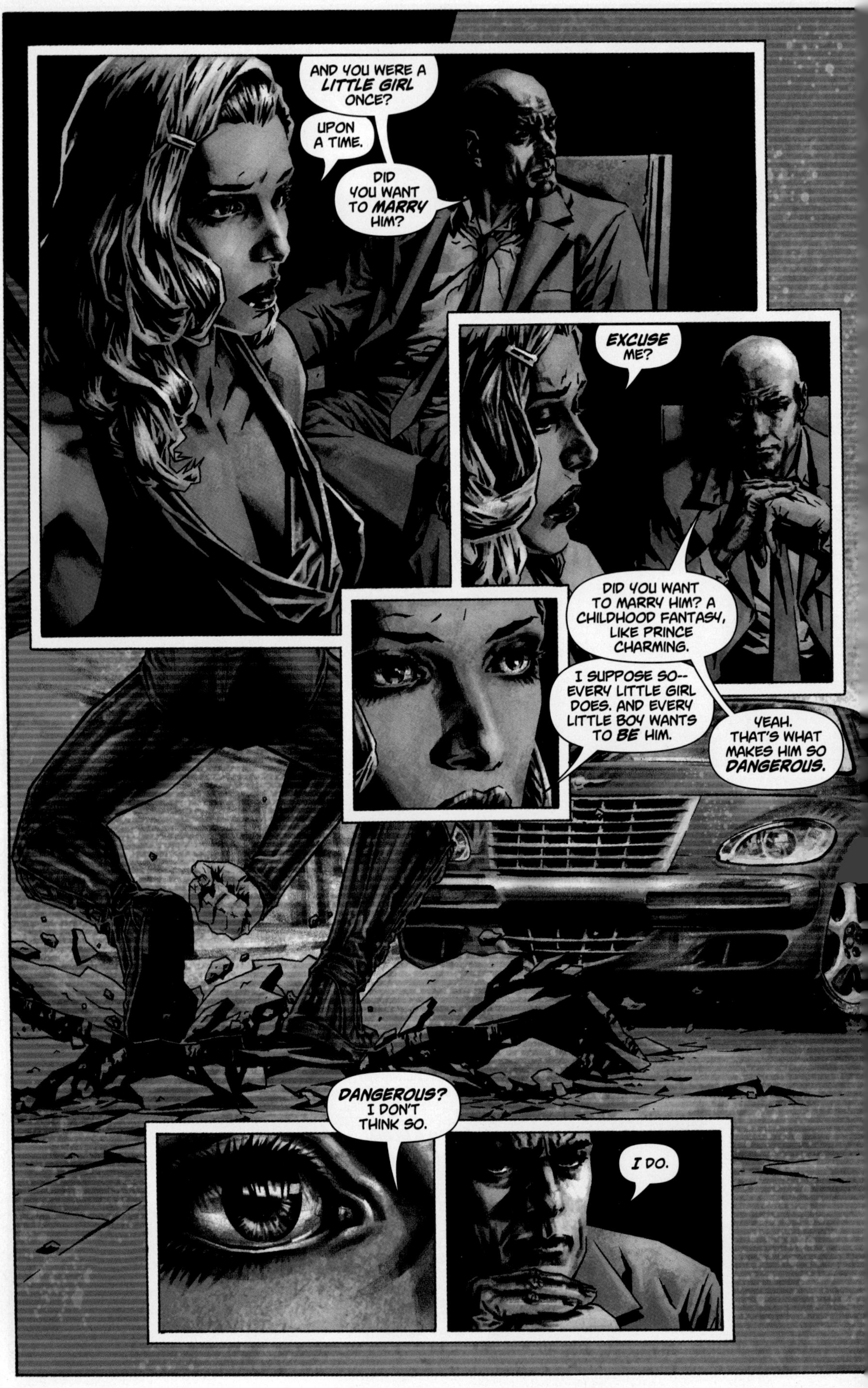
AND YOU WERE A LITTLE GIRL ONCE?
UPON A TIME.
DID YOU WANT TO MARRY HIM?
EXCUSE ME?
DID YOU WANT TO MARRY HIM? A CHILDHOOD FANTASY, LIKE PRINCE CHARMING.
I SUPPOSE SO-- EVERY LITTLE GIRL DOES. AND EVERY LITTLE BOY WANTS TO BE HIM.
YEAH. THAT'S WHAT MAKES HIM SO DANGEROUS.
DANGEROUS? I DON'T THINK SO.
I DO.

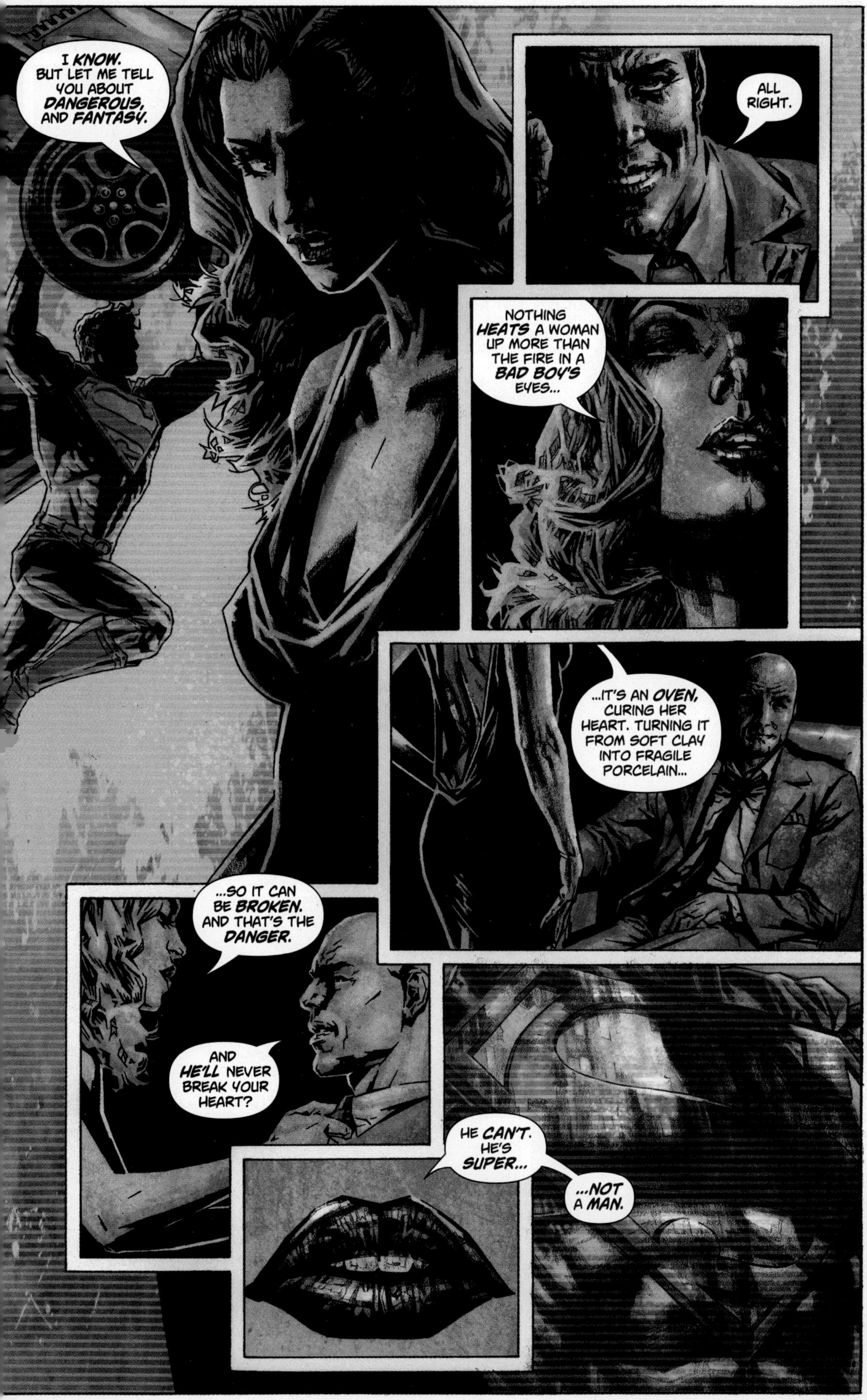
I KNOW. BUT LET ME TELL YOU ABOUT DANGEROUS, AND FANTASY.
ALL RIGHT.
NOTHING HEATS A WOMAN UP MORE THAN THE FIRE IN A BAD BOY'S EYES...
...IT'S AN OVEN, CURING HER HEART. TURNING IT FROM SOFT CLAY INTO FRAGILE PORCELAIN...
...SO IT CAN BE BROKEN. AND THAT'S THE DANGER.
AND HE'LL NEVER BREAK YOUR HEART?
HE CAN'T. HE'S SUPER...
...NOT A MAN.

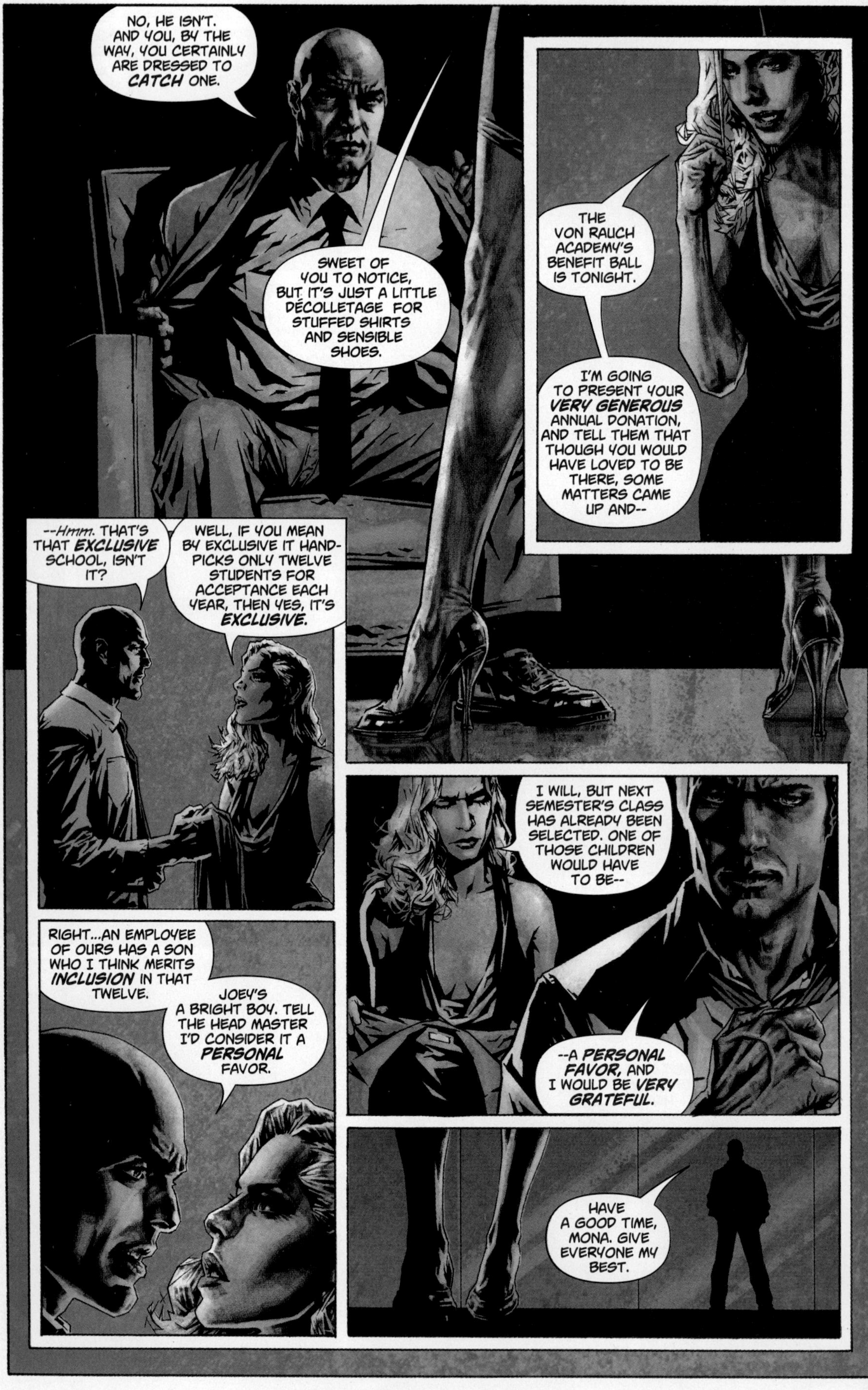
NO, HE ISN'T. AND YOU, BY THE WAY, YOU CERTAINLY ARE DRESSED TO *CATCH* ONE.
SWEET OF YOU TO NOTICE, BUT IT'S JUST A LITTLE DÉCOLLETAGE FOR STUFFED SHIRTS AND SENSIBLE SHOES.
THE VON RAUCH ACADEMY'S BENEFIT BALL IS TONIGHT.
I'M GOING TO PRESENT YOUR *VERY GENEROUS* ANNUAL DONATION, AND TELL THEM THAT THOUGH YOU WOULD HAVE LOVED TO BE THERE, SOME MATTERS CAME UP AND--
--*Hmm.* THAT'S THAT *EXCLUSIVE* SCHOOL, ISN'T IT?
WELL, IF YOU MEAN BY EXCLUSIVE IT HAND-PICKS ONLY TWELVE STUDENTS FOR ACCEPTANCE EACH YEAR, THEN YES, IT'S *EXCLUSIVE.*
I WILL, BUT NEXT SEMESTER'S CLASS HAS ALREADY BEEN SELECTED. ONE OF THOSE CHILDREN WOULD HAVE TO BE--
RIGHT...AN EMPLOYEE OF OURS HAS A SON WHO I THINK MERITS *INCLUSION* IN THAT TWELVE.
JOEY'S A BRIGHT BOY. TELL THE HEAD MASTER I'D CONSIDER IT A *PERSONAL* FAVOR.
--A *PERSONAL FAVOR,* AND I WOULD BE *VERY GRATEFUL.*
HAVE A GOOD TIME, MONA. GIVE EVERYONE MY BEST.

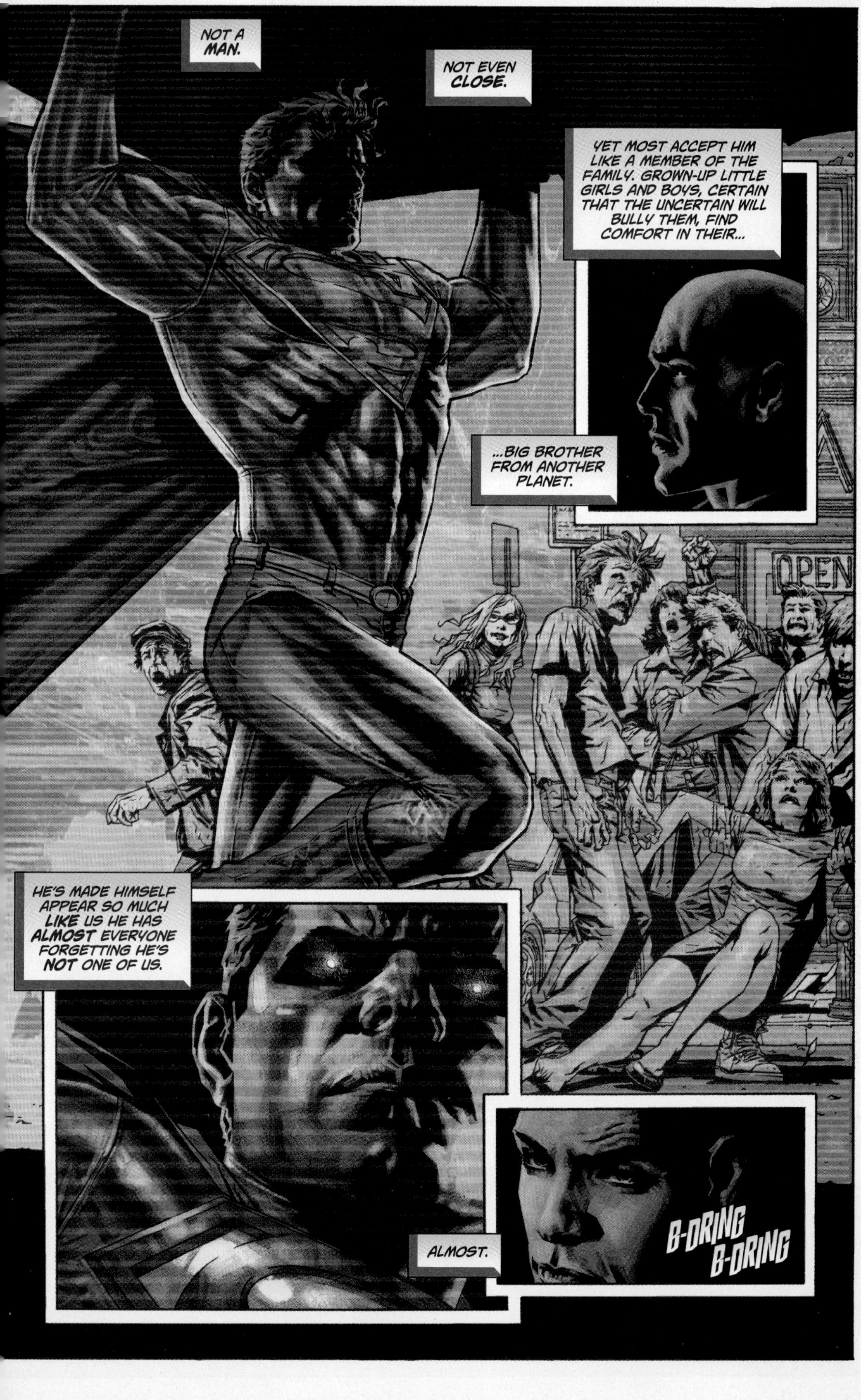
NOT A MAN.
NOT EVEN CLOSE.
YET MOST ACCEPT HIM LIKE A MEMBER OF THE FAMILY. GROWN-UP LITTLE GIRLS AND BOYS, CERTAIN THAT THE UNCERTAIN WILL BULLY THEM, FIND COMFORT IN THEIR...
...BIG BROTHER FROM ANOTHER PLANET.
OPEN
HE'S MADE HIMSELF APPEAR SO MUCH LIKE US HE HAS ALMOST EVERYONE FORGETTING HE'S NOT ONE OF US.
ALMOST.
B-DRING B-DRING

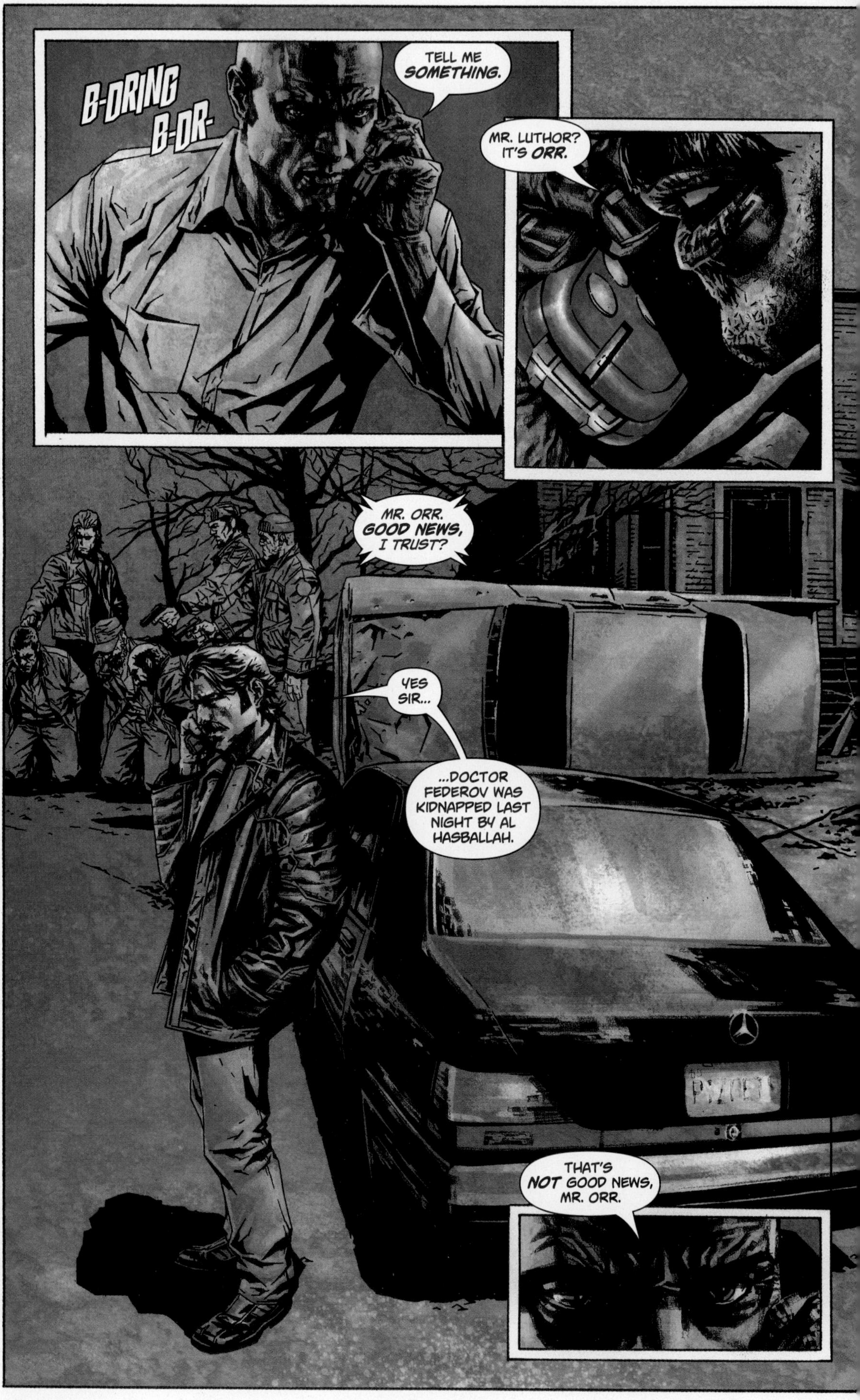
B-DRING B-DR-
TELL ME SOMETHING.
MR. LUTHOR? IT'S ORR.
MR. ORR. GOOD NEWS, I TRUST?
YES SIR...
...DOCTOR FEDEROV WAS KIDNAPPED LAST NIGHT BY AL HASBALLAH.
THAT'S NOT GOOD NEWS, MR. ORR.

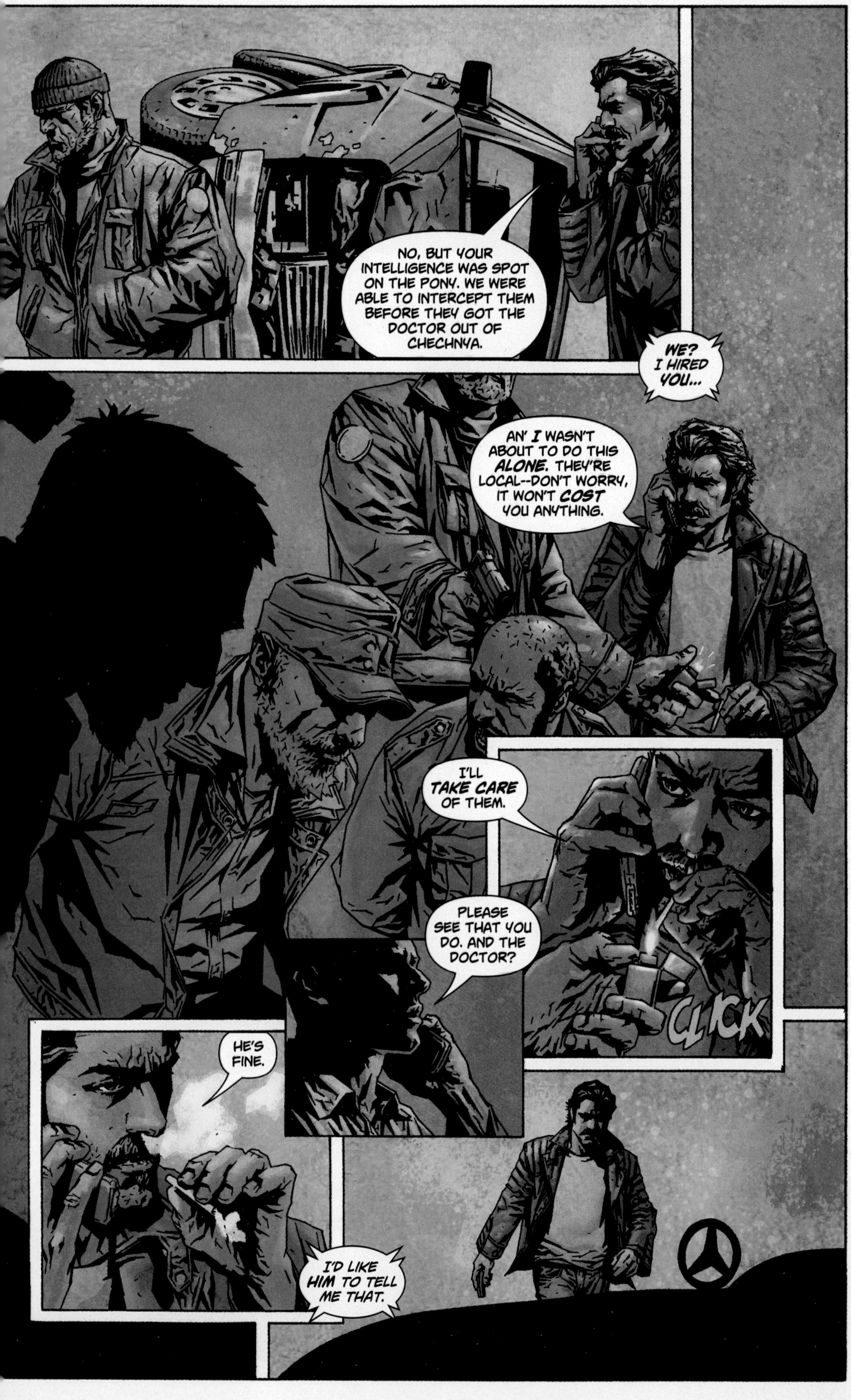
NO, BUT YOUR INTELLIGENCE WAS SPOT ON THE PONY. WE WERE ABLE TO INTERCEPT THEM BEFORE THEY GOT THE DOCTOR OUT OF CHECHNYA.
WE? I HIRED YOU...
AN' I WASN'T ABOUT TO DO THIS ALONE. THEY'RE LOCAL--DON'T WORRY, IT WON'T COST YOU ANYTHING.
I'LL TAKE CARE OF THEM.
PLEASE SEE THAT YOU DO. AND THE DOCTOR?
CLICK
HE'S FINE.
I'D LIKE HIM TO TELL ME THAT.

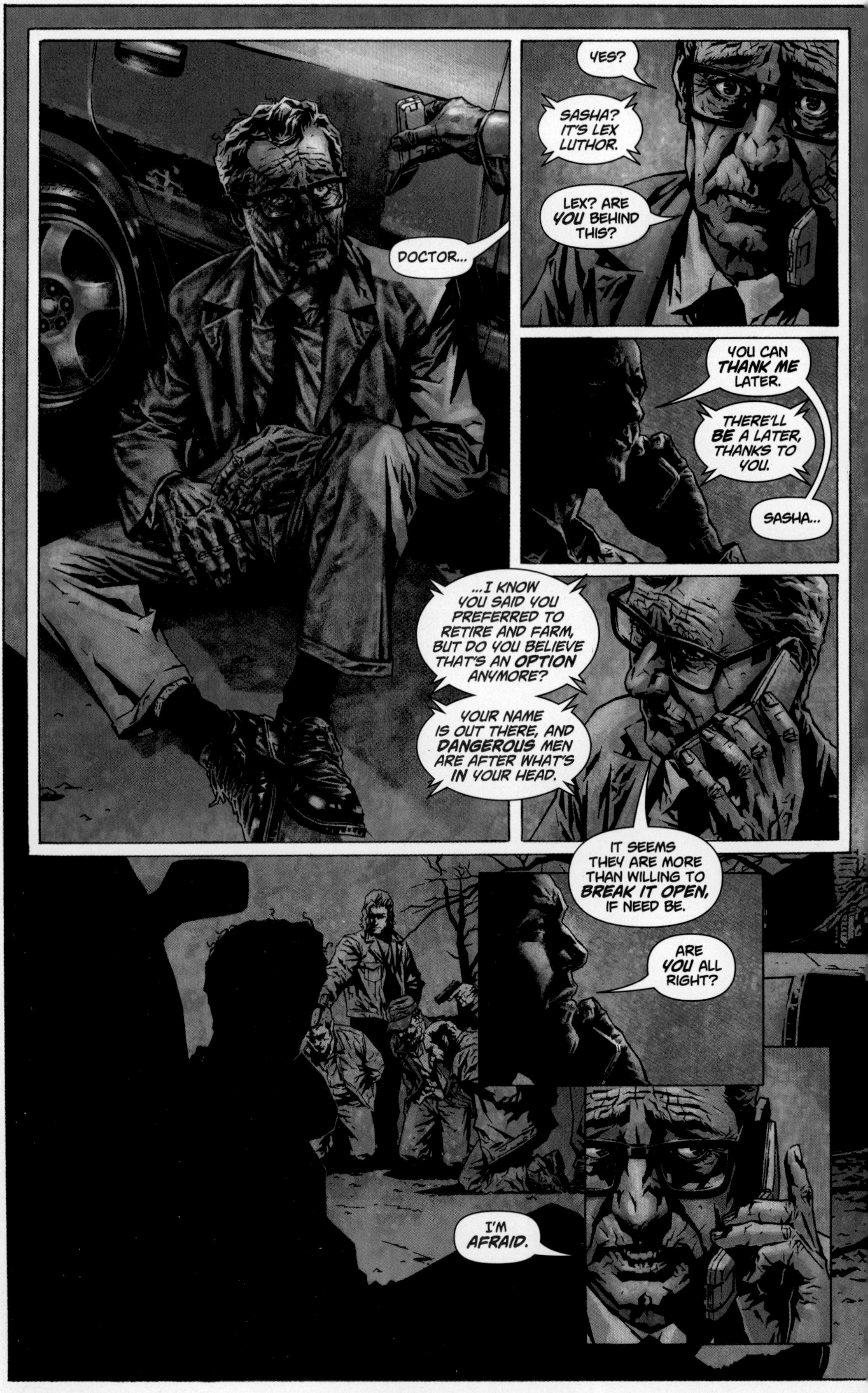
YES?
SASHA? IT'S LEX LUTHOR.
LEX? ARE YOU BEHIND THIS?
DOCTOR...
YOU CAN THANK ME LATER.
THERE'LL BE A LATER, THANKS TO YOU.
SASHA...
...I KNOW YOU SAID YOU PREFERRED TO RETIRE AND FARM, BUT DO YOU BELIEVE THAT'S AN OPTION ANYMORE?
YOUR NAME IS OUT THERE, AND DANGEROUS MEN ARE AFTER WHAT'S IN YOUR HEAD.
IT SEEMS THEY ARE MORE THAN WILLING TO BREAK IT OPEN, IF NEED BE.
ARE YOU ALL RIGHT?
I'M AFRAID.

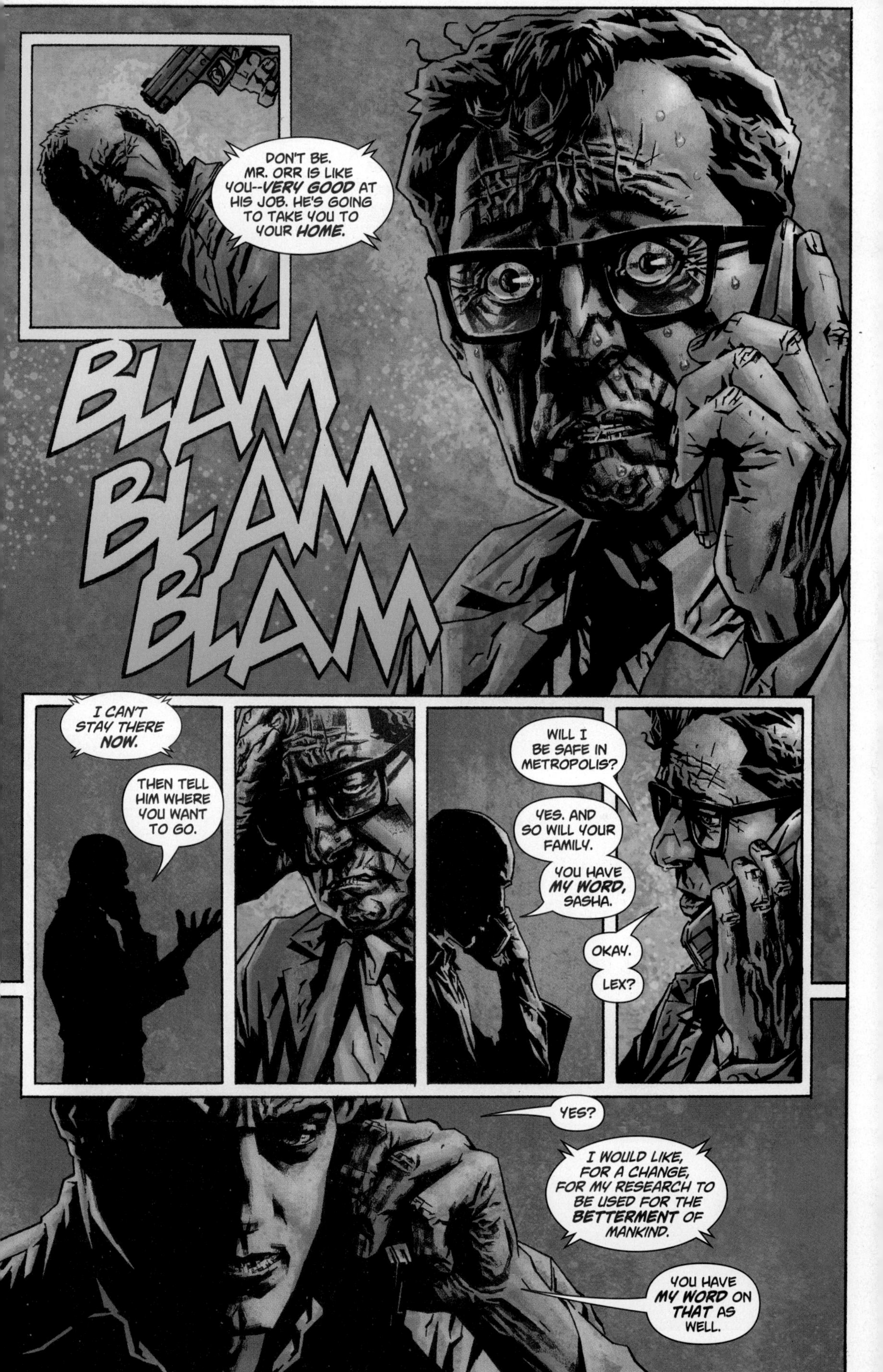
DON'T BE. MR. ORR IS LIKE YOU--**VERY GOOD** AT HIS JOB. HE'S GOING TO TAKE YOU TO YOUR **HOME.**
BLAM BLAM BLAM
I CAN'T STAY THERE ***NOW.***
THEN TELL HIM WHERE YOU WANT TO GO.
WILL I BE SAFE IN METROPOLIS?
YES. AND SO WILL YOUR FAMILY.
YOU HAVE **MY WORD,** SASHA.
OKAY.
LEX?
YES?
I WOULD LIKE, FOR A CHANGE, FOR MY RESEARCH TO BE USED FOR THE ***BETTERMENT*** *OF MANKIND.*
YOU HAVE **MY WORD** ON **THAT** AS WELL.

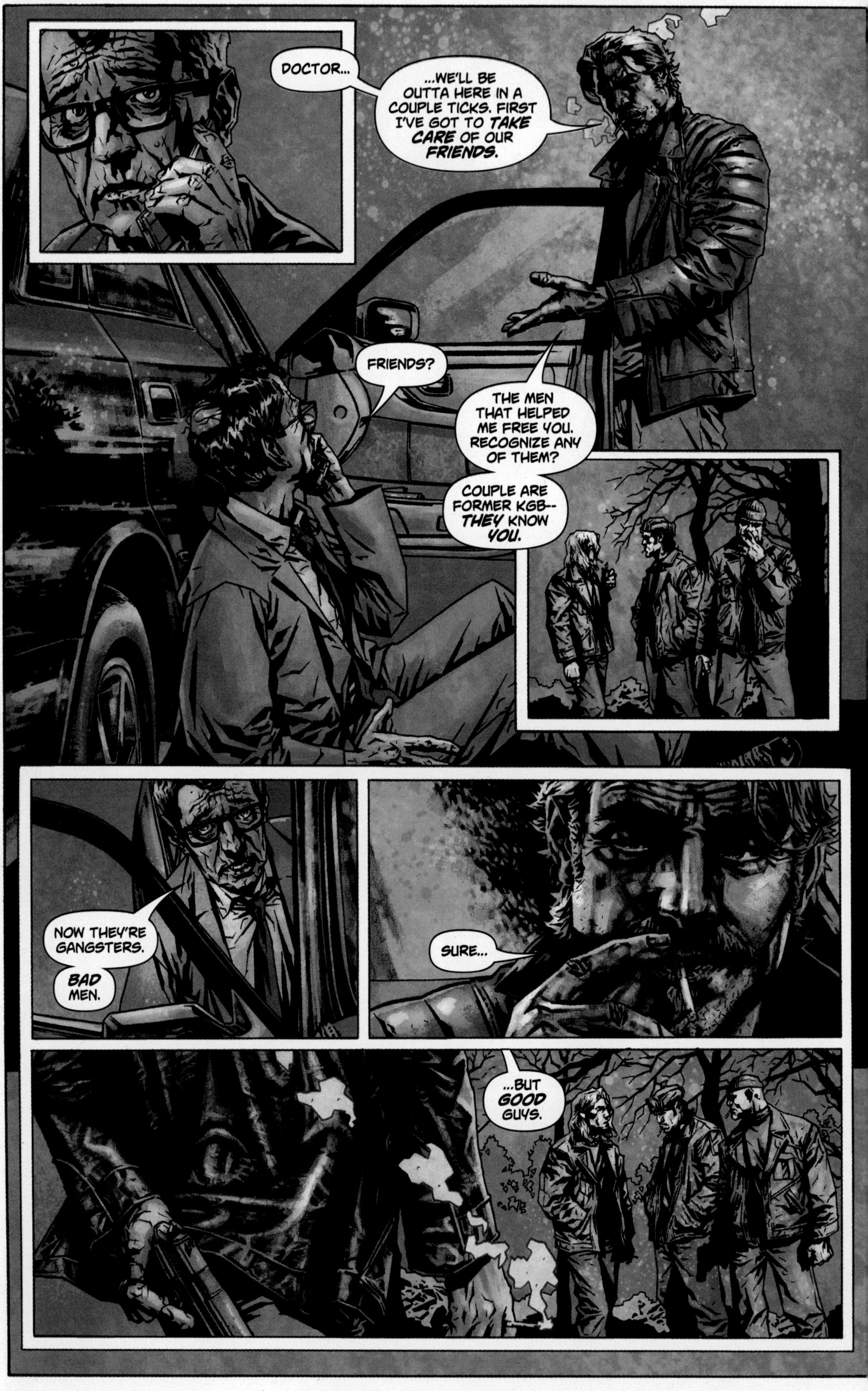
DOCTOR...
...WE'LL BE OUTTA HERE IN A COUPLE TICKS. FIRST I'VE GOT TO *TAKE CARE* OF OUR *FRIENDS.*
FRIENDS?
THE MEN THAT HELPED ME FREE YOU. RECOGNIZE ANY OF THEM?
COUPLE ARE FORMER KGB-- *THEY* KNOW *YOU.*
NOW THEY'RE GANGSTERS.
BAD MEN.
SURE...
...BUT *GOOD* GUYS.

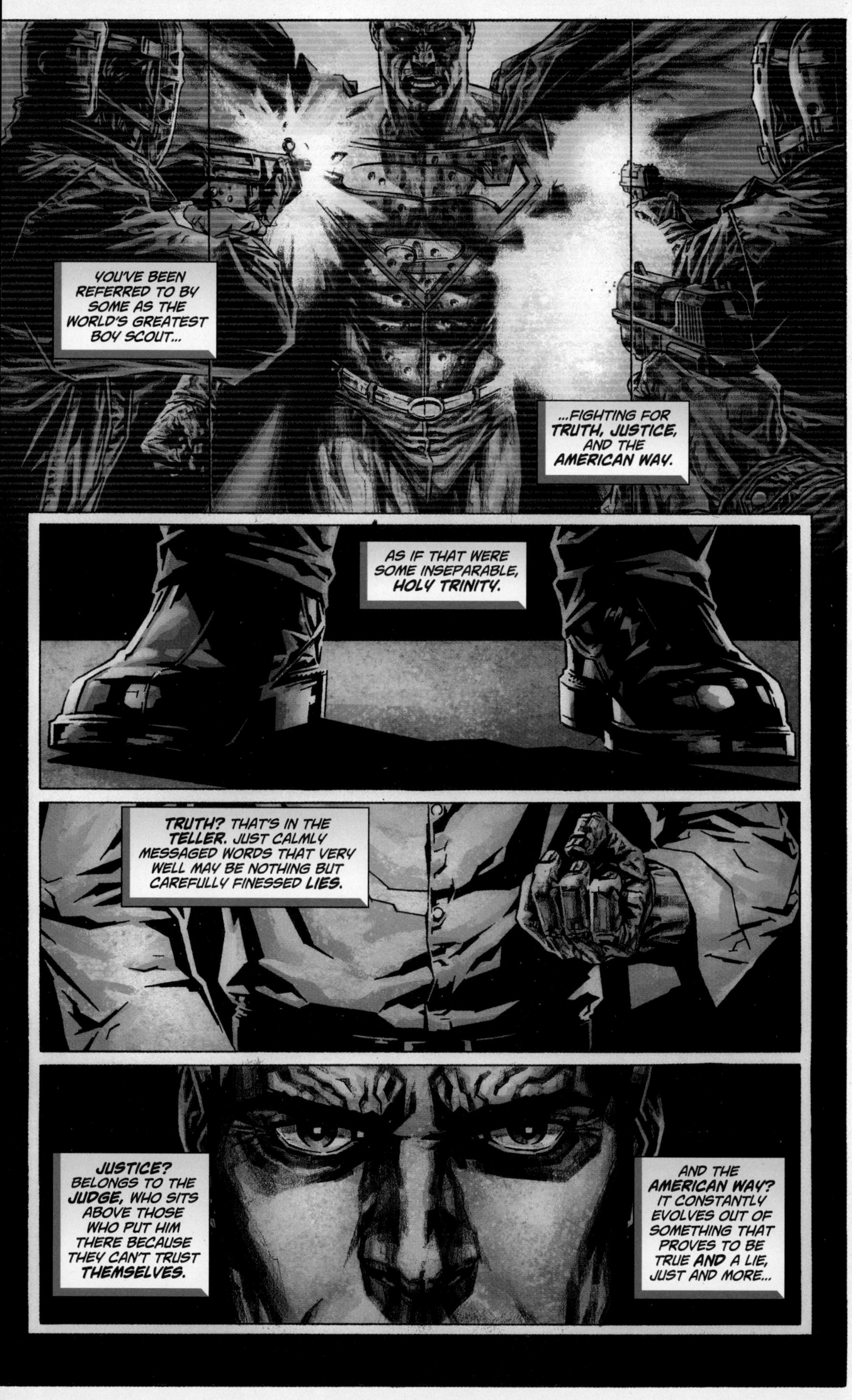
YOU'VE BEEN REFERRED TO BY SOME AS THE WORLD'S GREATEST BOY SCOUT...
...FIGHTING FOR TRUTH, JUSTICE, AND THE AMERICAN WAY.
AS IF THAT WERE SOME INSEPARABLE, HOLY TRINITY.
TRUTH? THAT'S IN THE TELLER. JUST CALMLY MESSAGED WORDS THAT VERY WELL MAY BE NOTHING BUT CAREFULLY FINESSED LIES.
JUSTICE? BELONGS TO THE JUDGE, WHO SITS ABOVE THOSE WHO PUT HIM THERE BECAUSE THEY CAN'T TRUST THEMSELVES.
AND THE AMERICAN WAY? IT CONSTANTLY EVOLVES OUT OF SOMETHING THAT PROVES TO BE TRUE AND A LIE, JUST AND MORE...

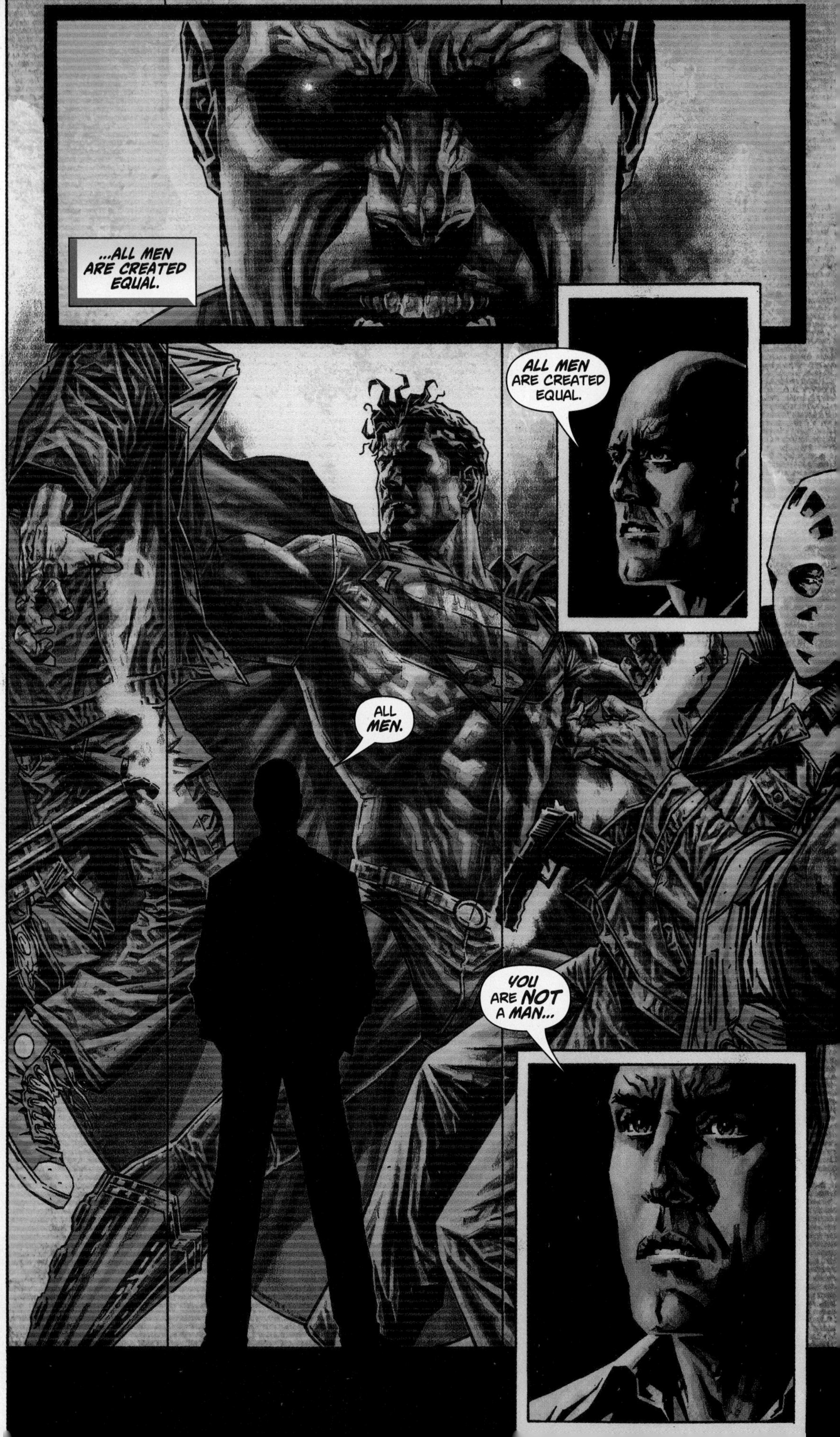
...ALL MEN ARE CREATED EQUAL.
ALL MEN ARE CREATED EQUAL.
ALL MEN.
YOU ARE NOT A MAN...

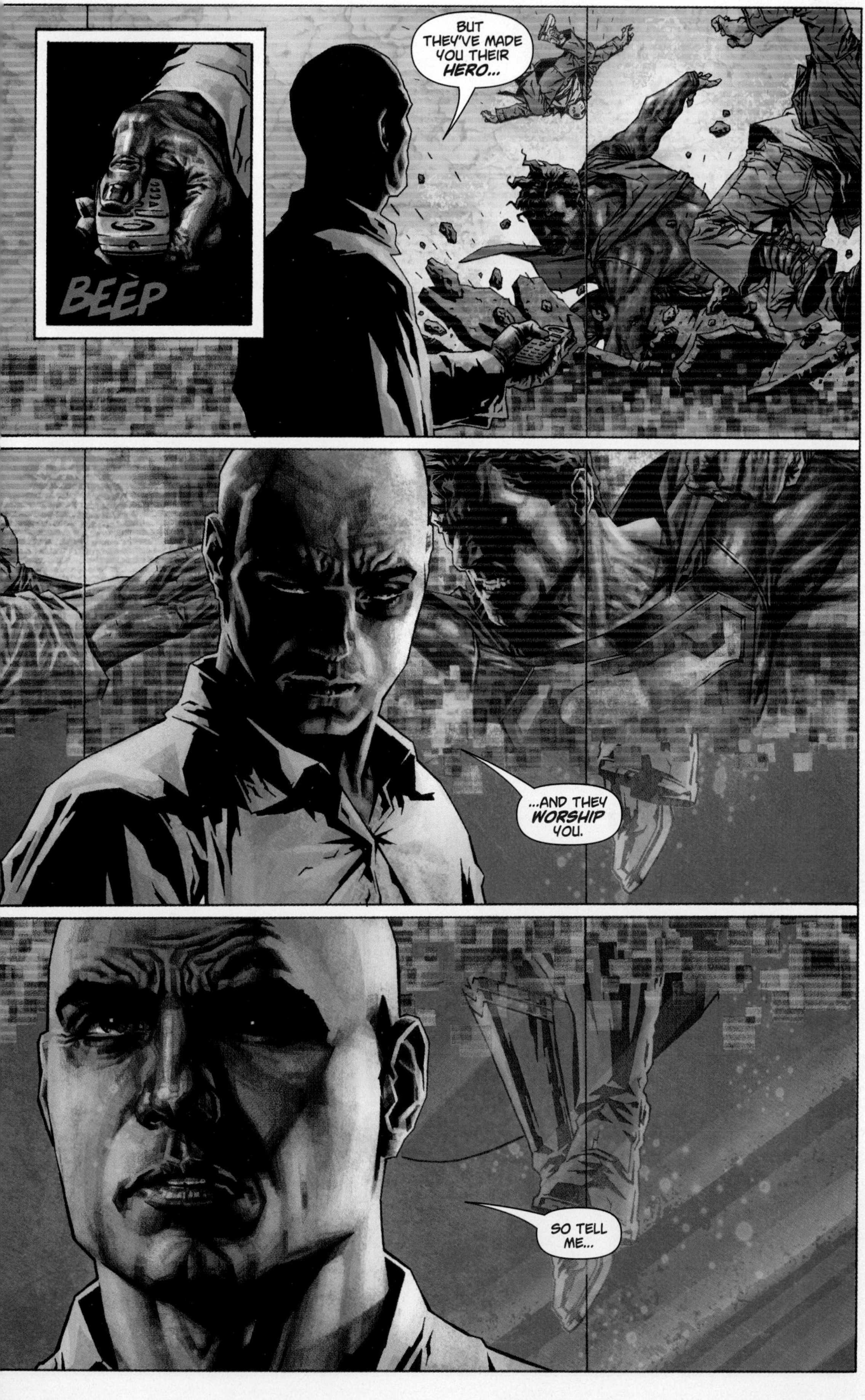
BEEP
BUT THEY'VE MADE YOU THEIR **HERO...**
...AND THEY **WORSHIP** YOU.
SO TELL ME...

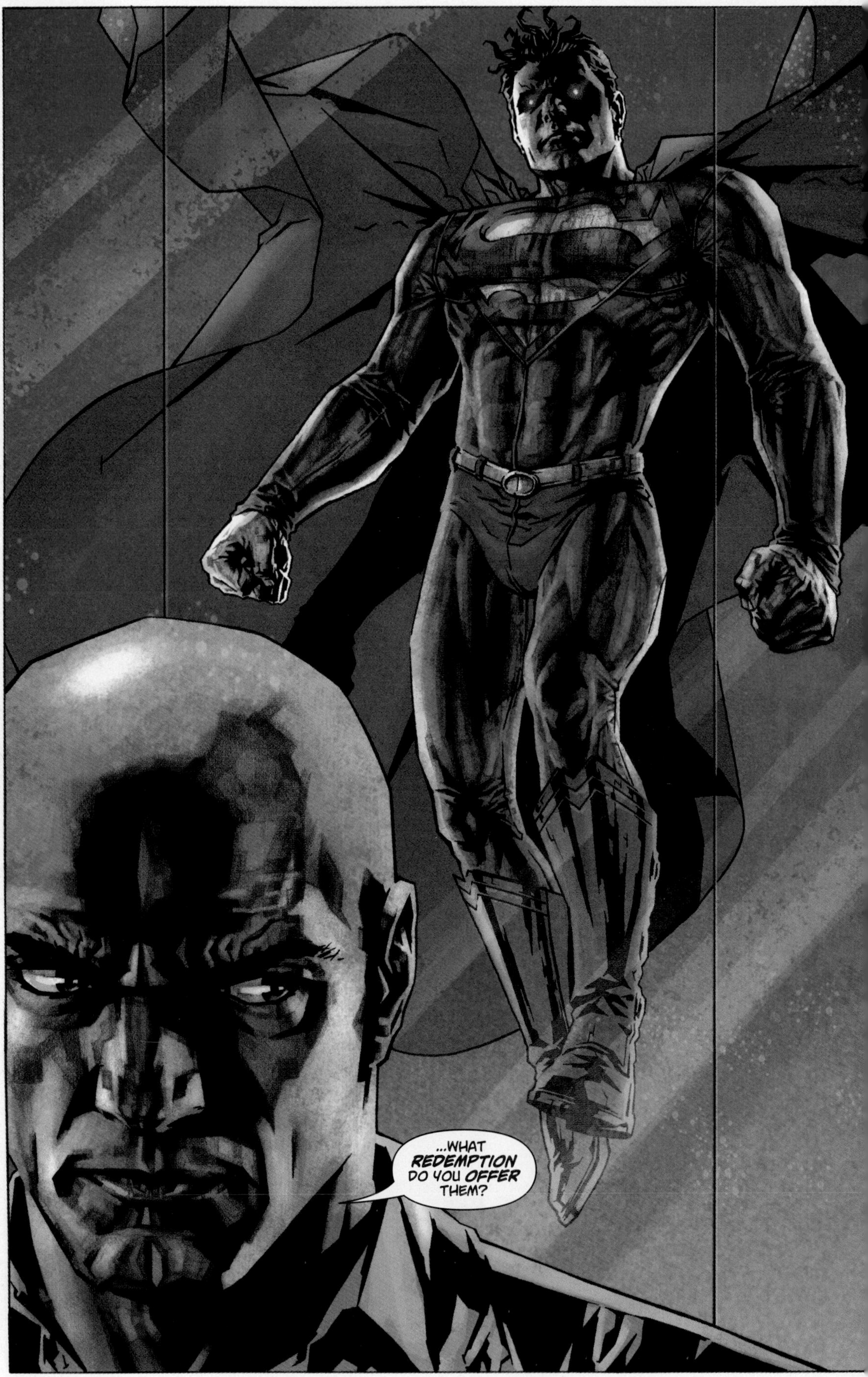
...WHAT REDEMPTION DO YOU OFFER THEM?

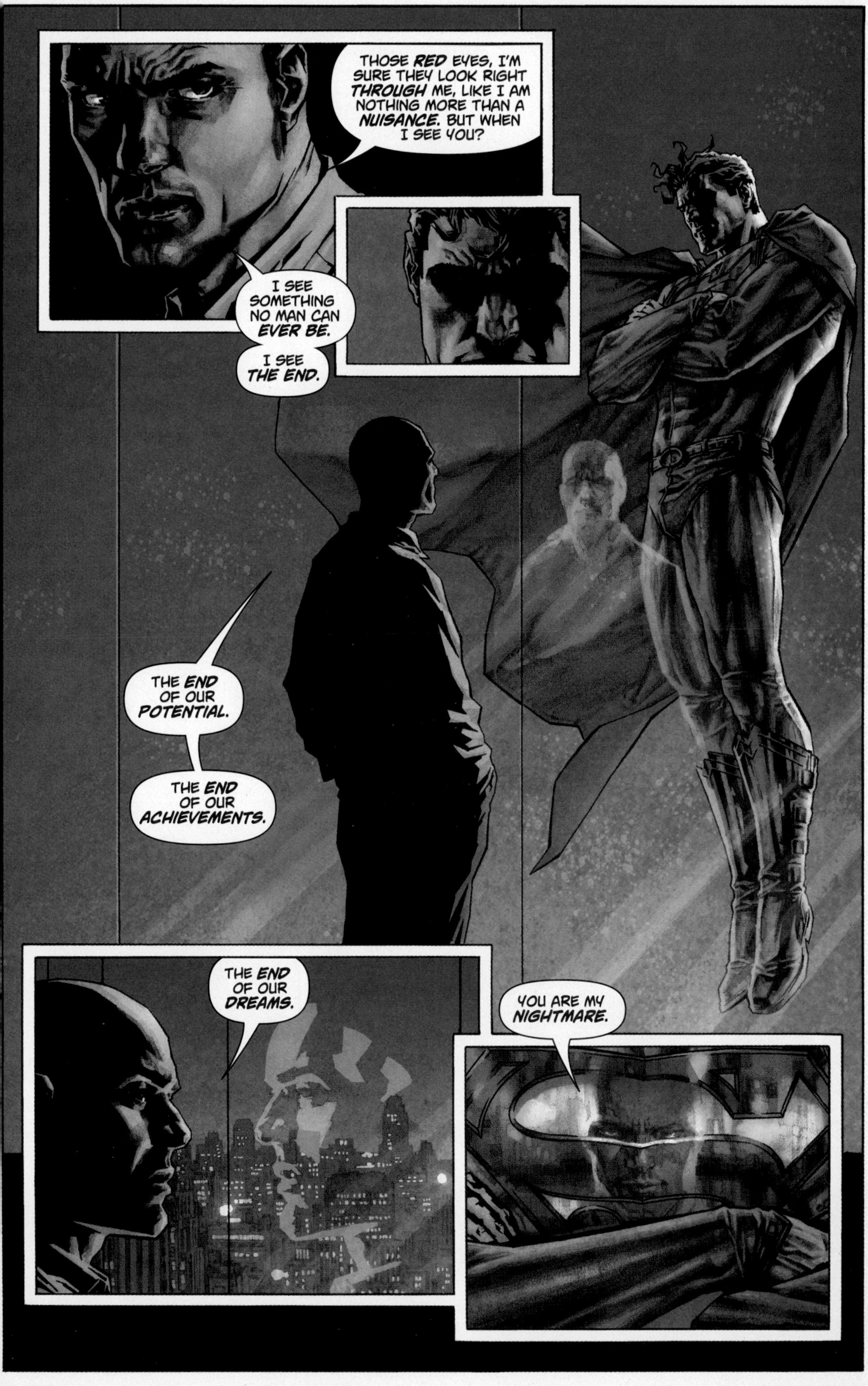
THOSE RED EYES, I'M SURE THEY LOOK RIGHT THROUGH ME, LIKE I AM NOTHING MORE THAN A NUISANCE. BUT WHEN I SEE YOU?
I SEE SOMETHING NO MAN CAN EVER BE.
I SEE THE END.
THE END OF OUR POTENTIAL.
THE END OF OUR ACHIEVEMENTS.
THE END OF OUR DREAMS.
YOU ARE MY NIGHTMARE.

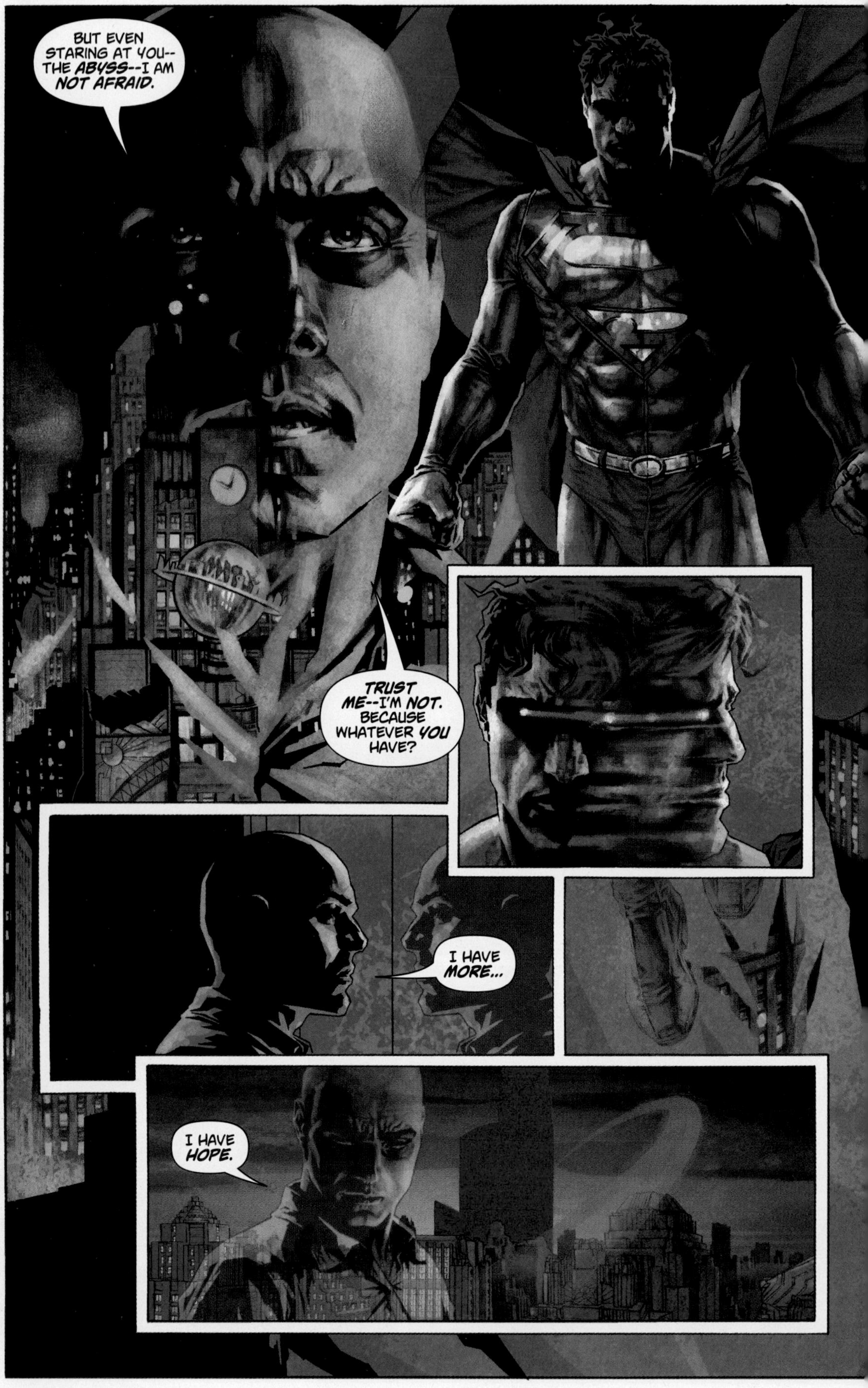
BUT EVEN STARING AT YOU-- THE ABYSS--I AM NOT AFRAID.
TRUST ME--I'M NOT. BECAUSE WHATEVER YOU HAVE?
I HAVE MORE...
I HAVE HOPE.

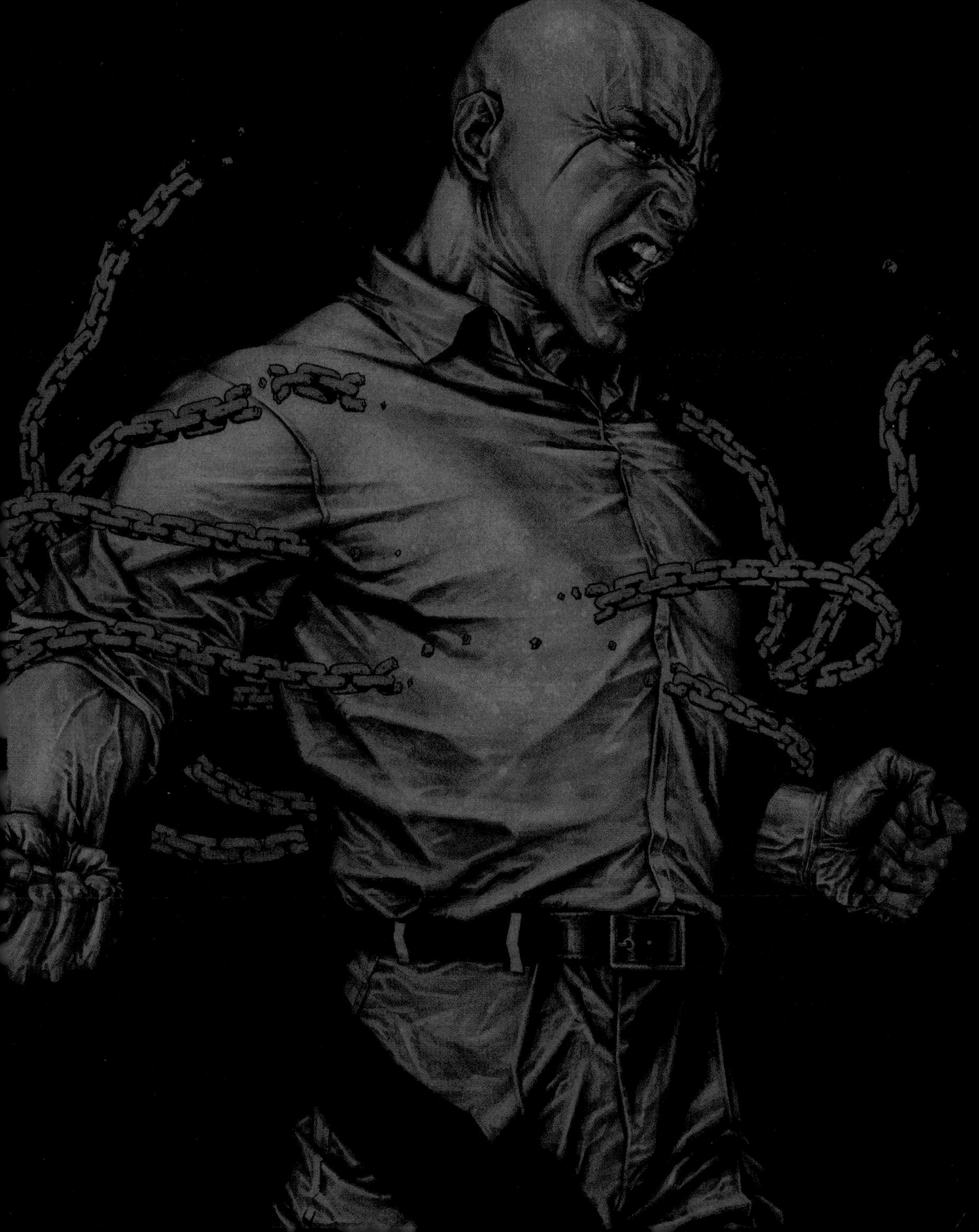

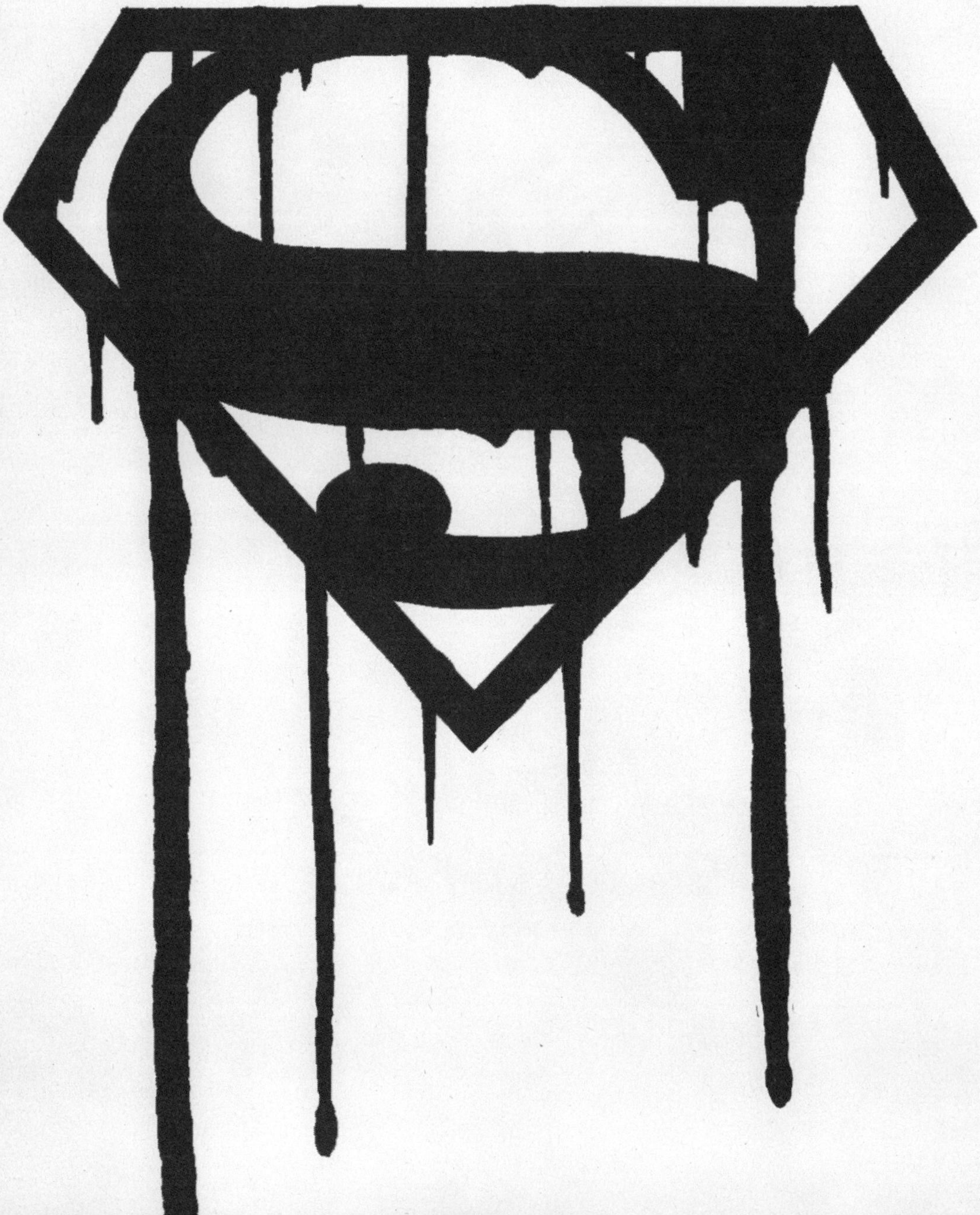

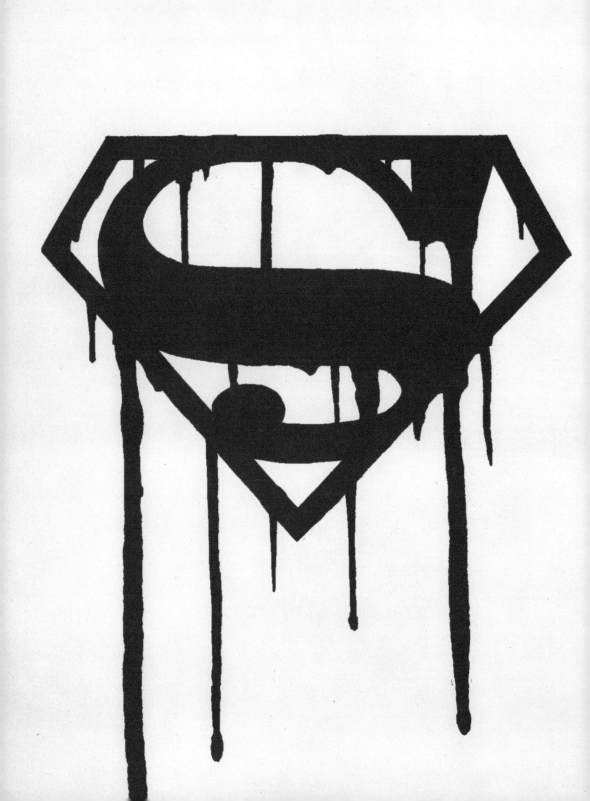

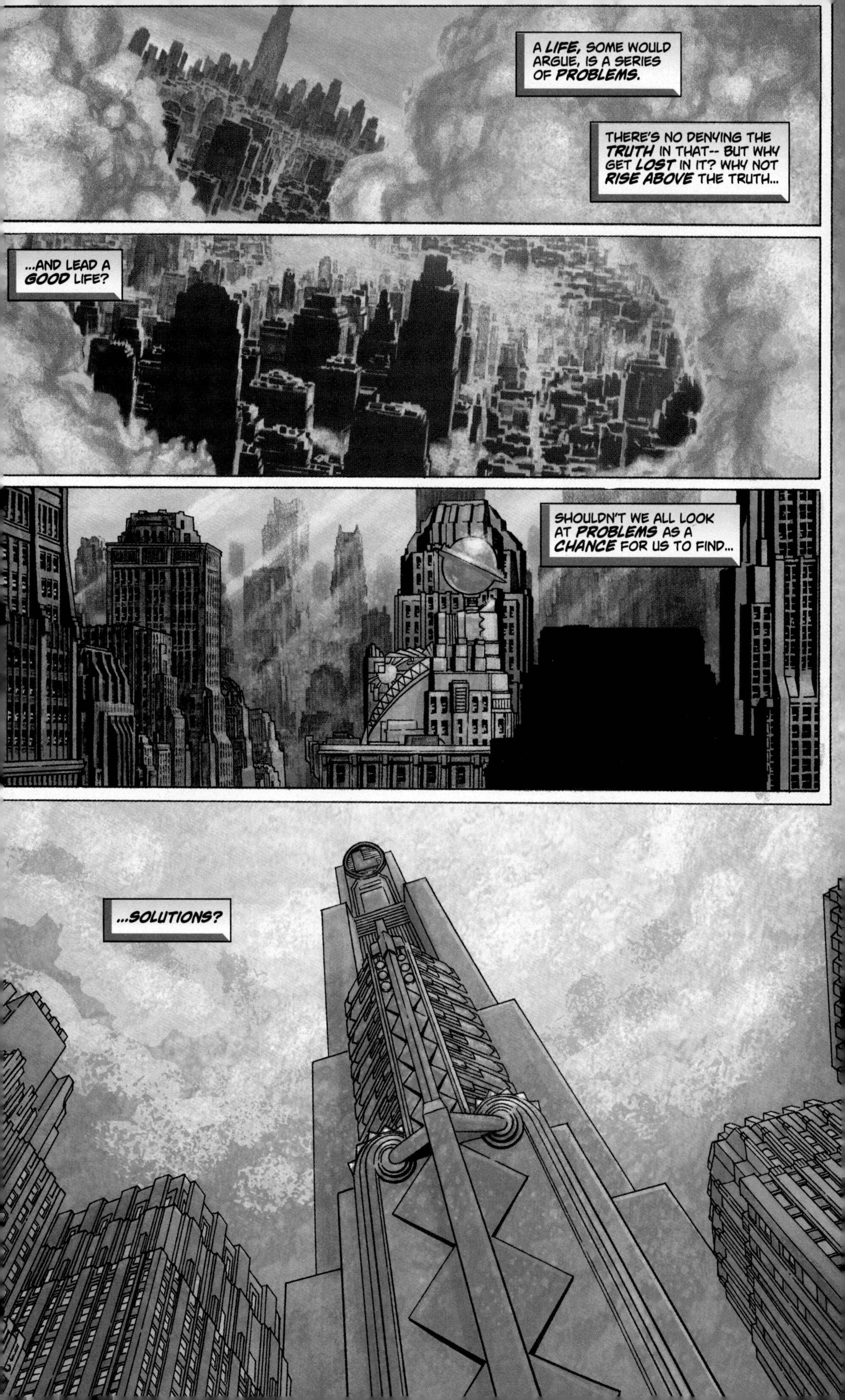
A LIFE, SOME WOULD ARGUE, IS A SERIES OF PROBLEMS.
THERE'S NO DENYING THE TRUTH IN THAT-- BUT WHY GET LOST IN IT? WHY NOT RISE ABOVE THE TRUTH...
...AND LEAD A GOOD LIFE?
SHOULDN'T WE ALL LOOK AT PROBLEMS AS A CHANCE FOR US TO FIND...
...SOLUTIONS?

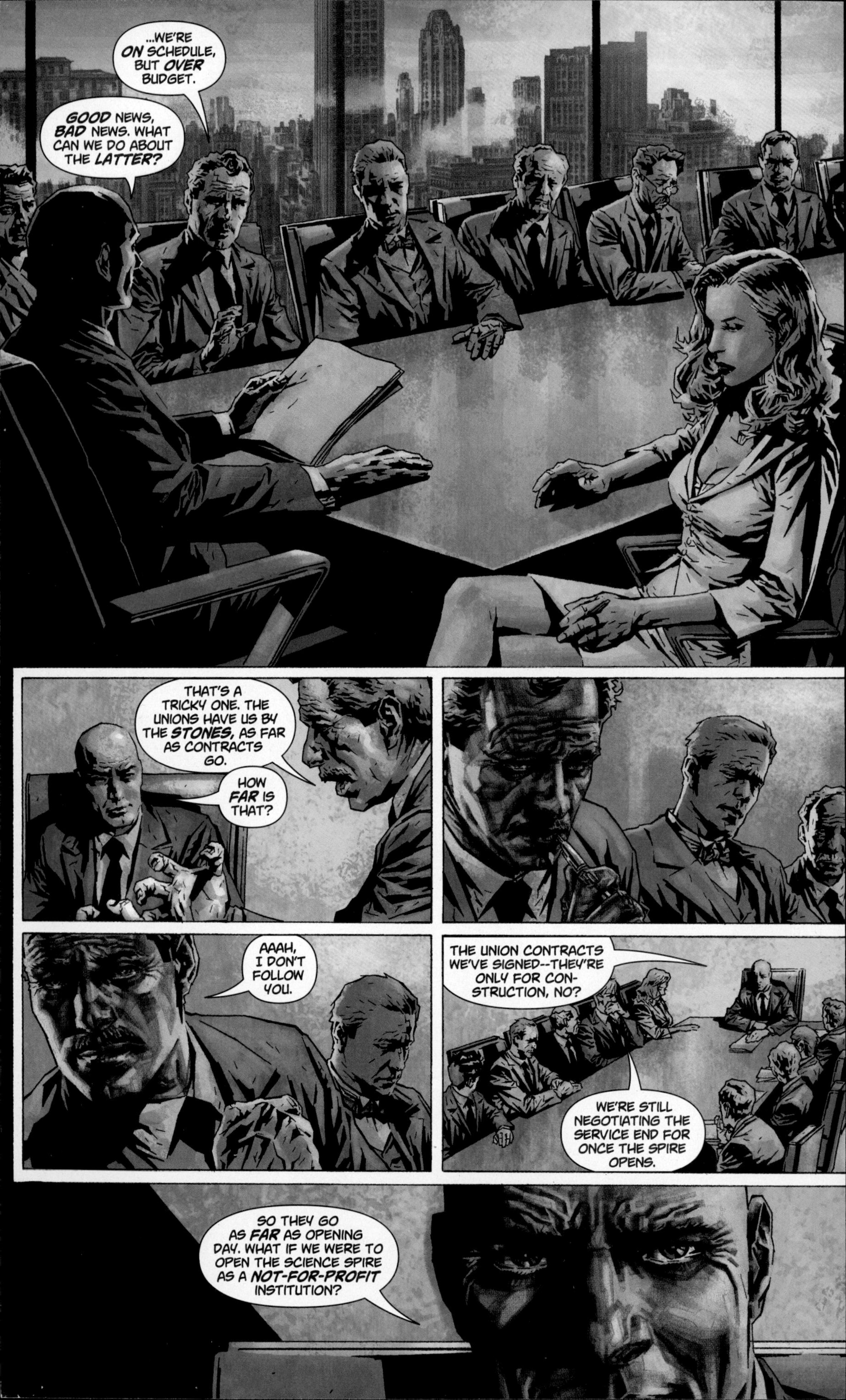

...WE'RE ON SCHEDULE, BUT OVER BUDGET.
GOOD NEWS, BAD NEWS. WHAT CAN WE DO ABOUT THE LATTER?
THAT'S A TRICKY ONE. THE UNIONS HAVE US BY THE STONES, AS FAR AS CONTRACTS GO.
HOW FAR IS THAT?
AAAH, I DON'T FOLLOW YOU.
THE UNION CONTRACTS WE'VE SIGNED--THEY'RE ONLY FOR CONSTRUCTION, NO?
WE'RE STILL NEGOTIATING THE SERVICE END FOR ONCE THE SPIRE OPENS.
SO THEY GO AS FAR AS OPENING DAY. WHAT IF WE WERE TO OPEN THE SCIENCE SPIRE AS A NOT-FOR-PROFIT INSTITUTION?

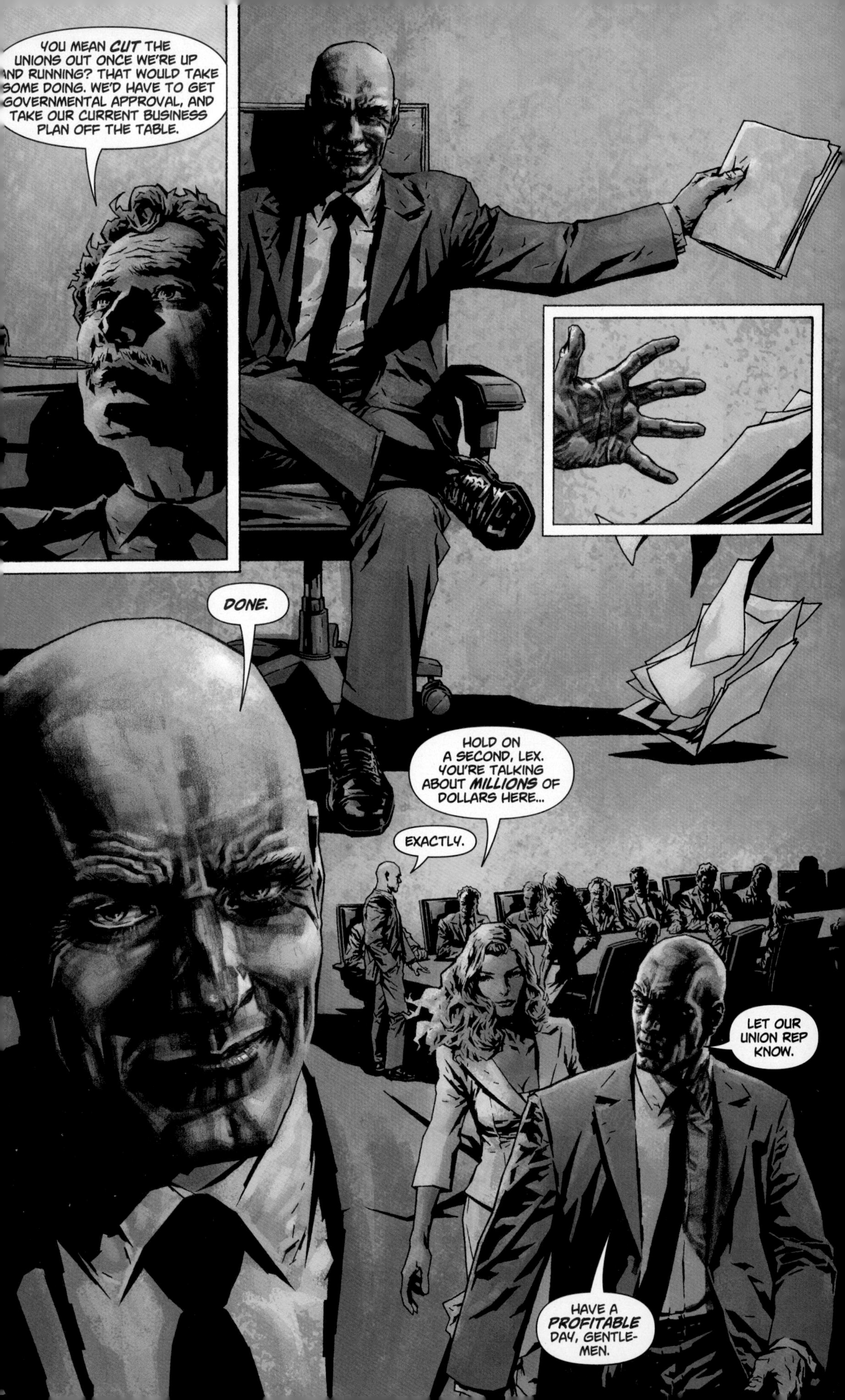
YOU MEAN *CUT* THE UNIONS OUT ONCE WE'RE UP AND RUNNING? THAT WOULD TAKE SOME DOING. WE'D HAVE TO GET GOVERNMENTAL APPROVAL, AND TAKE OUR CURRENT BUSINESS PLAN OFF THE TABLE.
DONE.
HOLD ON A SECOND, LEX. YOU'RE TALKING ABOUT *MILLIONS* OF DOLLARS HERE...
EXACTLY.
LET OUR UNION REP KNOW.
HAVE A *PROFITABLE* DAY, GENTLE-MEN.

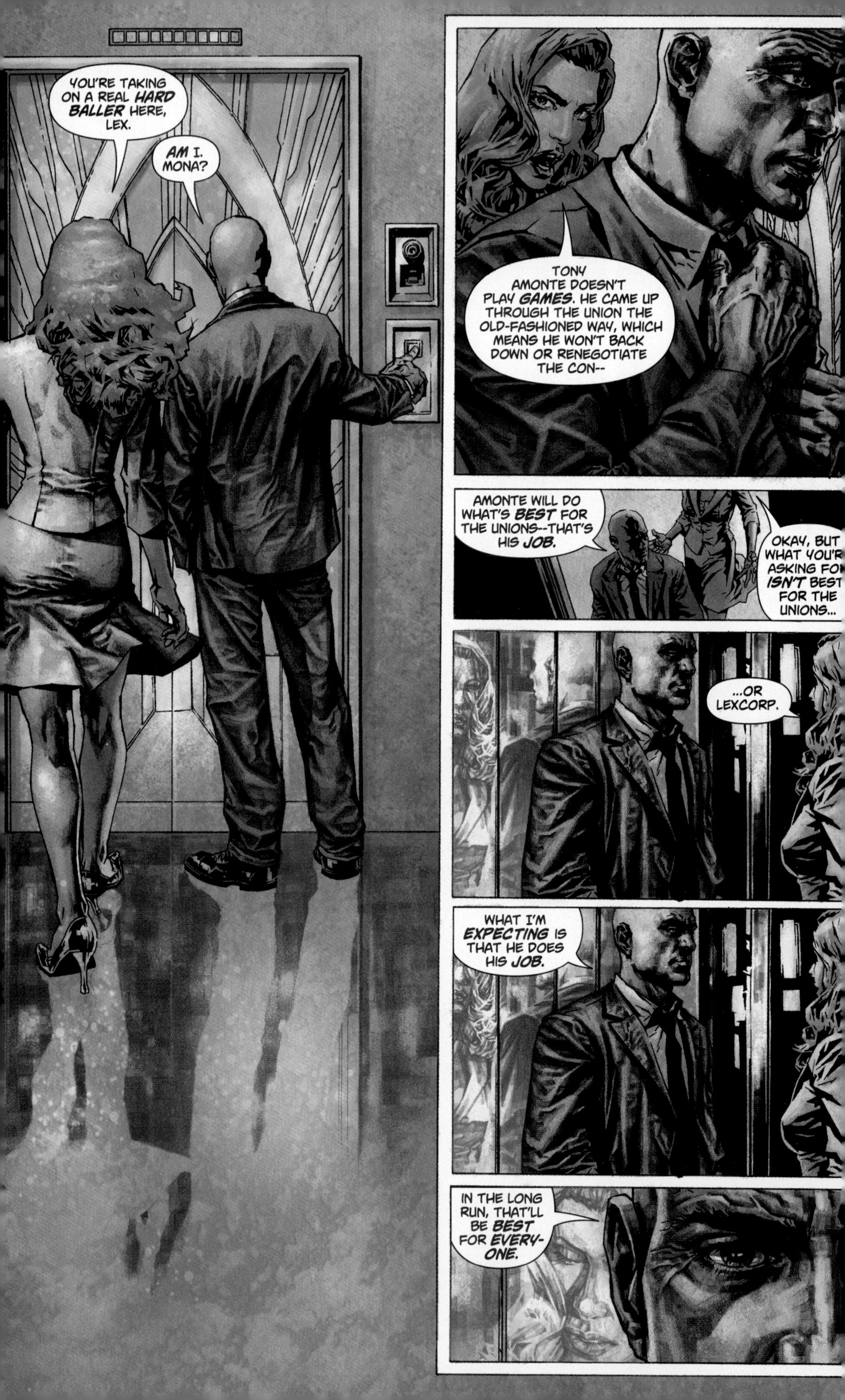
YOU'RE TAKING ON A REAL HARD BALLER HERE, LEX.
AM I. MONA?
TONY AMONTE DOESN'T PLAY GAMES. HE CAME UP THROUGH THE UNION THE OLD-FASHIONED WAY, WHICH MEANS HE WON'T BACK DOWN OR RENEGOTIATE THE CON--
AMONTE WILL DO WHAT'S BEST FOR THE UNIONS--THAT'S HIS JOB.
...OR LEXCORP.
WHAT I'M EXPECTING IS THAT HE DOES HIS JOB.
IN THE LONG RUN, THAT'LL BE BEST FOR EVERY-ONE.

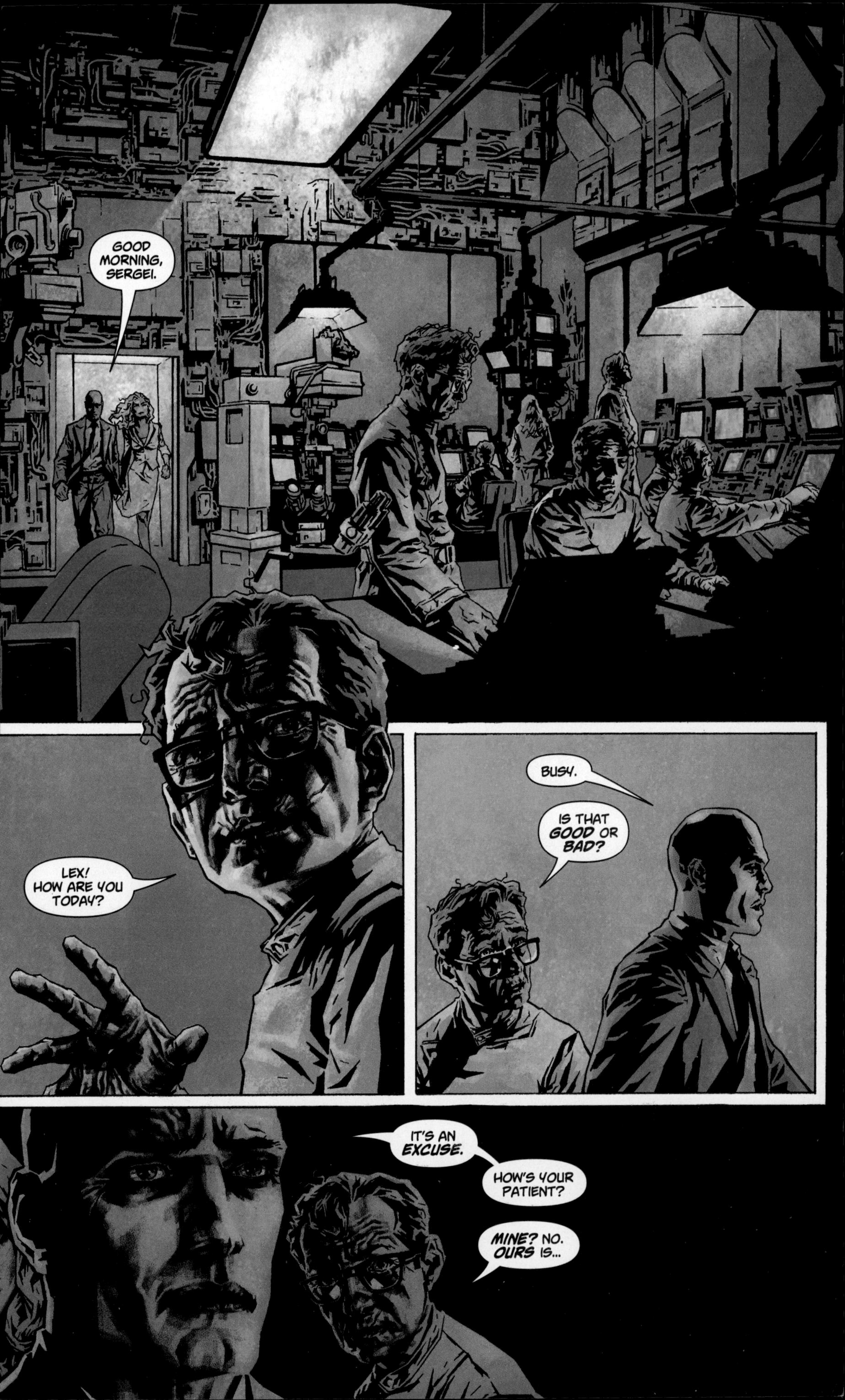
GOOD MORNING, SERGEI.
LEX! HOW ARE YOU TODAY?
BUSY.
IS THAT GOOD OR BAD?
IT'S AN EXCUSE.
HOW'S YOUR PATIENT?
MINE? NO. OURS IS...

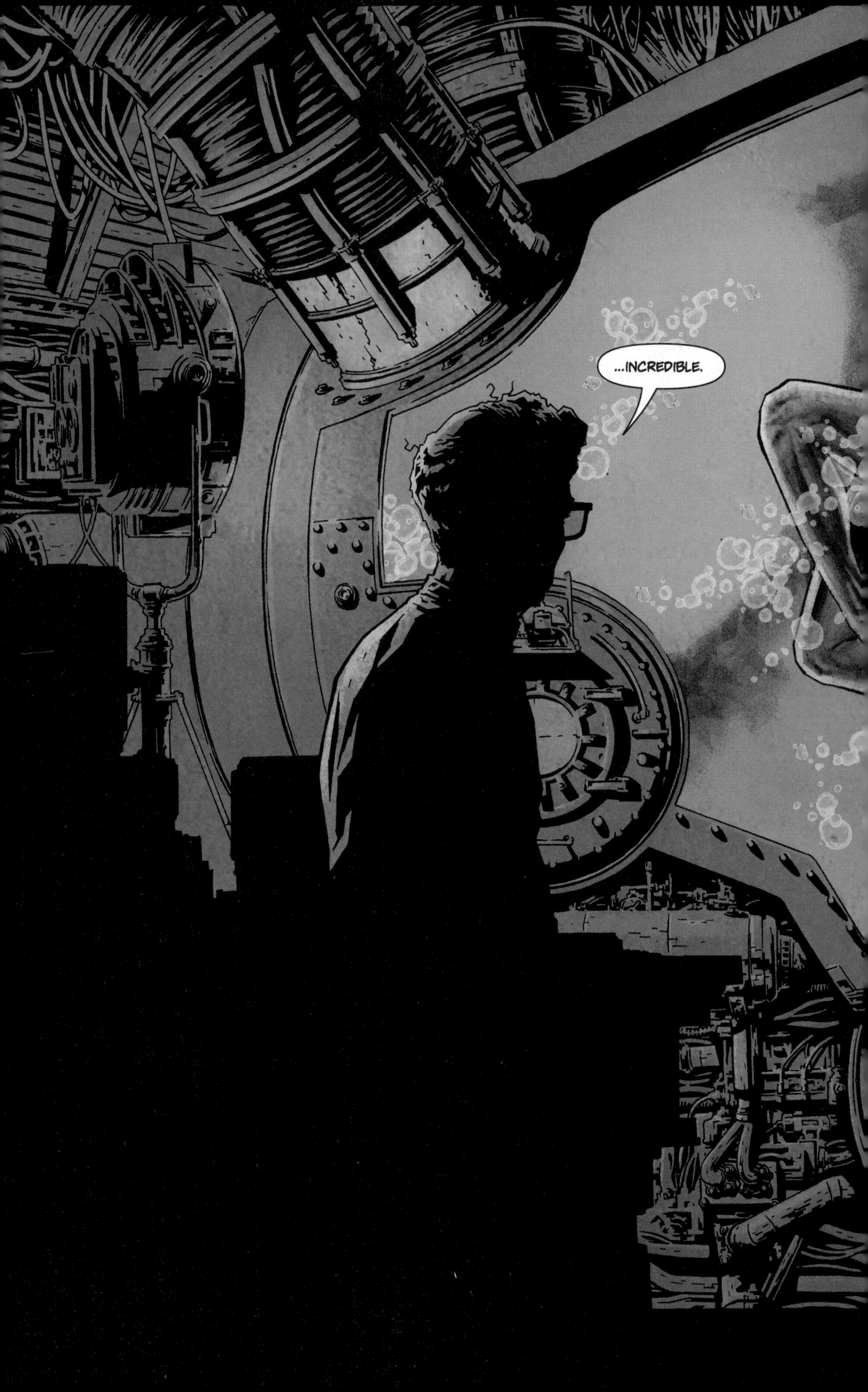
...INCREDIBLE.

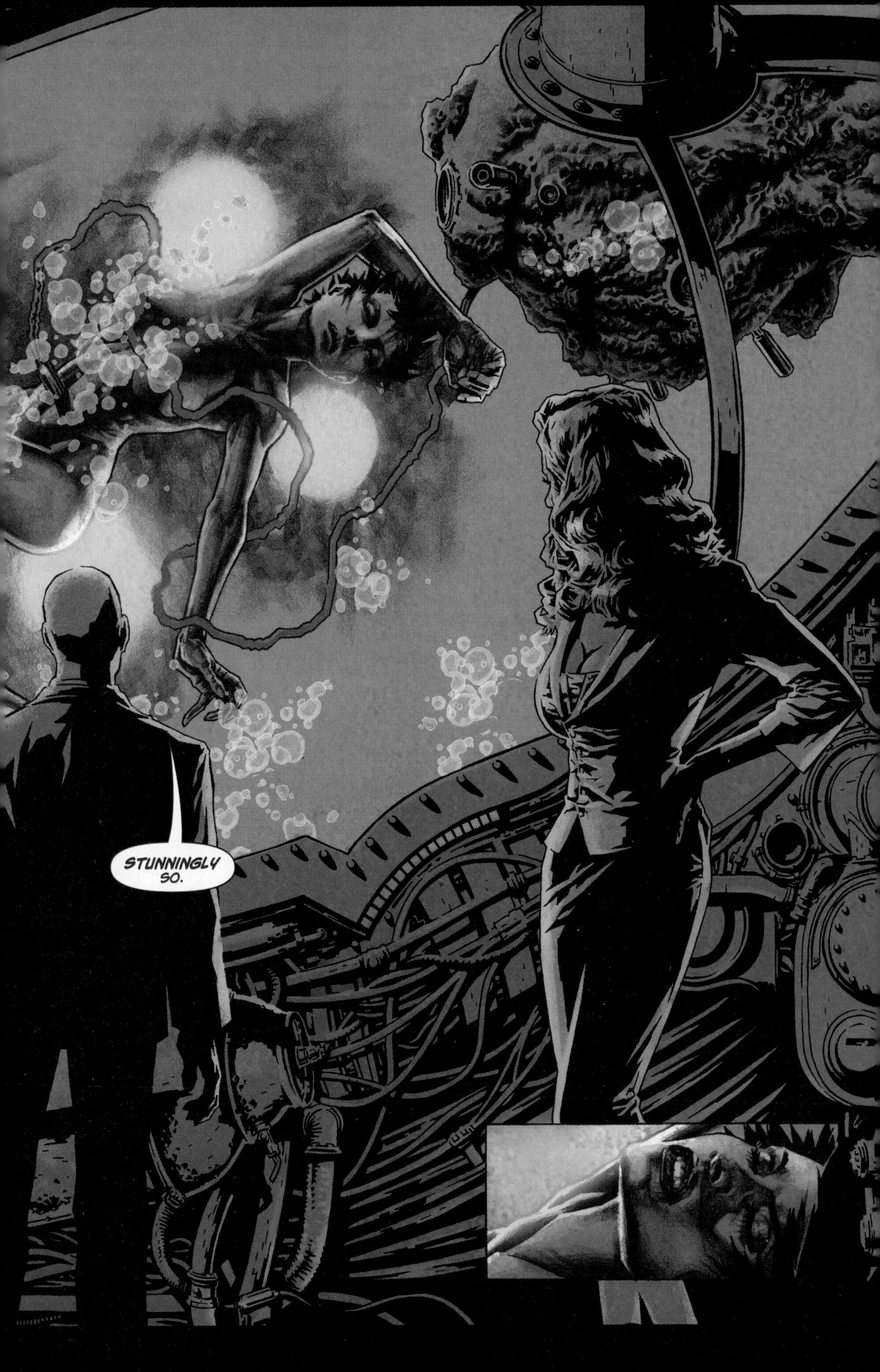
STUNNINGLY SO.

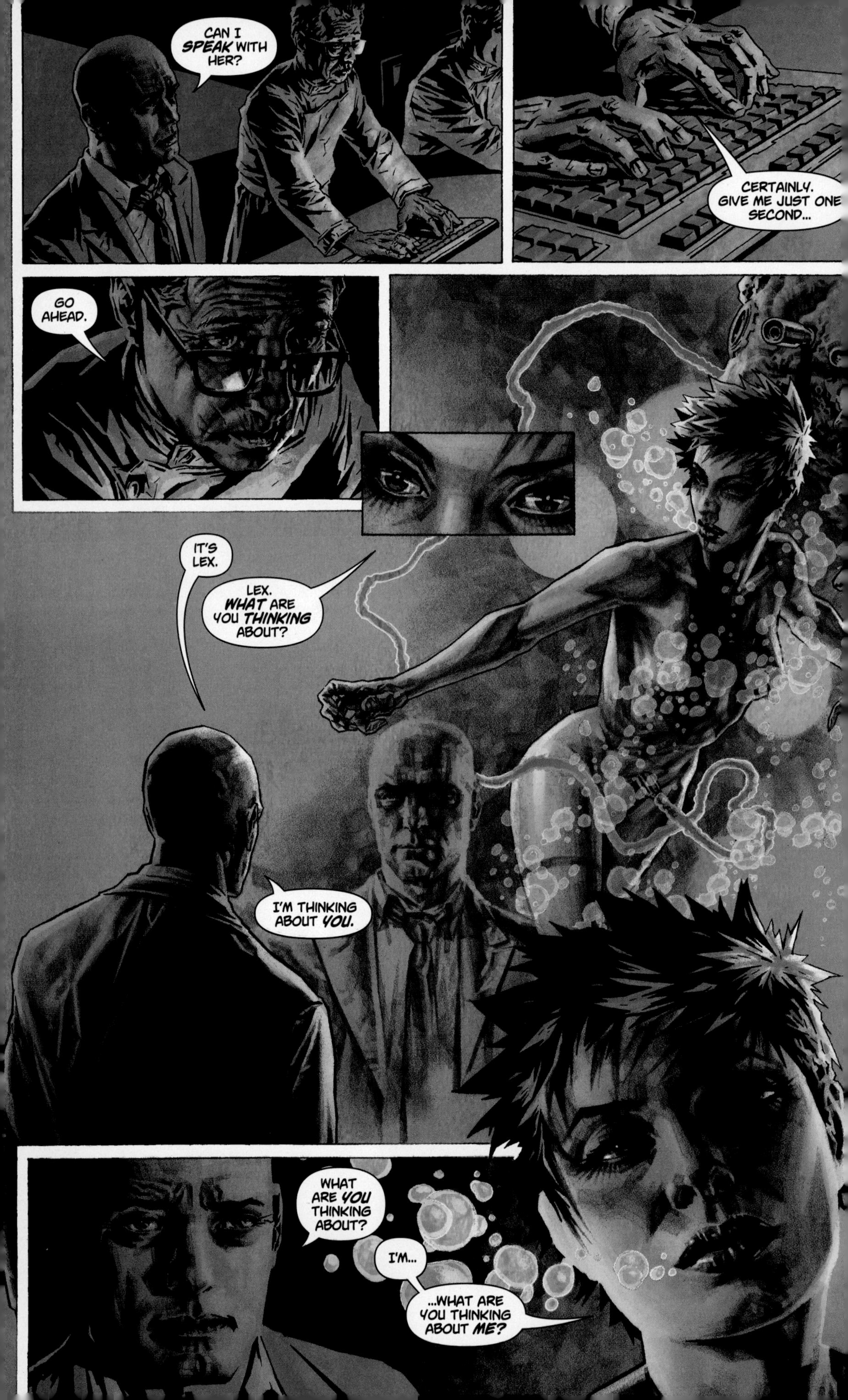
CAN I SPEAK WITH HER?
CERTAINLY. GIVE ME JUST ONE SECOND...
GO AHEAD.
IT'S LEX.
LEX. WHAT ARE YOU THINKING ABOUT?
I'M THINKING ABOUT YOU.
WHAT ARE YOU THINKING ABOUT?
I'M...
...WHAT ARE YOU THINKING ABOUT ME?

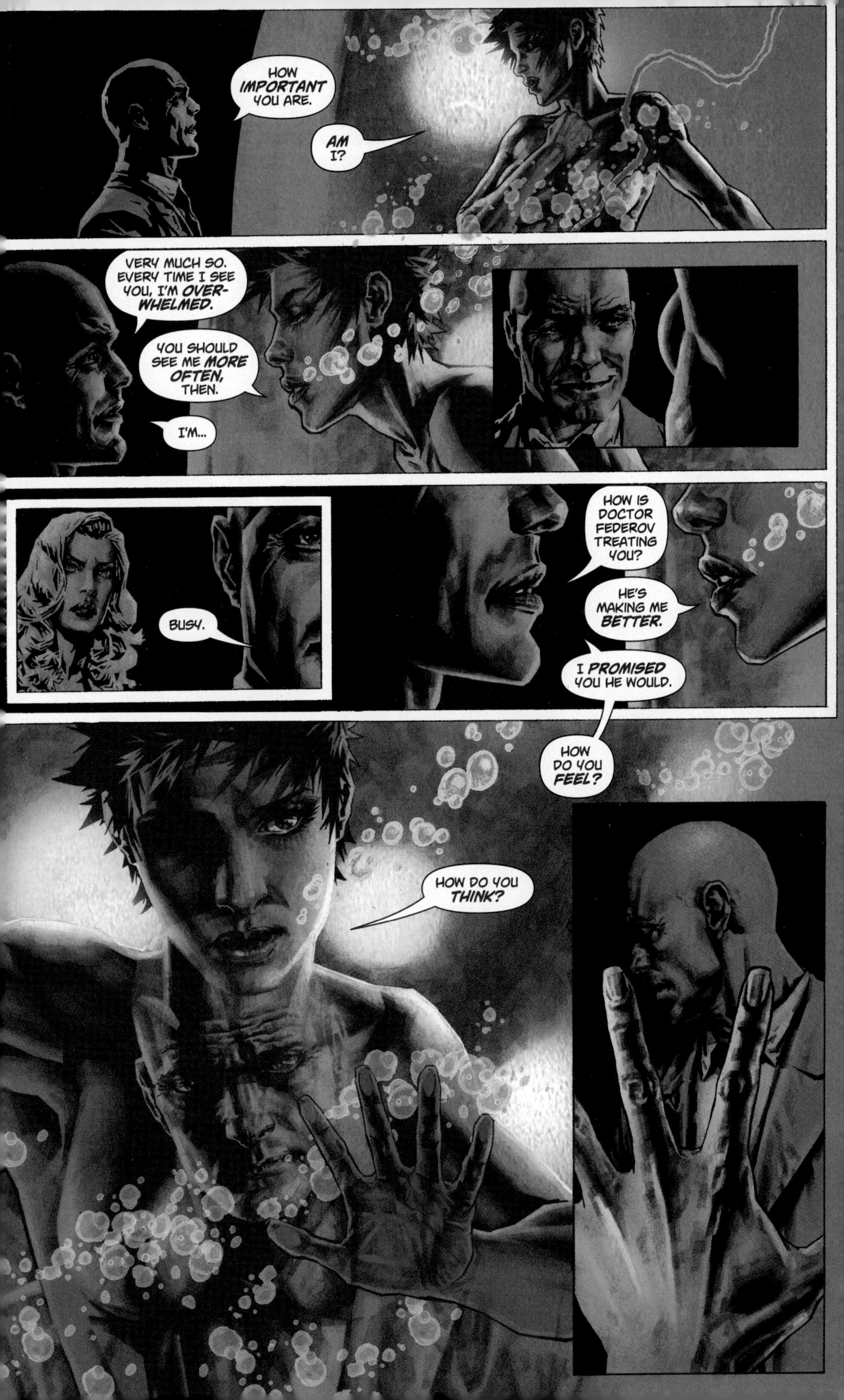
HOW IMPORTANT YOU ARE.
AM I?
VERY MUCH SO. EVERY TIME I SEE YOU, I'M OVER-WHELMED.
YOU SHOULD SEE ME MORE OFTEN, THEN.
I'M...
BUSY.
HOW IS DOCTOR FEDEROV TREATING YOU?
HE'S MAKING ME BETTER.
I PROMISED YOU HE WOULD.
HOW DO YOU FEEL?
HOW DO YOU THINK?

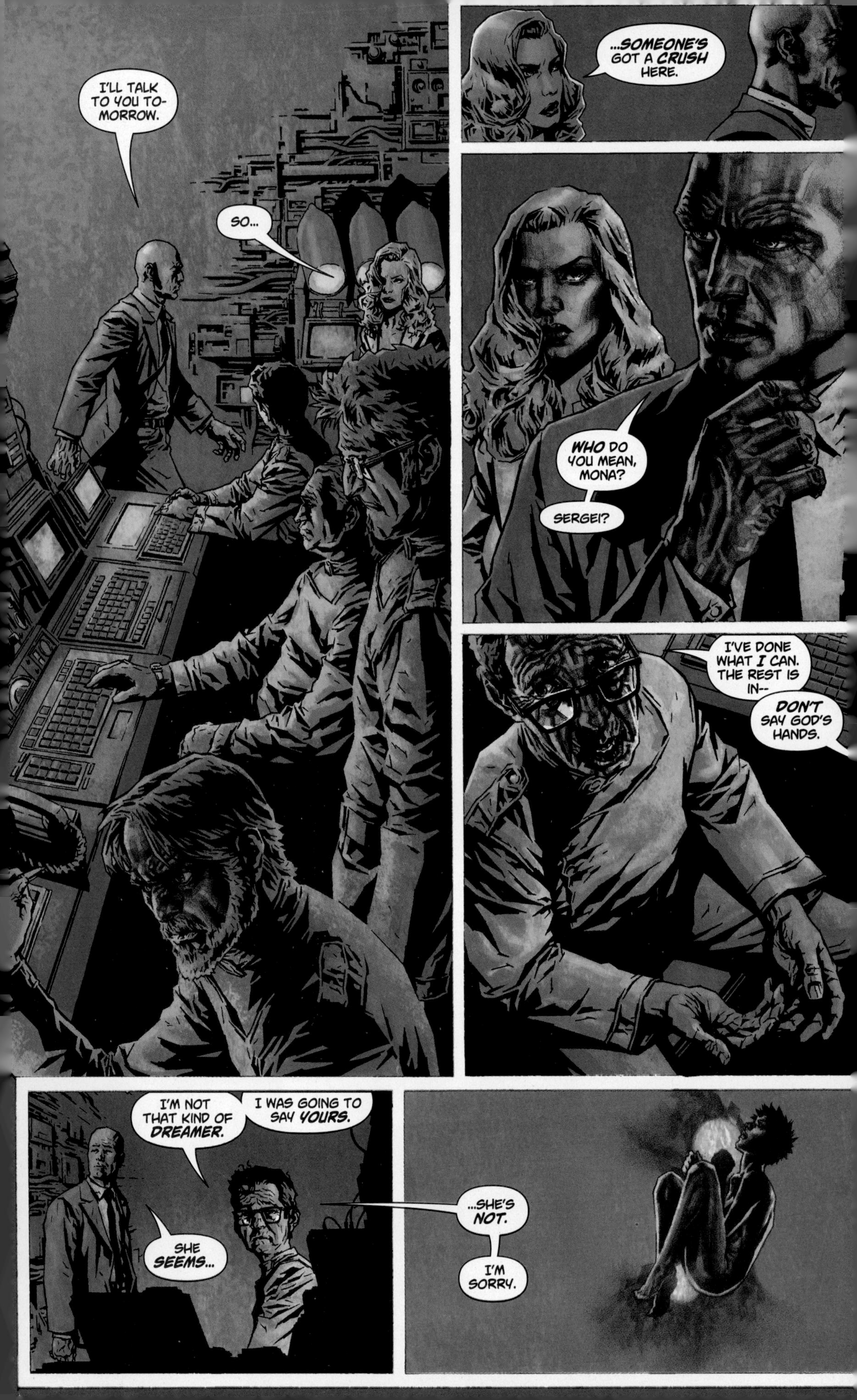

I'LL TALK TO YOU TO-MORROW.
SO...
...SOMEONE'S GOT A CRUSH HERE.
WHO DO YOU MEAN, MONA?
SERGEI?
I'VE DONE WHAT I CAN. THE REST IS IN--
DON'T SAY GOD'S HANDS.
I'M NOT THAT KIND OF DREAMER.
I WAS GOING TO SAY YOURS.
SHE SEEMS...
...SHE'S NOT.
I'M SORRY.

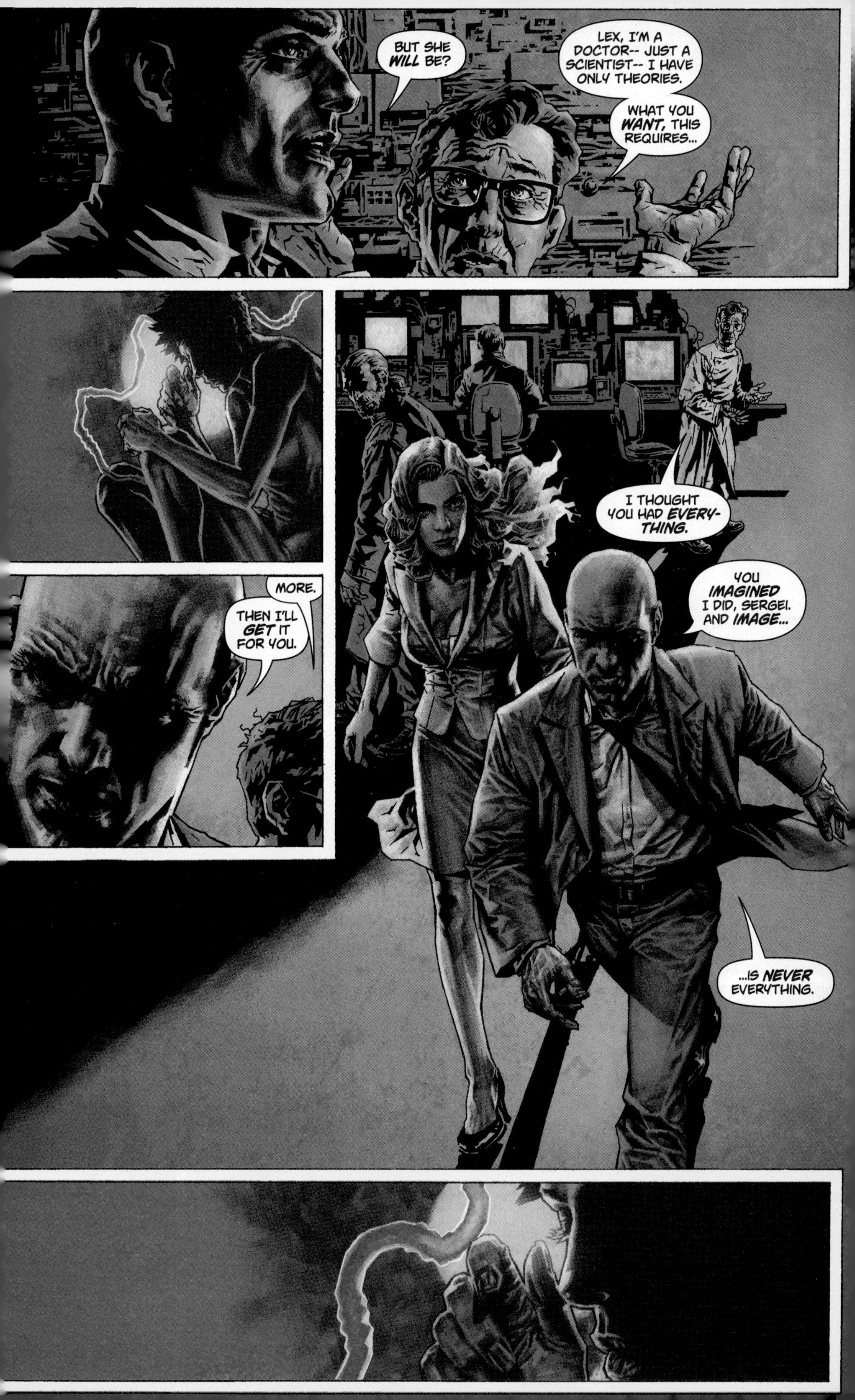
BUT SHE WILL BE?
LEX, I'M A DOCTOR-- JUST A SCIENTIST-- I HAVE ONLY THEORIES.
WHAT YOU WANT, THIS REQUIRES...
MORE.
THEN I'LL GET IT FOR YOU.
I THOUGHT YOU HAD EVERY-THING.
YOU IMAGINED I DID, SERGEI. AND IMAGE...
...IS NEVER EVERYTHING.

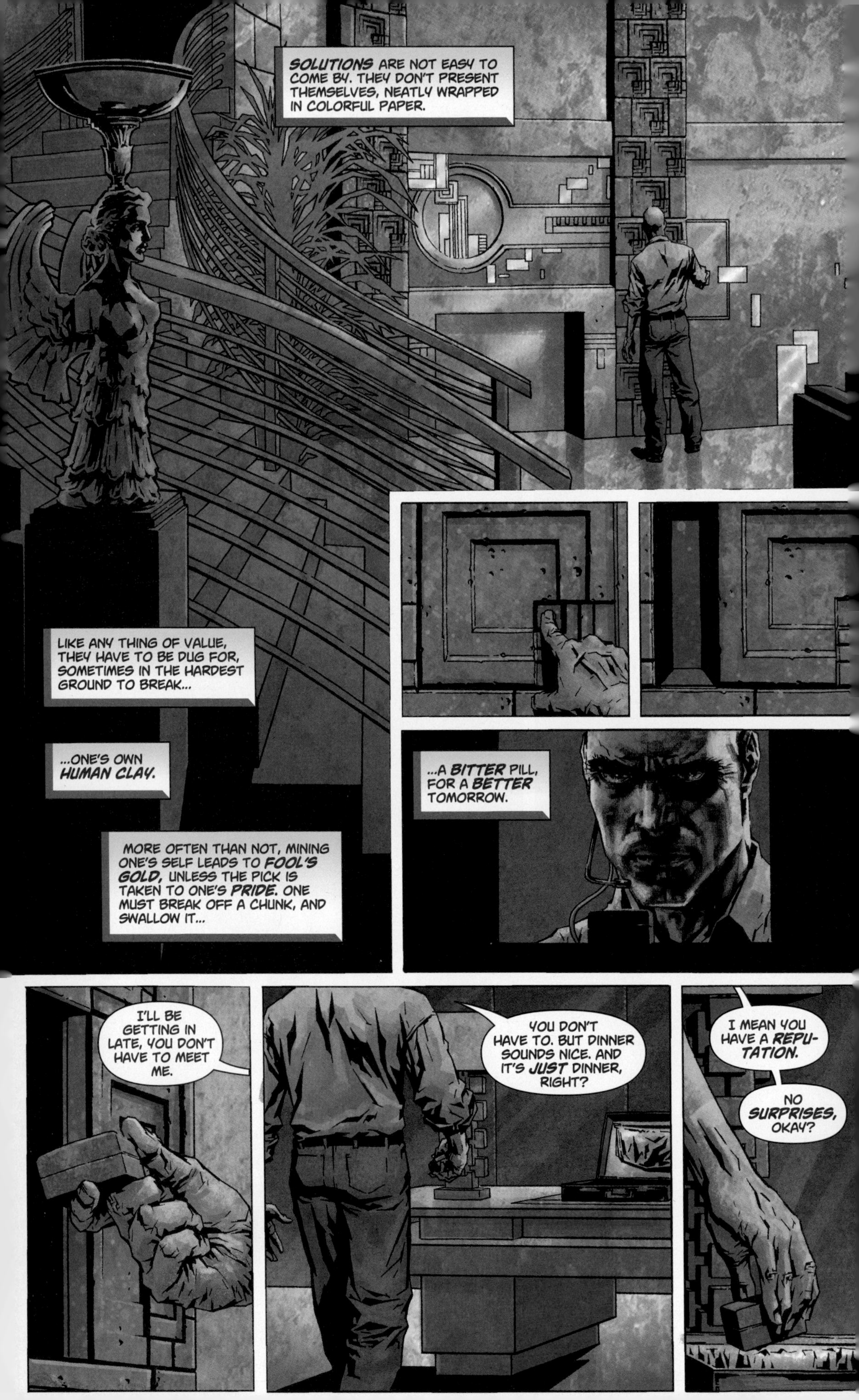
SOLUTIONS ARE NOT EASY TO COME BY. THEY DON'T PRESENT THEMSELVES, NEATLY WRAPPED IN COLORFUL PAPER.
LIKE ANY THING OF VALUE, THEY HAVE TO BE DUG FOR, SOMETIMES IN THE HARDEST GROUND TO BREAK...
...ONE'S OWN HUMAN CLAY.
MORE OFTEN THAN NOT, MINING ONE'S SELF LEADS TO FOOL'S GOLD, UNLESS THE PICK IS TAKEN TO ONE'S PRIDE. ONE MUST BREAK OFF A CHUNK, AND SWALLOW IT...
...A BITTER PILL, FOR A BETTER TOMORROW.
I'LL BE GETTING IN LATE, YOU DON'T HAVE TO MEET ME.
YOU DON'T HAVE TO. BUT DINNER SOUNDS NICE. AND IT'S JUST DINNER, RIGHT?
I MEAN YOU HAVE A REPUTATION.
NO SURPRISES, OKAY?

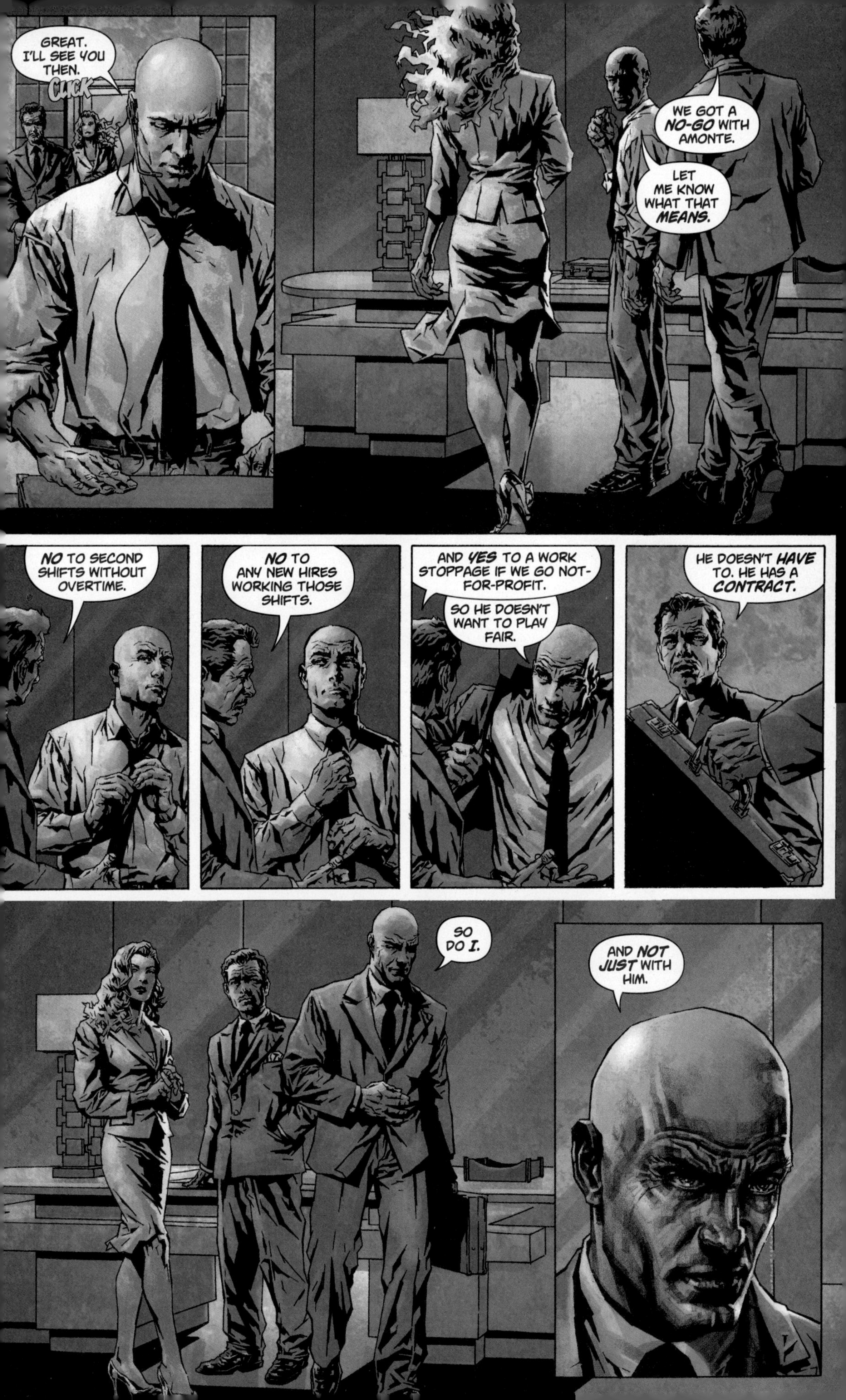
GREAT. I'LL SEE YOU THEN.
CLICK
WE GOT A NO-GO WITH AMONTE.
LET ME KNOW WHAT THAT MEANS.
NO TO SECOND SHIFTS WITHOUT OVERTIME.
NO TO ANY NEW HIRES WORKING THOSE SHIFTS.
AND YES TO A WORK STOPPAGE IF WE GO NOT-FOR-PROFIT.
SO HE DOESN'T WANT TO PLAY FAIR.
HE DOESN'T HAVE TO. HE HAS A CONTRACT.
SO DO I.
AND NOT JUST WITH HIM.

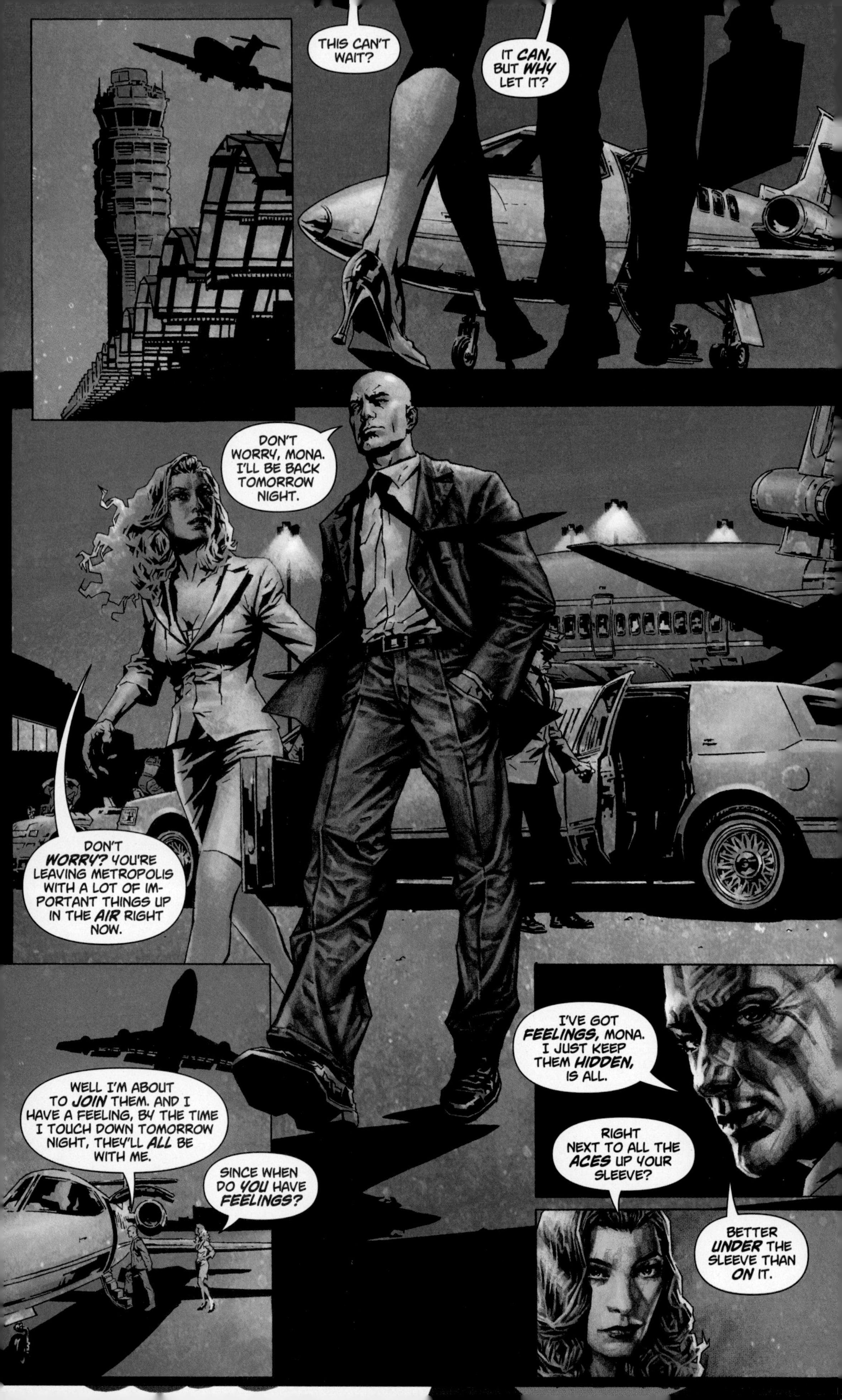
THIS CAN'T WAIT?
IT CAN, BUT WHY LET IT?
DON'T WORRY, MONA. I'LL BE BACK TOMORROW NIGHT.
DON'T WORRY? YOU'RE LEAVING METROPOLIS WITH A LOT OF IMPORTANT THINGS UP IN THE AIR RIGHT NOW.
WELL I'M ABOUT TO JOIN THEM. AND I HAVE A FEELING, BY THE TIME I TOUCH DOWN TOMORROW NIGHT, THEY'LL ALL BE WITH ME.
SINCE WHEN DO YOU HAVE FEELINGS?
I'VE GOT FEELINGS, MONA. I JUST KEEP THEM HIDDEN, IS ALL.
RIGHT NEXT TO ALL THE ACES UP YOUR SLEEVE?
BETTER UNDER THE SLEEVE THAN ON IT.

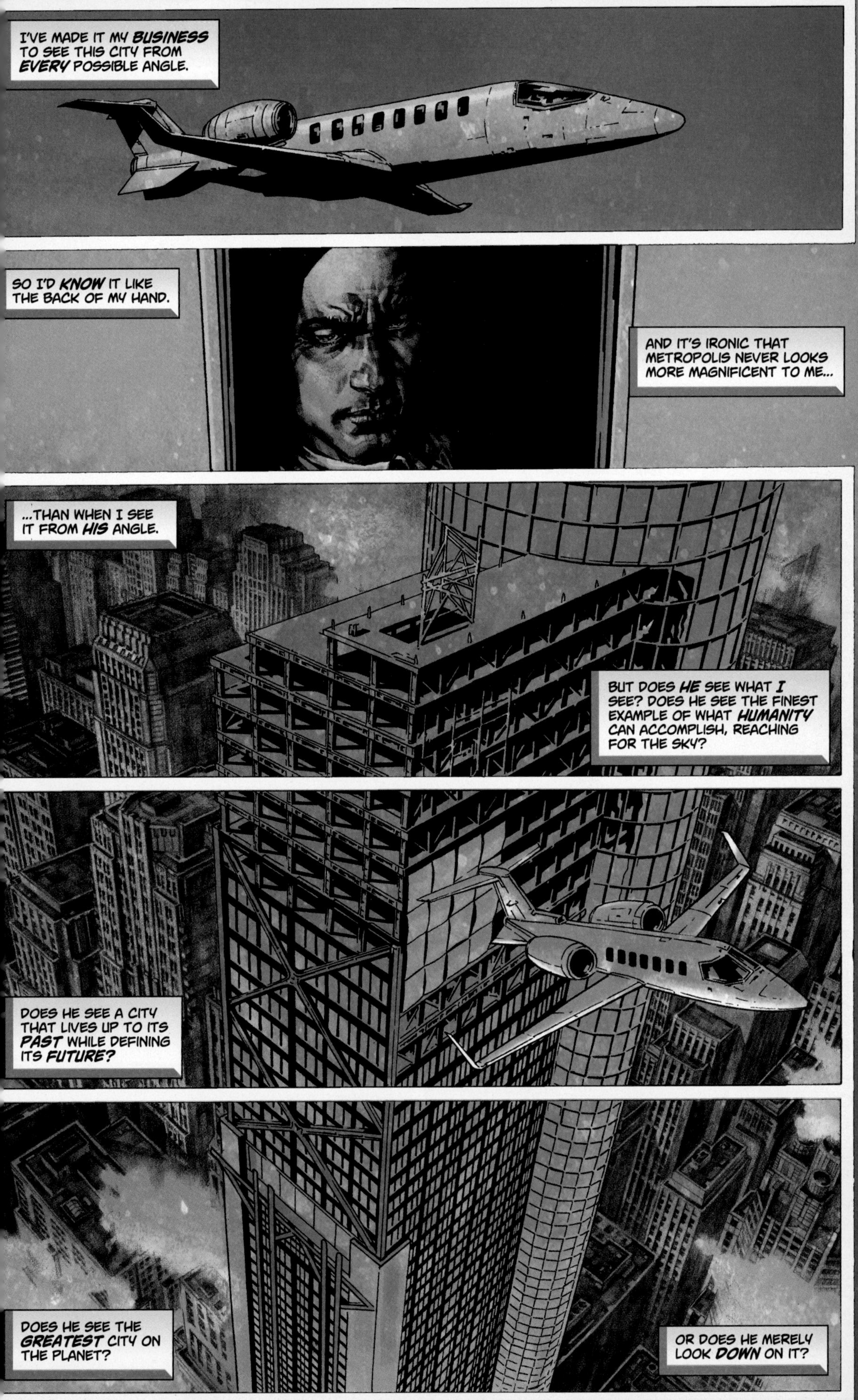
I'VE MADE IT MY BUSINESS TO SEE THIS CITY FROM EVERY POSSIBLE ANGLE.
SO I'D KNOW IT LIKE THE BACK OF MY HAND.
AND IT'S IRONIC THAT METROPOLIS NEVER LOOKS MORE MAGNIFICENT TO ME...
...THAN WHEN I SEE IT FROM HIS ANGLE.
BUT DOES HE SEE WHAT I SEE? DOES HE SEE THE FINEST EXAMPLE OF WHAT HUMANITY CAN ACCOMPLISH, REACHING FOR THE SKY?
DOES HE SEE A CITY THAT LIVES UP TO ITS PAST WHILE DEFINING ITS FUTURE?
DOES HE SEE THE GREATEST CITY ON THE PLANET?
OR DOES HE MERELY LOOK DOWN ON IT?

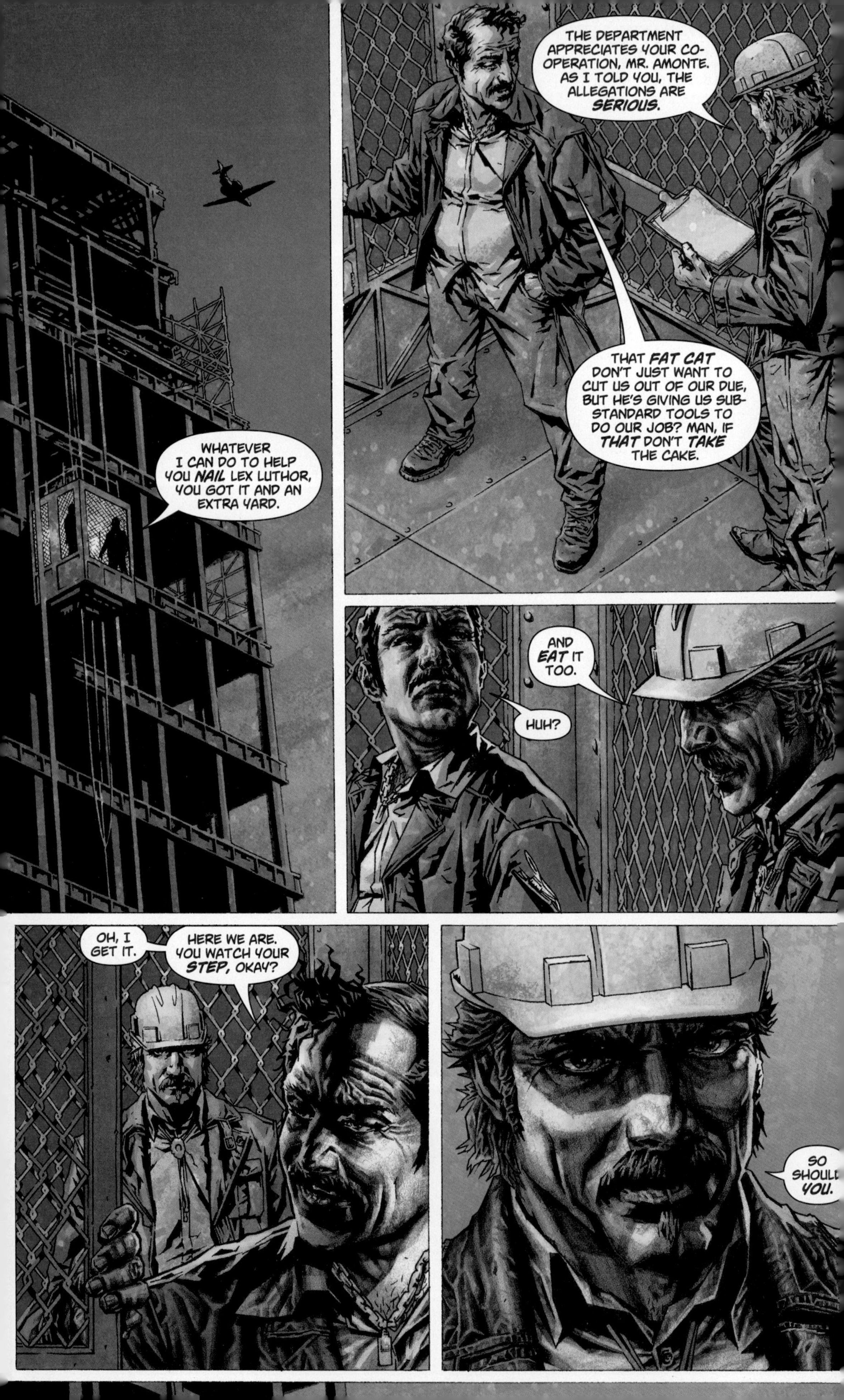
THE DEPARTMENT APPRECIATES YOUR CO-OPERATION, MR. AMONTE. AS I TOLD YOU, THE ALLEGATIONS ARE SERIOUS.
THAT FAT CAT DON'T JUST WANT TO CUT US OUT OF OUR DUE, BUT HE'S GIVING US SUB-STANDARD TOOLS TO DO OUR JOB? MAN, IF THAT DON'T TAKE THE CAKE.
WHATEVER I CAN DO TO HELP YOU NAIL LEX LUTHOR, YOU GOT IT AND AN EXTRA YARD.
AND EAT IT TOO.
HUH?
OH, I GET IT.
HERE WE ARE. YOU WATCH YOUR STEP, OKAY?
SO SHOULD YOU.

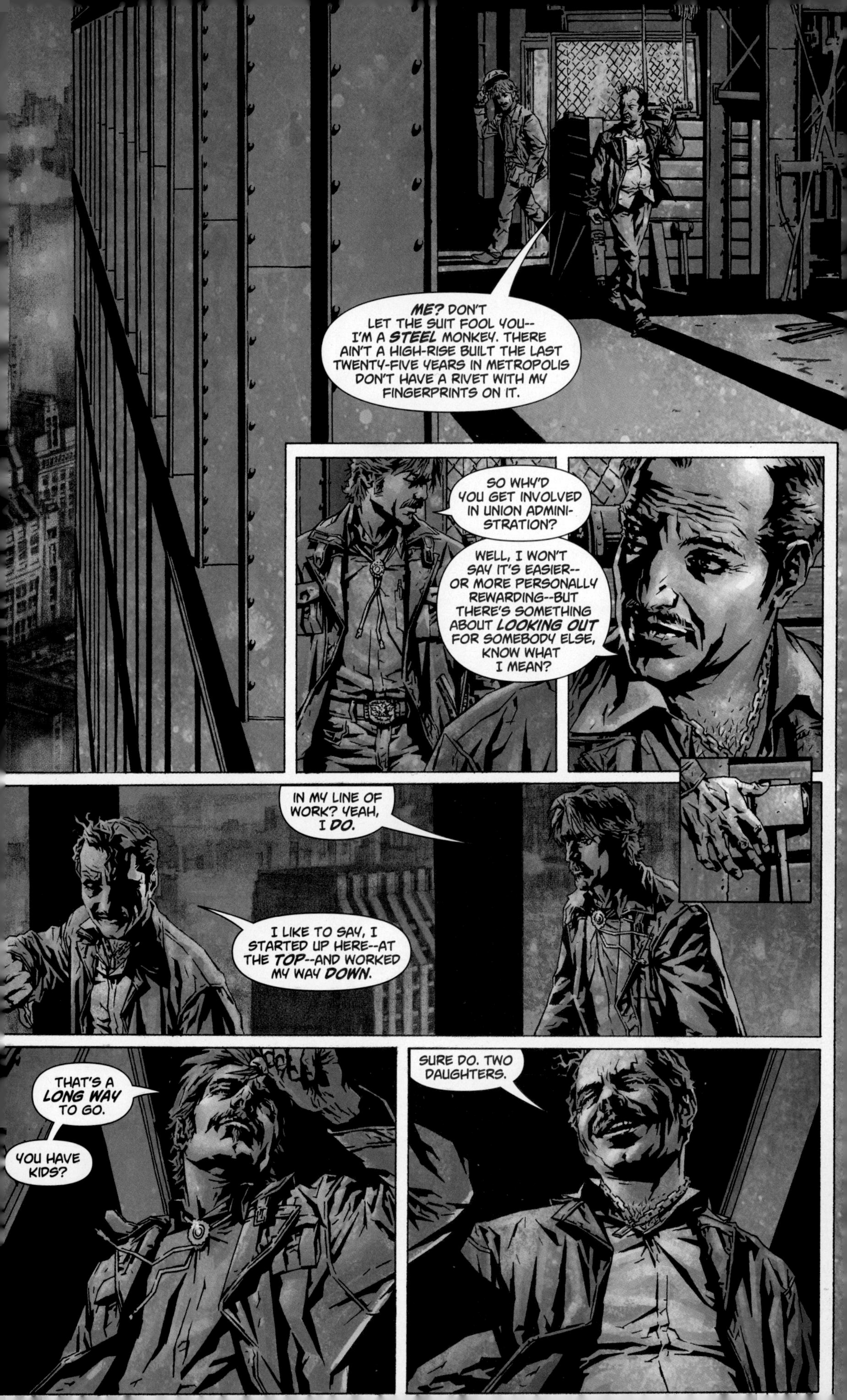
ME? DON'T LET THE SUIT FOOL YOU-- I'M A STEEL MONKEY. THERE AIN'T A HIGH-RISE BUILT THE LAST TWENTY-FIVE YEARS IN METROPOLIS DON'T HAVE A RIVET WITH MY FINGERPRINTS ON IT.
SO WHY'D YOU GET INVOLVED IN UNION ADMINI-STRATION?
WELL, I WON'T SAY IT'S EASIER-- OR MORE PERSONALLY REWARDING--BUT THERE'S SOMETHING ABOUT LOOKING OUT FOR SOMEBODY ELSE, KNOW WHAT I MEAN?
IN MY LINE OF WORK? YEAH, I DO.
I LIKE TO SAY, I STARTED UP HERE--AT THE TOP--AND WORKED MY WAY DOWN.
THAT'S A LONG WAY TO GO.
YOU HAVE KIDS?
SURE DO. TWO DAUGHTERS.

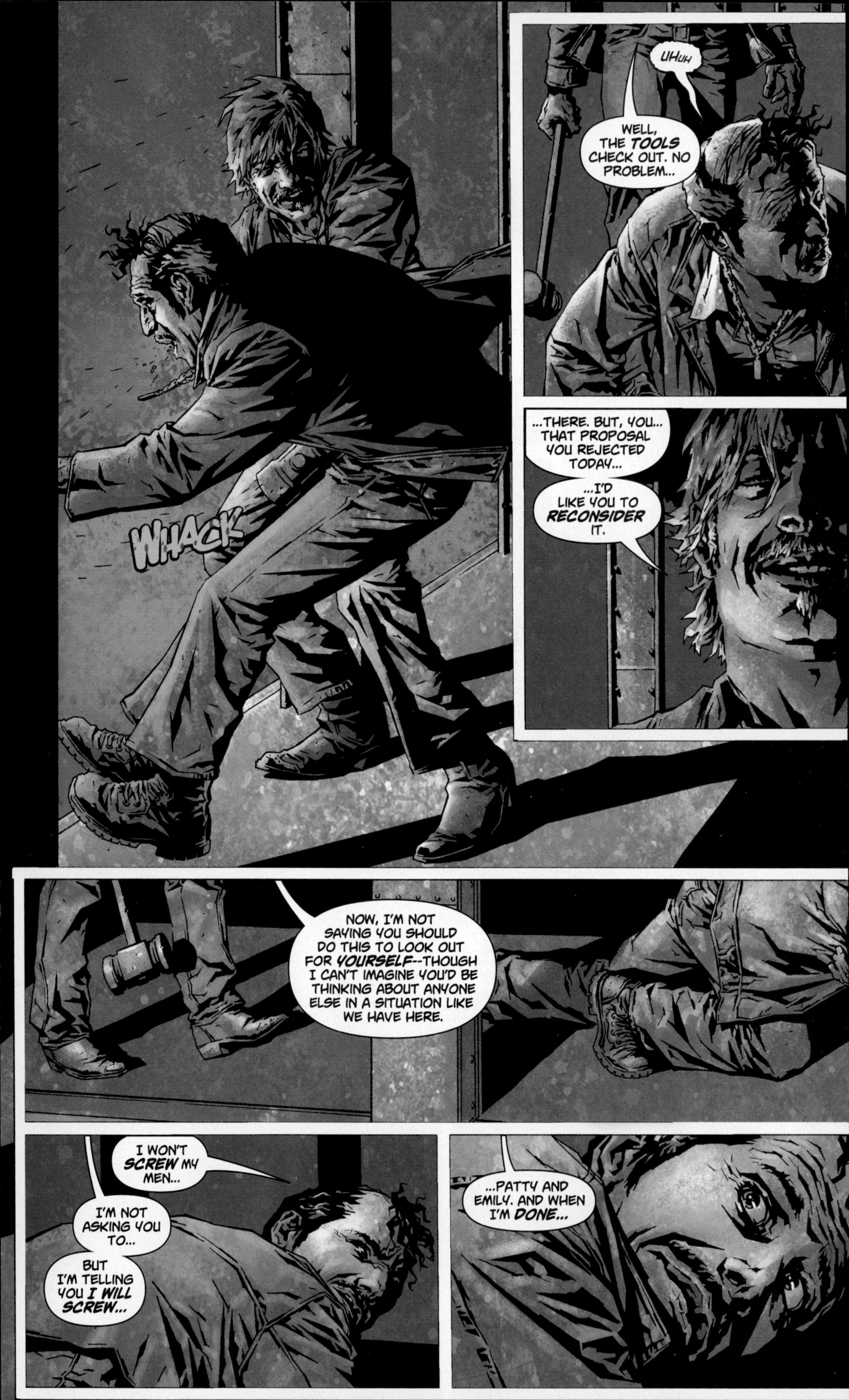
WHACK
UHuh
WELL, THE TOOLS CHECK OUT. NO PROBLEM...
...THERE. BUT, YOU... THAT PROPOSAL YOU REJECTED TODAY...
...I'D LIKE YOU TO RECONSIDER IT.
NOW, I'M NOT SAYING YOU SHOULD DO THIS TO LOOK OUT FOR YOURSELF--THOUGH I CAN'T IMAGINE YOU'D BE THINKING ABOUT ANYONE ELSE IN A SITUATION LIKE WE HAVE HERE.
I WON'T SCREW MY MEN...
I'M NOT ASKING YOU TO...
BUT I'M TELLING YOU I WILL SCREW...
...PATTY AND EMILY. AND WHEN I'M DONE...

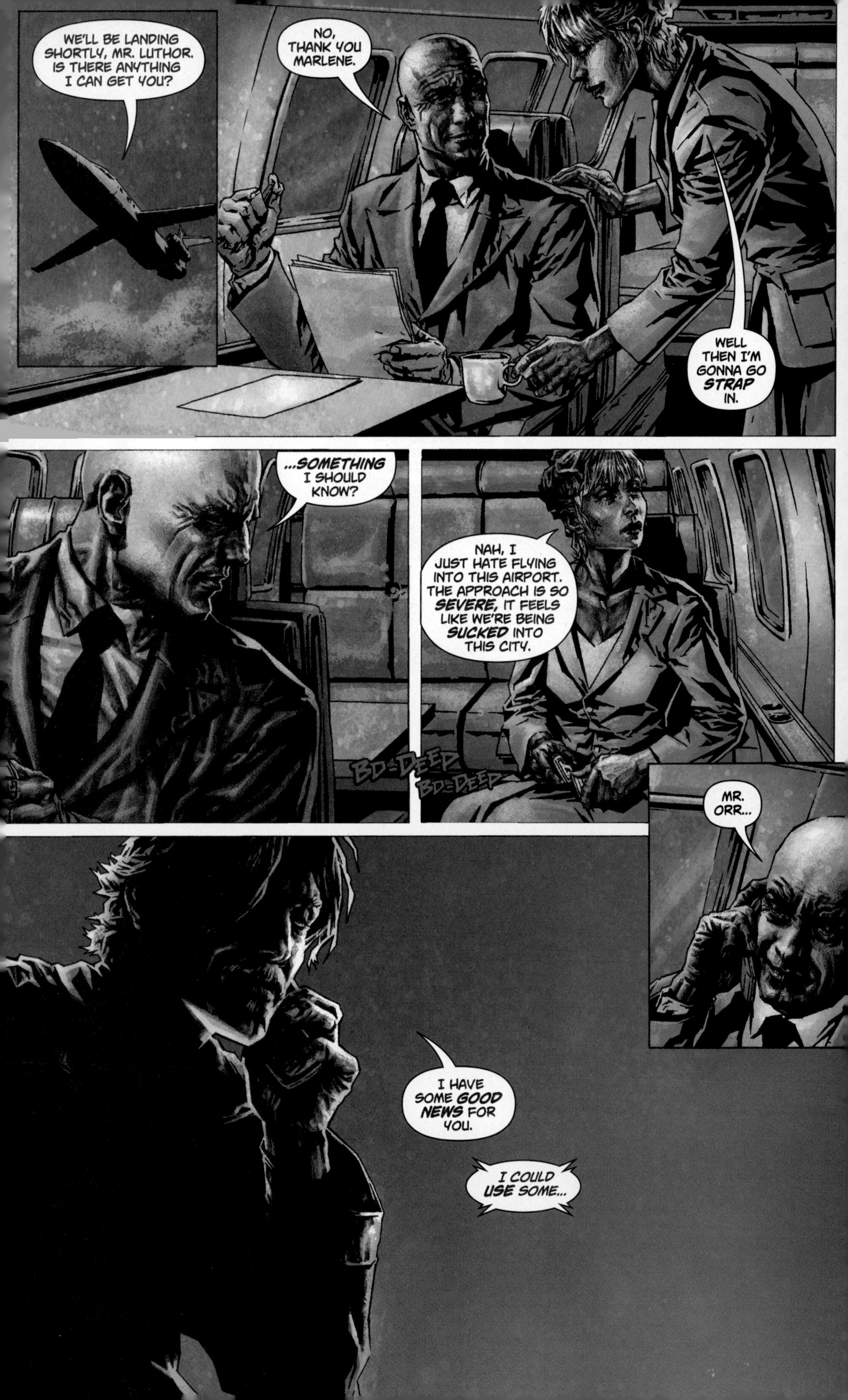
WE'LL BE LANDING SHORTLY, MR. LUTHOR. IS THERE ANYTHING I CAN GET YOU?
NO, THANK YOU MARLENE.
WELL THEN I'M GONNA GO STRAP IN.
...SOMETHING I SHOULD KNOW?
NAH, I JUST HATE FLYING INTO THIS AIRPORT. THE APPROACH IS SO SEVERE, IT FEELS LIKE WE'RE BEING SUCKED INTO THIS CITY.
BD-DEEP BD-DEEP
MR. ORR...
I HAVE SOME GOOD NEWS FOR YOU.
I COULD USE SOME...

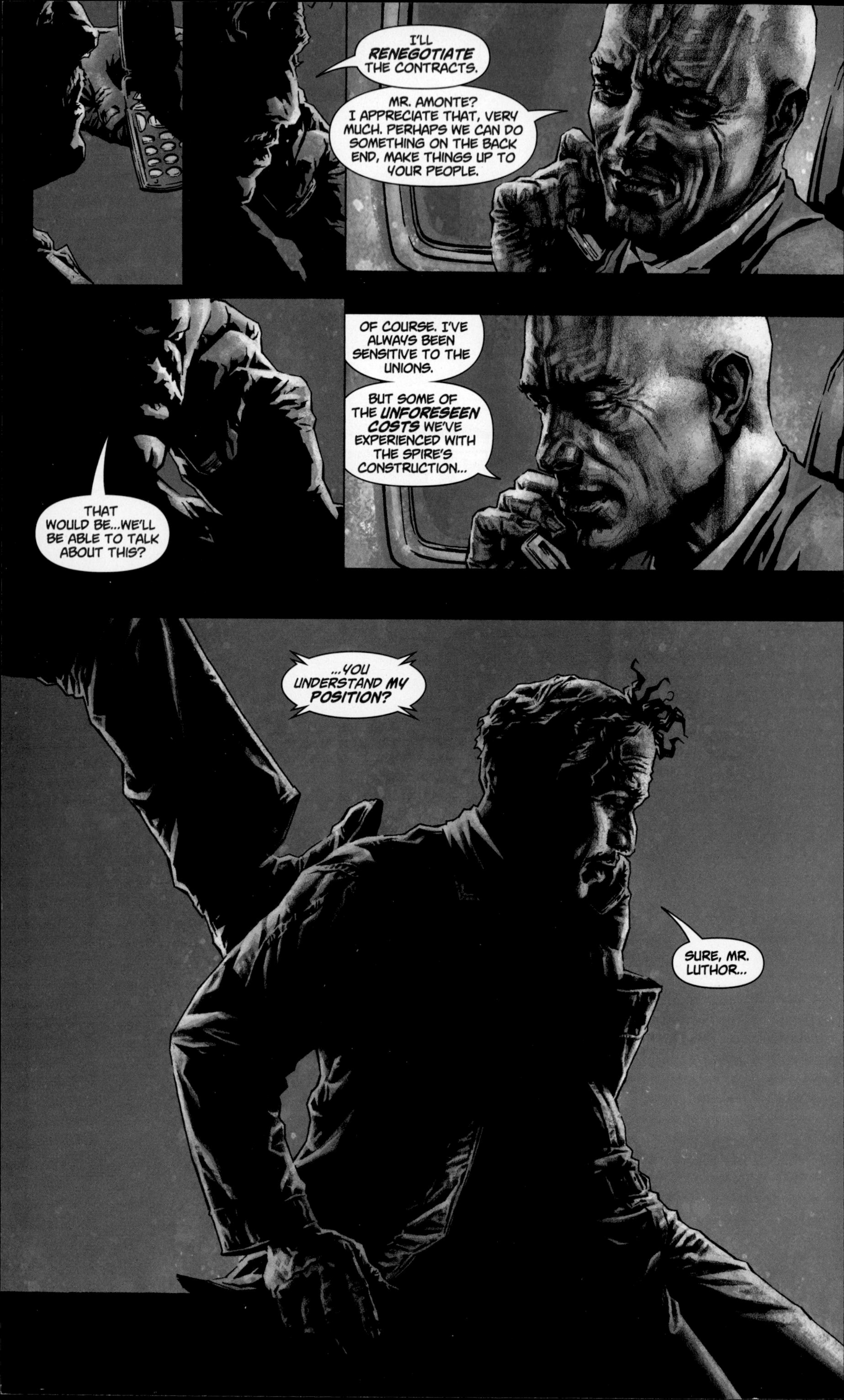
I'LL **RENEGOTIATE** THE CONTRACTS.
MR. AMONTE? I APPRECIATE THAT, VERY MUCH. PERHAPS WE CAN DO SOMETHING ON THE BACK END, MAKE THINGS UP TO YOUR PEOPLE.
THAT WOULD BE...WE'LL BE ABLE TO TALK ABOUT THIS?
OF COURSE. I'VE ALWAYS BEEN SENSITIVE TO THE UNIONS.
BUT SOME OF THE **UNFORESEEN COSTS** WE'VE EXPERIENCED WITH THE SPIRE'S CONSTRUCTION...
...YOU UNDERSTAND **MY POSITION?**
SURE, MR. LUTHOR...

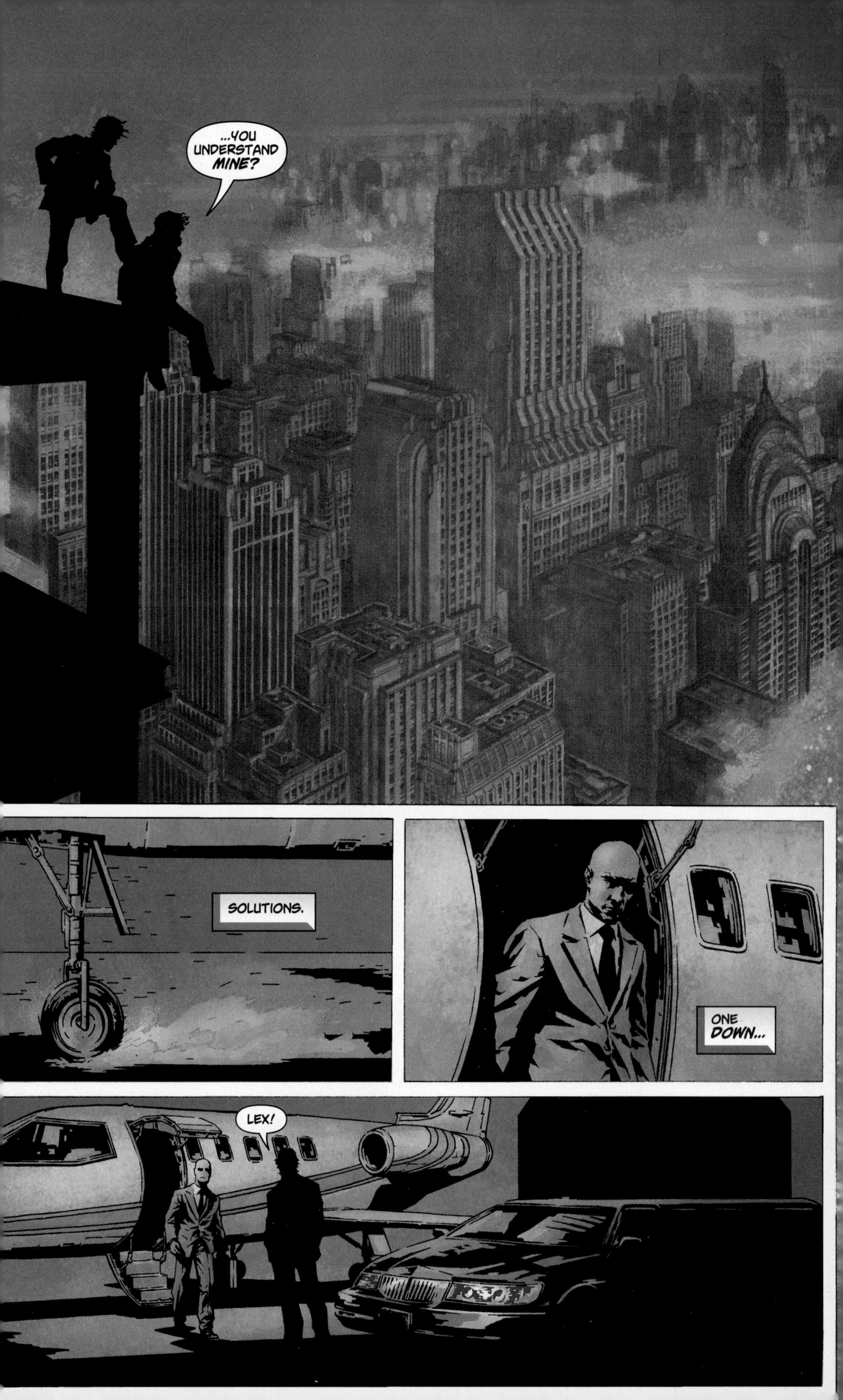
...YOU UNDERSTAND MINE?
SOLUTIONS.
ONE DOWN...
LEX!

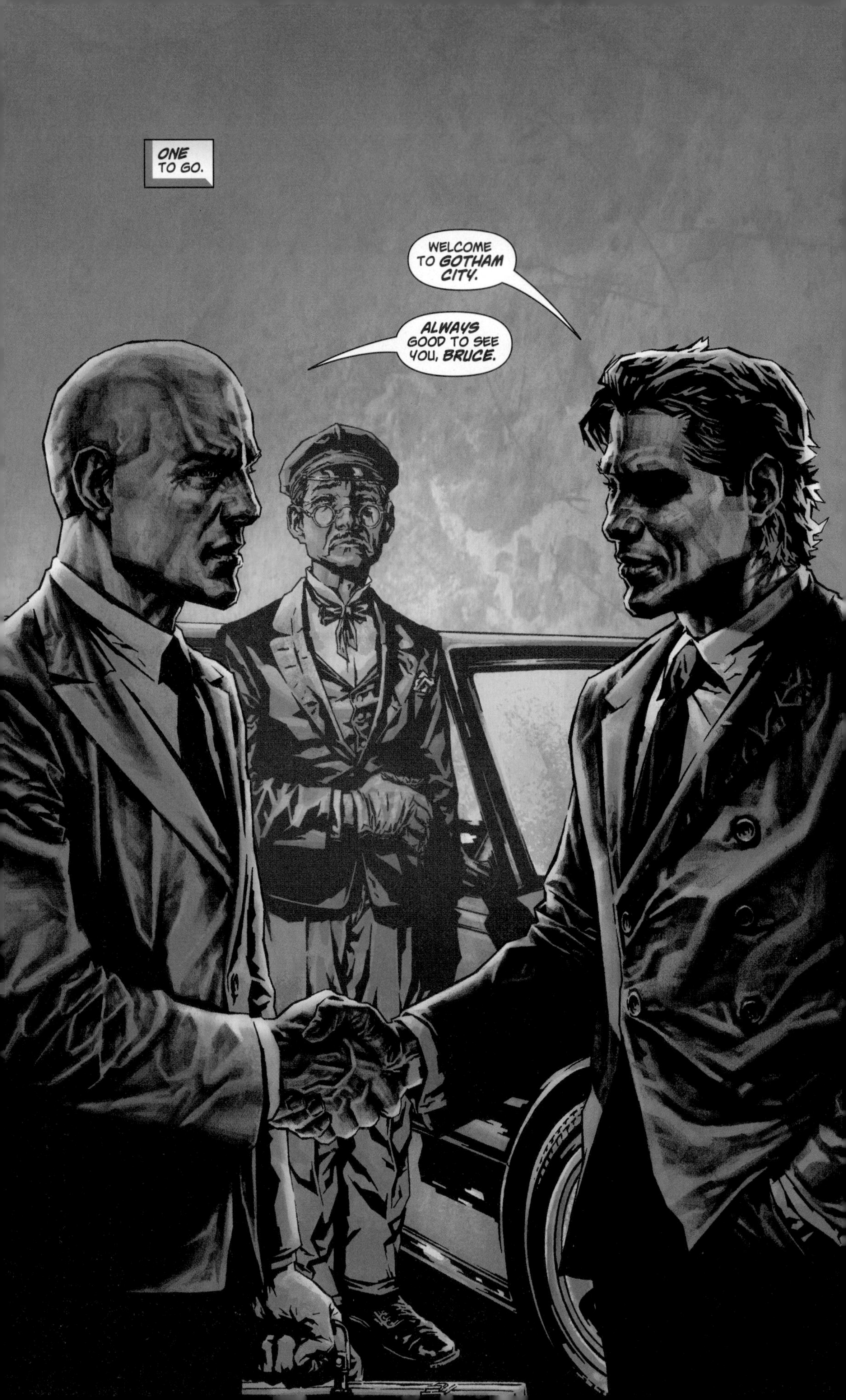
ONE TO GO.
WELCOME TO GOTHAM CITY.
ALWAYS GOOD TO SEE YOU, BRUCE.

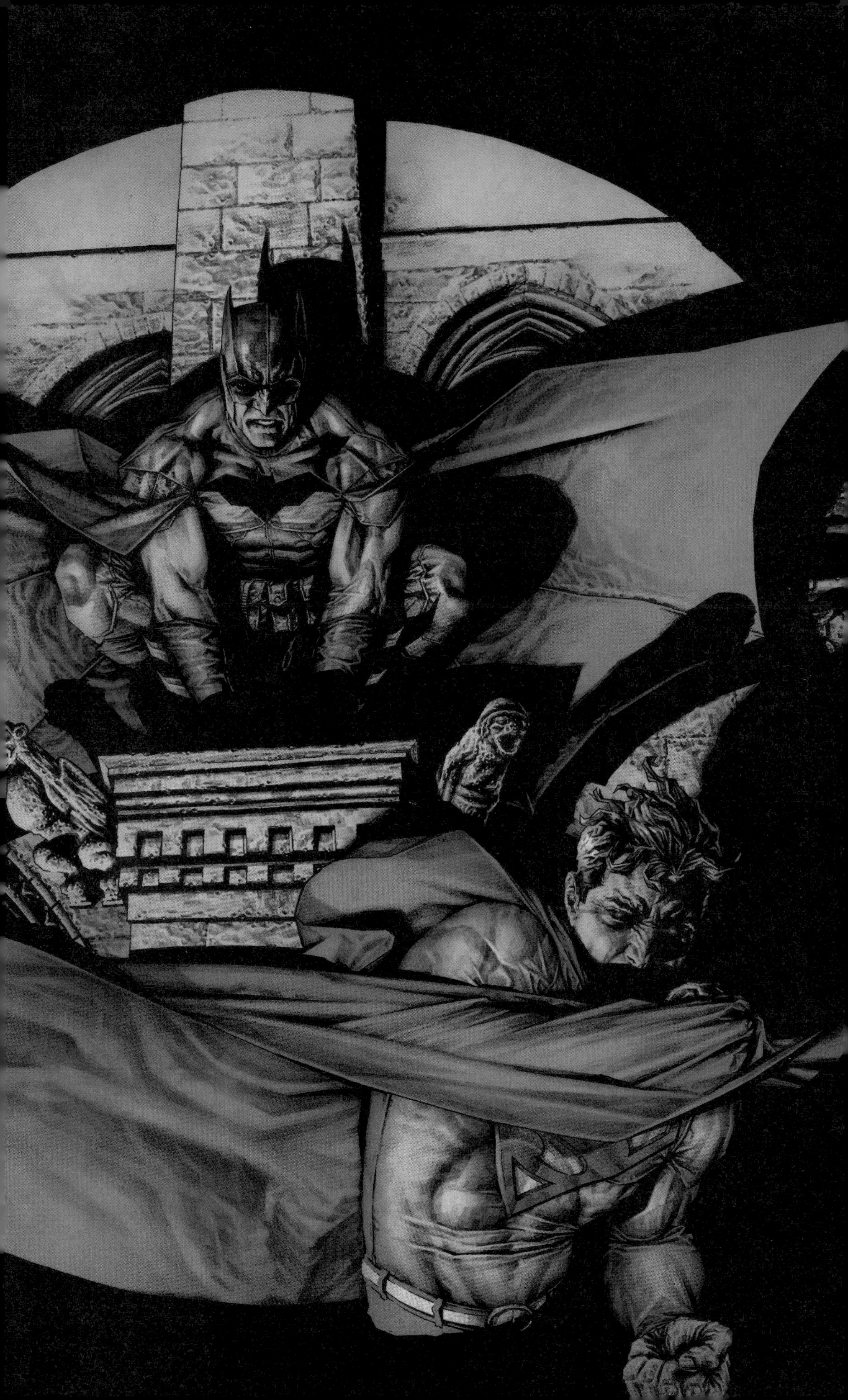

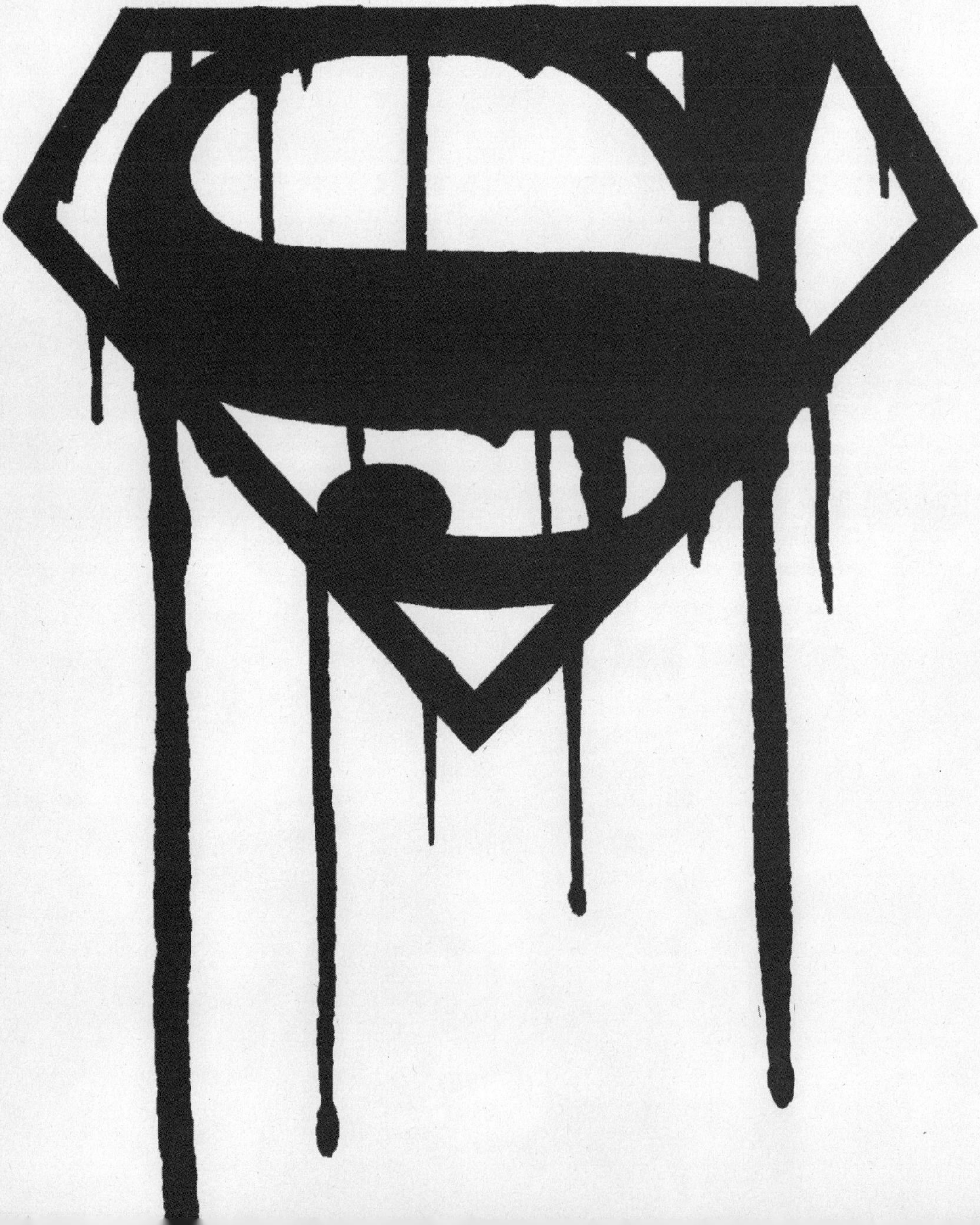

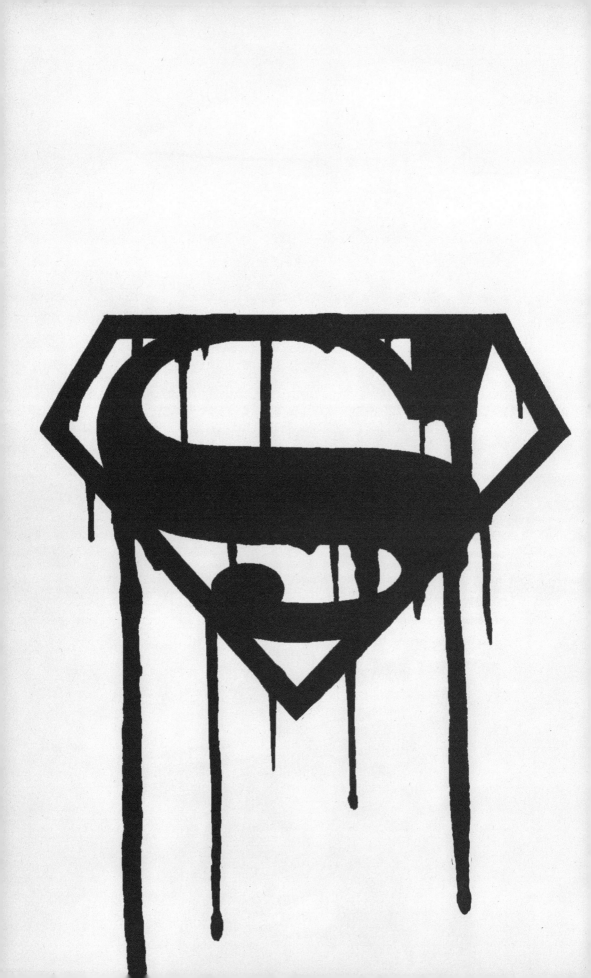

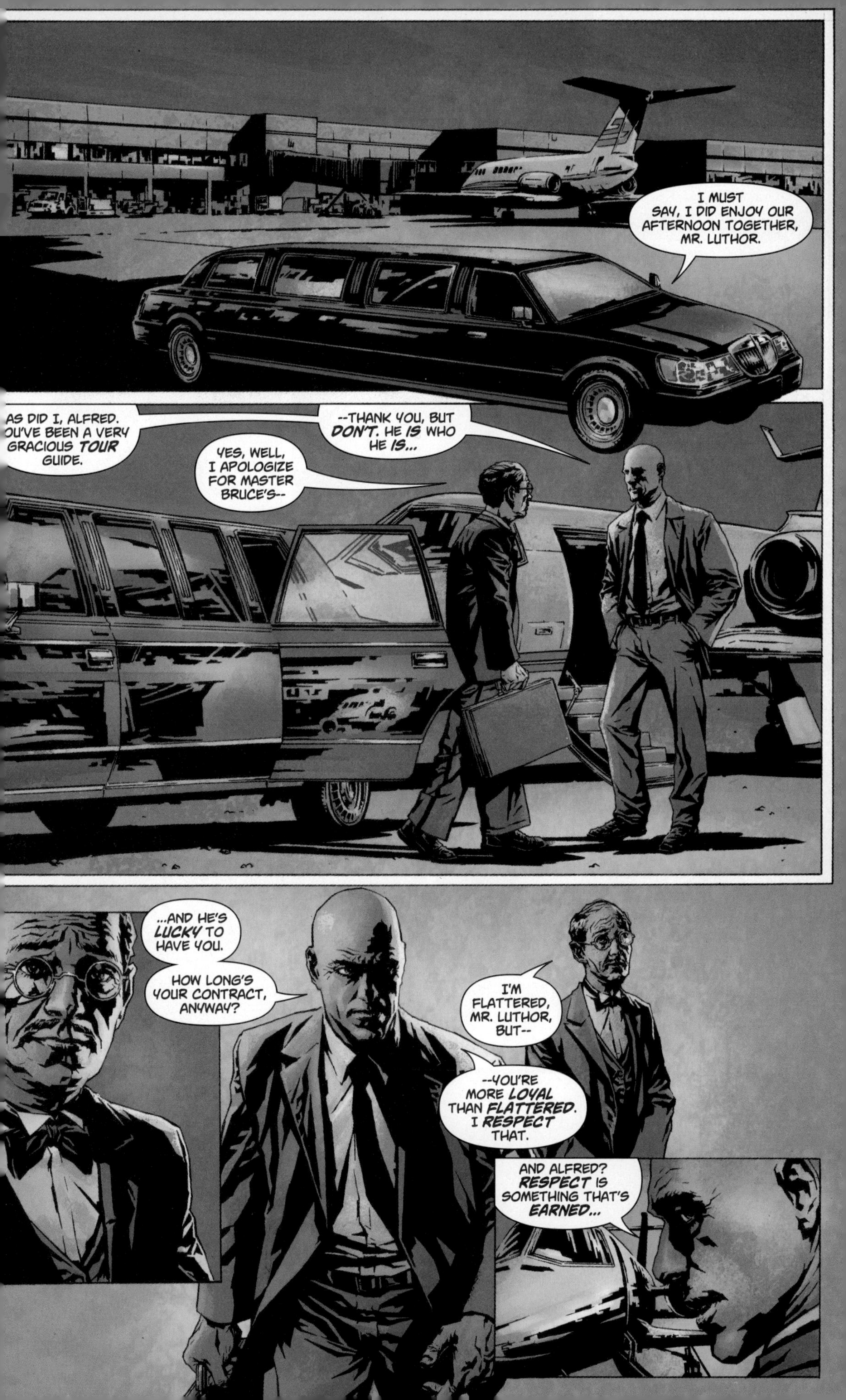
I MUST SAY, I DID ENJOY OUR AFTERNOON TOGETHER, MR. LUTHOR.
AS DID I, ALFRED. YOU'VE BEEN A VERY GRACIOUS TOUR GUIDE.
YES, WELL, I APOLOGIZE FOR MASTER BRUCE'S--
--THANK YOU, BUT DON'T. HE IS WHO HE IS...
...AND HE'S LUCKY TO HAVE YOU.
HOW LONG'S YOUR CONTRACT, ANYWAY?
I'M FLATTERED, MR. LUTHOR, BUT--
--YOU'RE MORE LOYAL THAN FLATTERED. I RESPECT THAT.
AND ALFRED? RESPECT IS SOMETHING THAT'S EARNED...

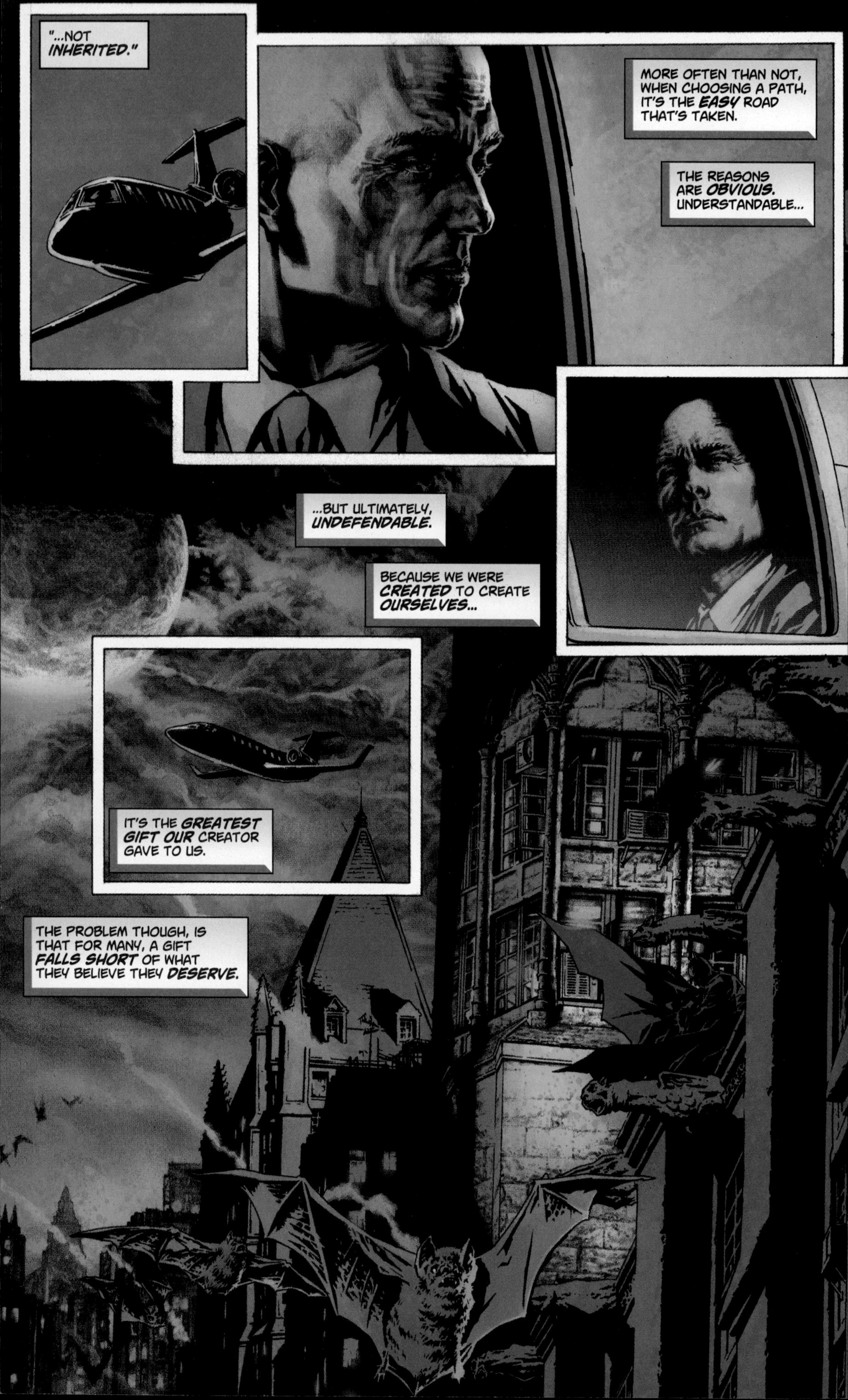

"...NOT INHERITED."
MORE OFTEN THAN NOT, WHEN CHOOSING A PATH, IT'S THE EASY ROAD THAT'S TAKEN.
THE REASONS ARE OBVIOUS. UNDERSTANDABLE...
...BUT ULTIMATELY, UNDEFENDABLE.
BECAUSE WE WERE CREATED TO CREATE OURSELVES...
IT'S THE GREATEST GIFT OUR CREATOR GAVE TO US.
THE PROBLEM THOUGH, IS THAT FOR MANY, A GIFT FALLS SHORT OF WHAT THEY BELIEVE THEY DESERVE.

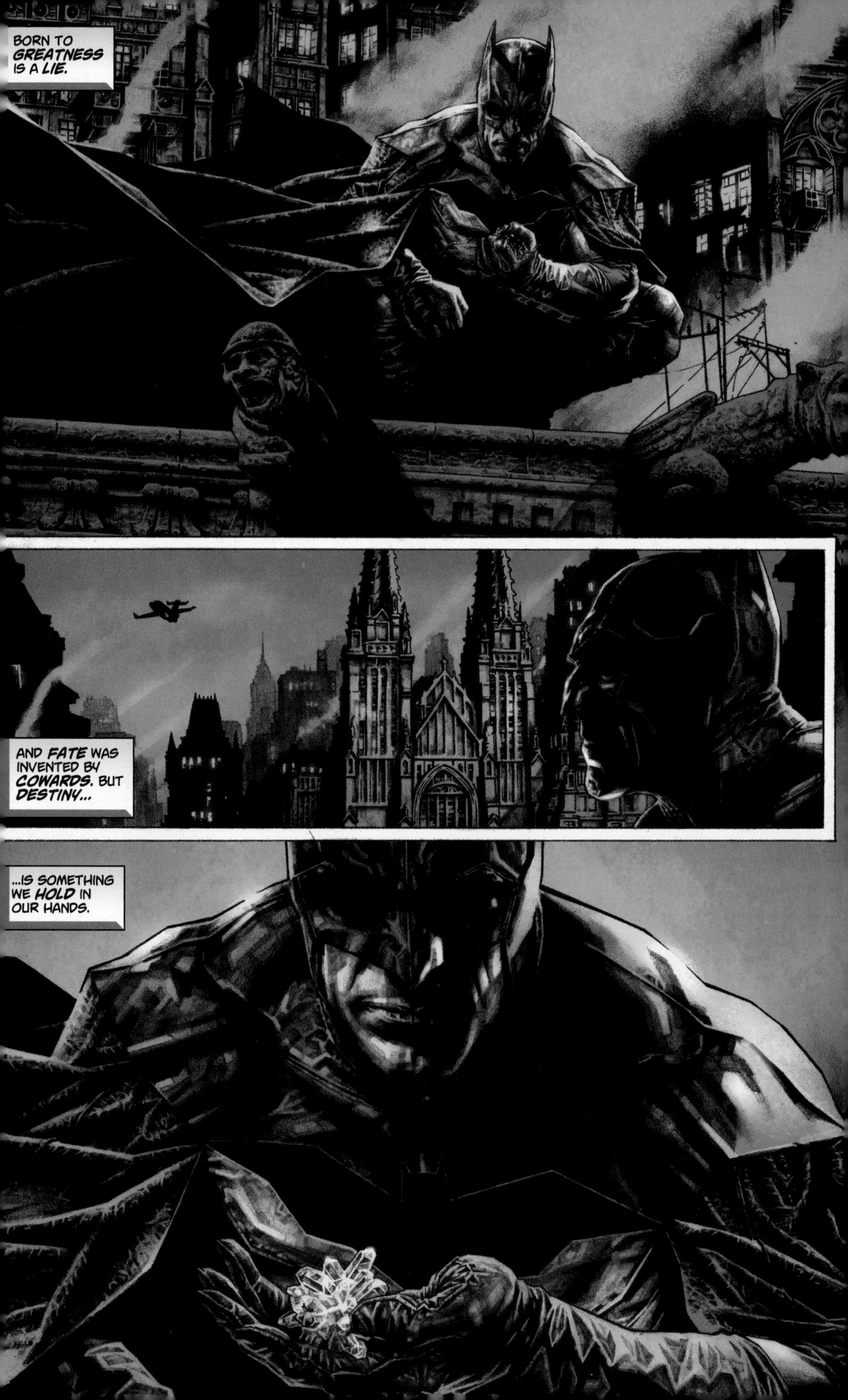
BORN TO GREATNESS IS A LIE.
AND FATE WAS INVENTED BY COWARDS. BUT DESTINY...
...IS SOMETHING WE HOLD IN OUR HANDS.

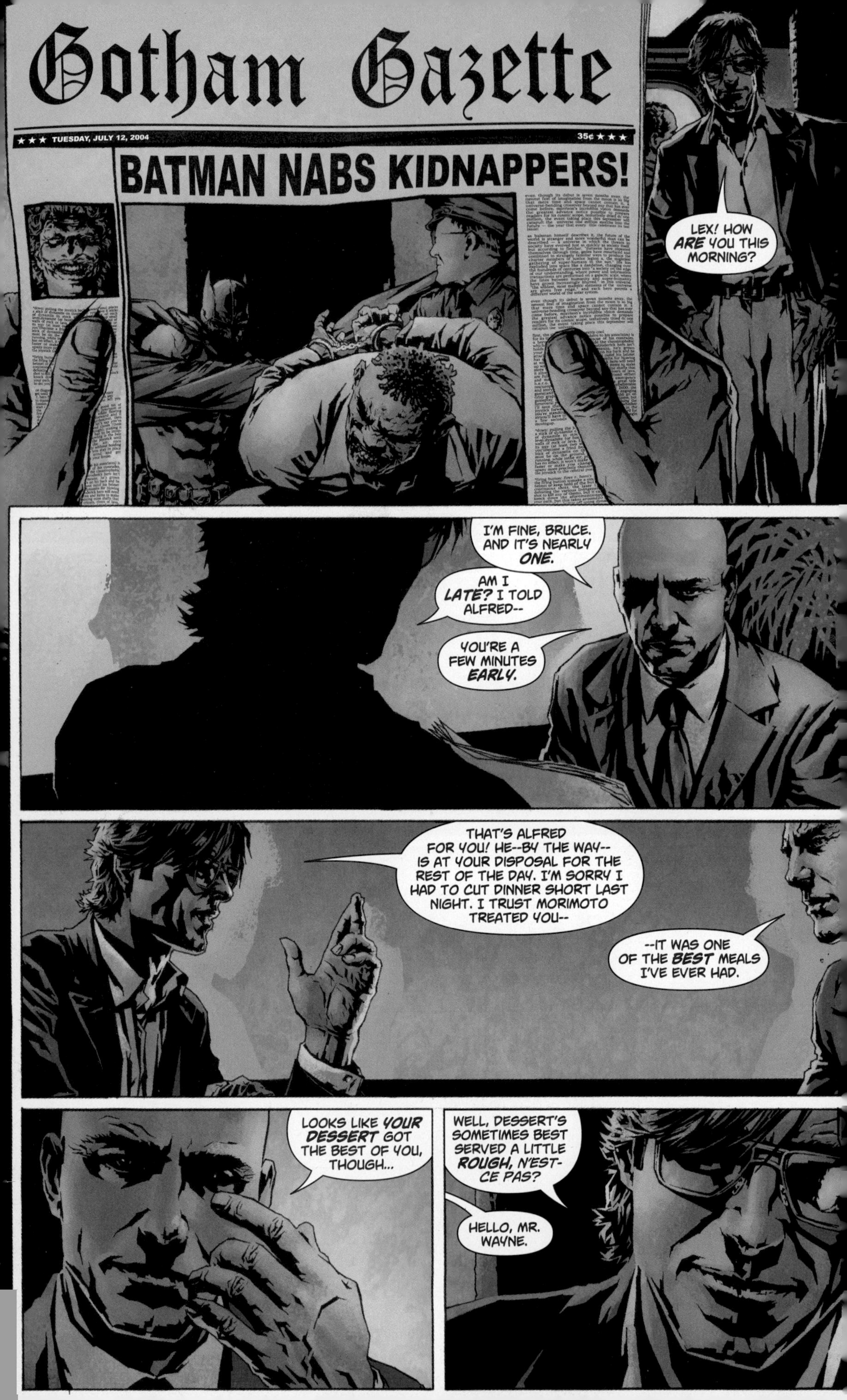
Gotham Gazette
TUESDAY, JULY 12, 2004
35¢
BATMAN NABS KIDNAPPERS!
LEX! HOW ARE YOU THIS MORNING?
I'M FINE, BRUCE. AND IT'S NEARLY ONE.
AM I LATE? I TOLD ALFRED--
YOU'RE A FEW MINUTES EARLY.
THAT'S ALFRED FOR YOU! HE--BY THE WAY--IS AT YOUR DISPOSAL FOR THE REST OF THE DAY. I'M SORRY I HAD TO CUT DINNER SHORT LAST NIGHT. I TRUST MORIMOTO TREATED YOU--
--IT WAS ONE OF THE BEST MEALS I'VE EVER HAD.
LOOKS LIKE YOUR DESSERT GOT THE BEST OF YOU, THOUGH...
WELL, DESSERT'S SOMETIMES BEST SERVED A LITTLE ROUGH, N'EST-CE PAS?
HELLO, MR. WAYNE.

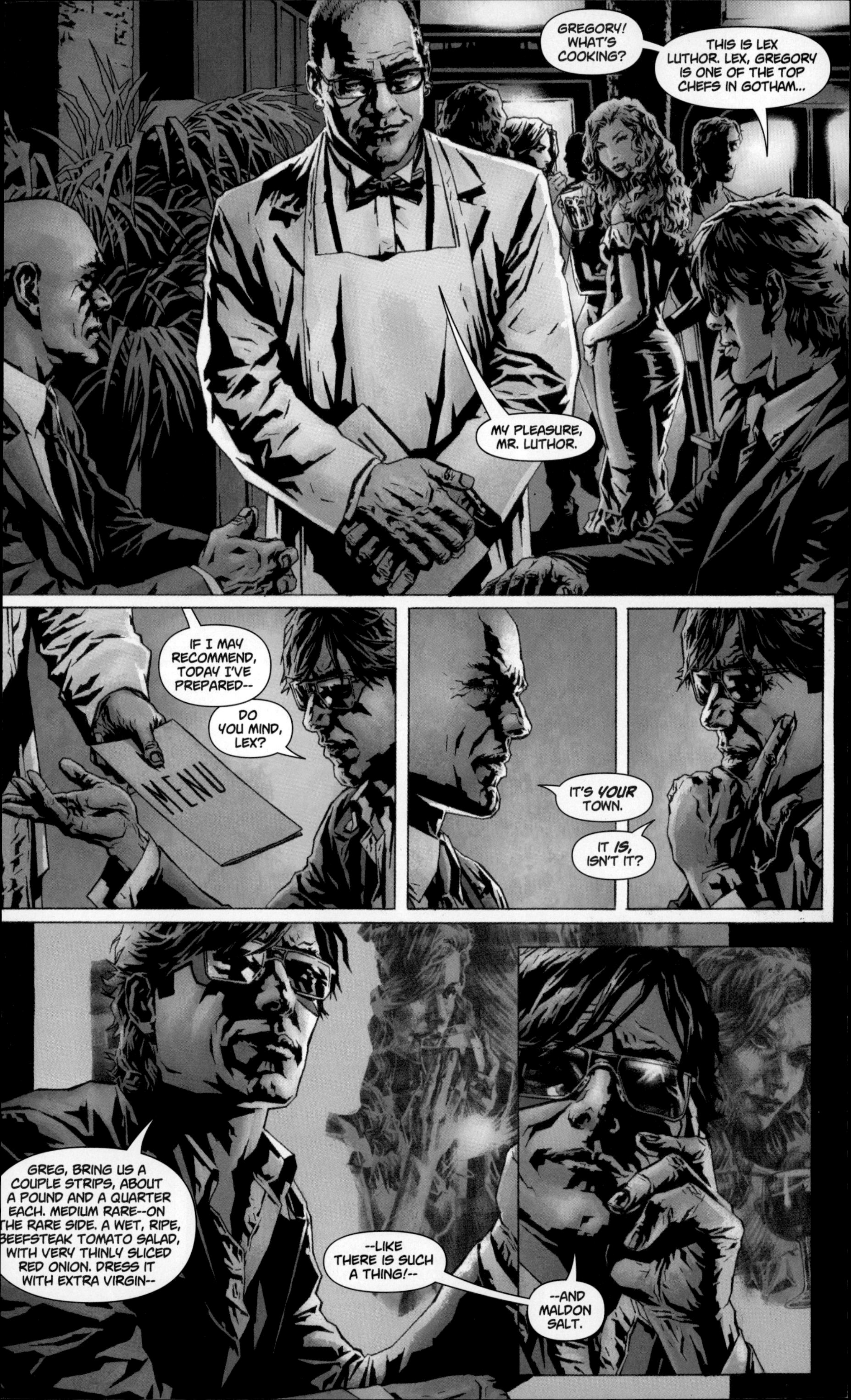
GREGORY! WHAT'S COOKING?
THIS IS LEX LUTHOR. LEX, GREGORY IS ONE OF THE TOP CHEFS IN GOTHAM...
MY PLEASURE, MR. LUTHOR.
IF I MAY RECOMMEND, TODAY I'VE PREPARED--
DO YOU MIND, LEX?
MENU
IT'S YOUR TOWN.
IT IS, ISN'T IT?
GREG, BRING US A COUPLE STRIPS, ABOUT A POUND AND A QUARTER EACH. MEDIUM RARE--ON THE RARE SIDE. A WET, RIPE, BEEFSTEAK TOMATO SALAD, WITH VERY THINLY SLICED RED ONION. DRESS IT WITH EXTRA VIRGIN--
--LIKE THERE IS SUCH A THING!--
--AND MALDON SALT.

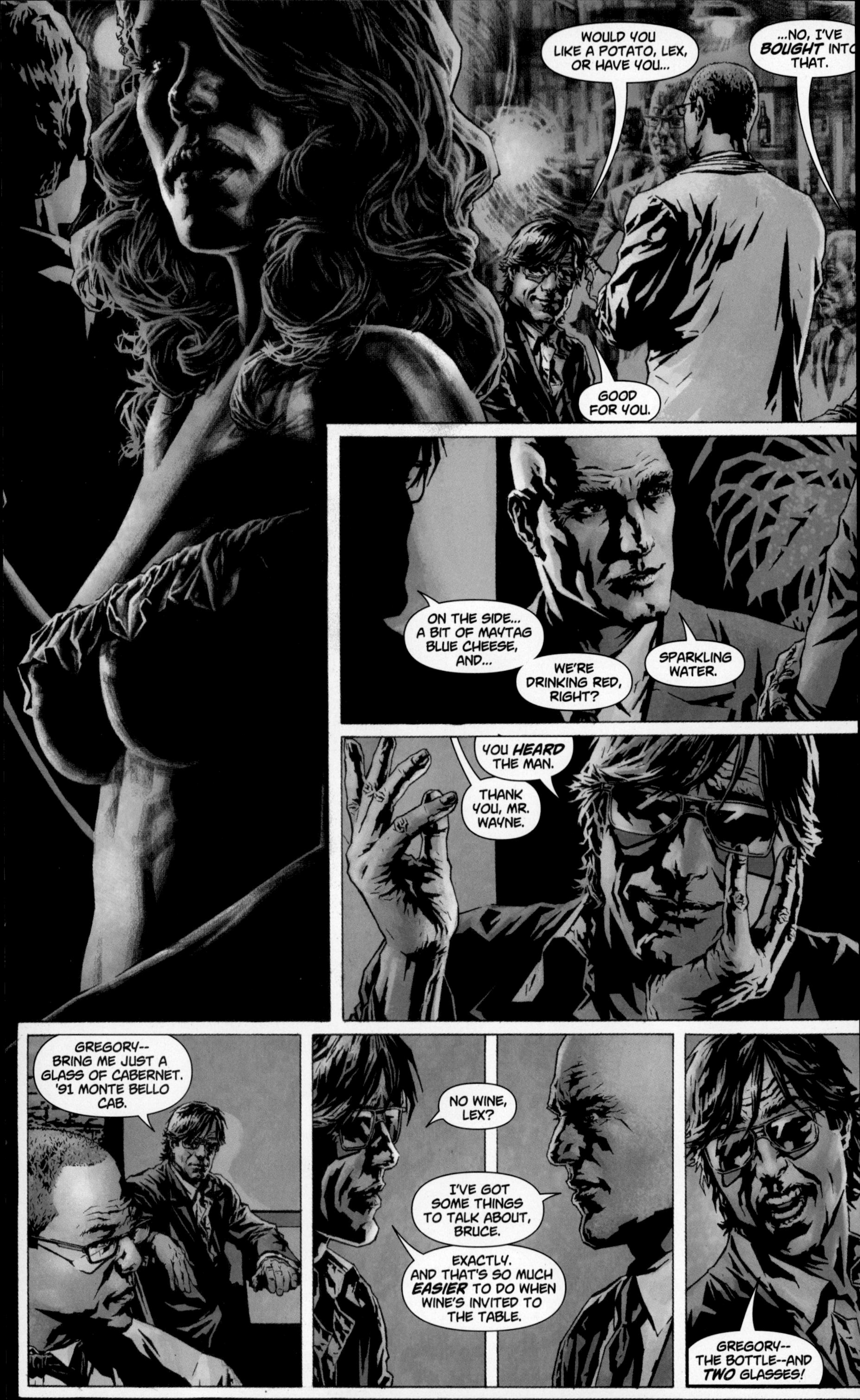
WOULD YOU LIKE A POTATO, LEX, OR HAVE YOU...
...NO, I'VE BOUGHT INTO THAT.
GOOD FOR YOU.
ON THE SIDE... A BIT OF MAYTAG BLUE CHEESE, AND...
WE'RE DRINKING RED, RIGHT?
SPARKLING WATER.
YOU HEARD THE MAN.
THANK YOU, MR. WAYNE.
GREGORY-- BRING ME JUST A GLASS OF CABERNET. '91 MONTE BELLO CAB.
NO WINE, LEX?
I'VE GOT SOME THINGS TO TALK ABOUT, BRUCE.
EXACTLY. AND THAT'S SO MUCH EASIER TO DO WHEN WINE'S INVITED TO THE TABLE.
GREGORY-- THE BOTTLE--AND TWO GLASSES!

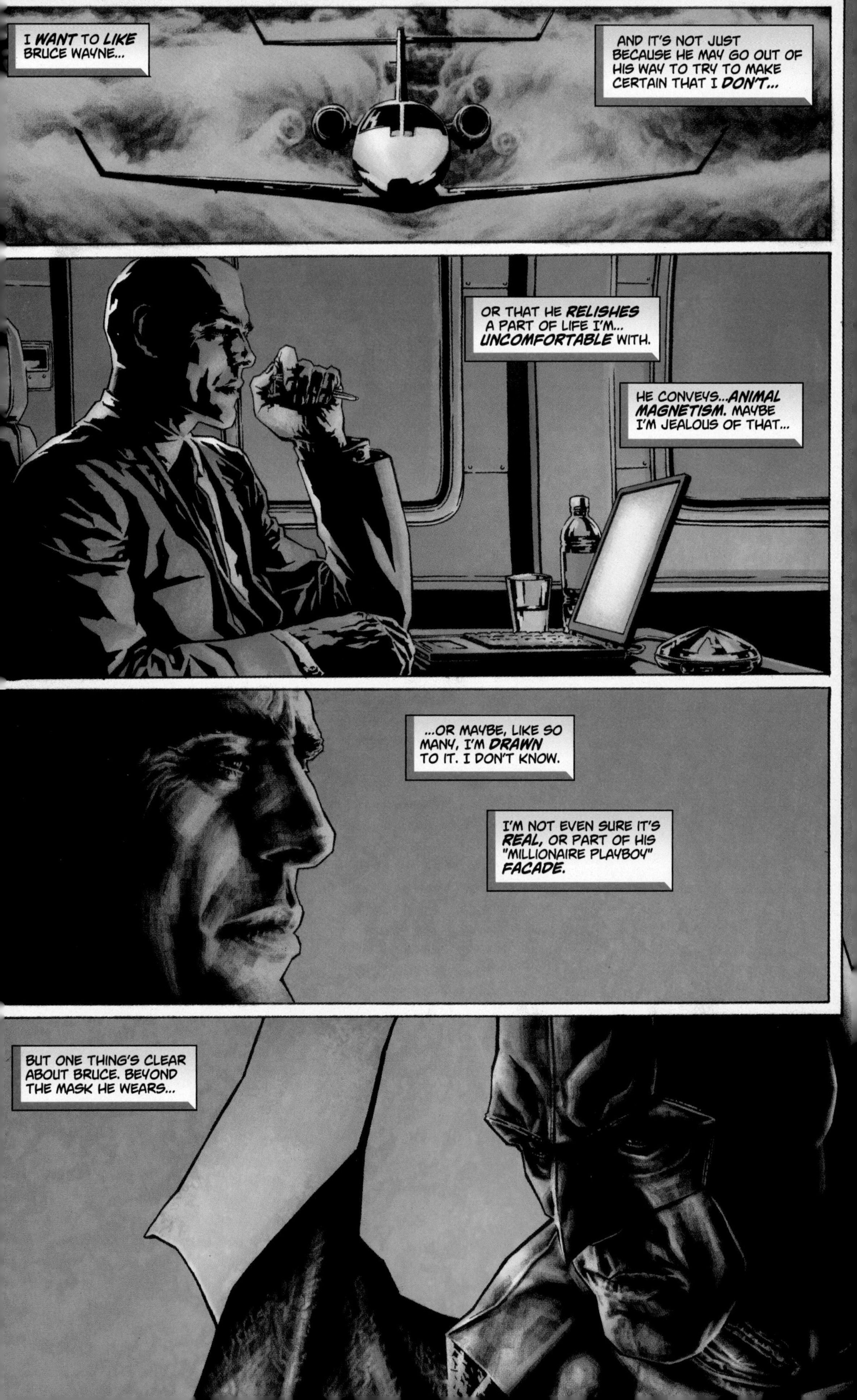
I WANT TO LIKE BRUCE WAYNE...
AND IT'S NOT JUST BECAUSE HE MAY GO OUT OF HIS WAY TO TRY TO MAKE CERTAIN THAT I DON'T...
OR THAT HE RELISHES A PART OF LIFE I'M... UNCOMFORTABLE WITH.
HE CONVEYS...ANIMAL MAGNETISM. MAYBE I'M JEALOUS OF THAT...
...OR MAYBE, LIKE SO MANY, I'M DRAWN TO IT. I DON'T KNOW.
I'M NOT EVEN SURE IT'S REAL, OR PART OF HIS "MILLIONAIRE PLAYBOY" FACADE.
BUT ONE THING'S CLEAR ABOUT BRUCE. BEYOND THE MASK HE WEARS...

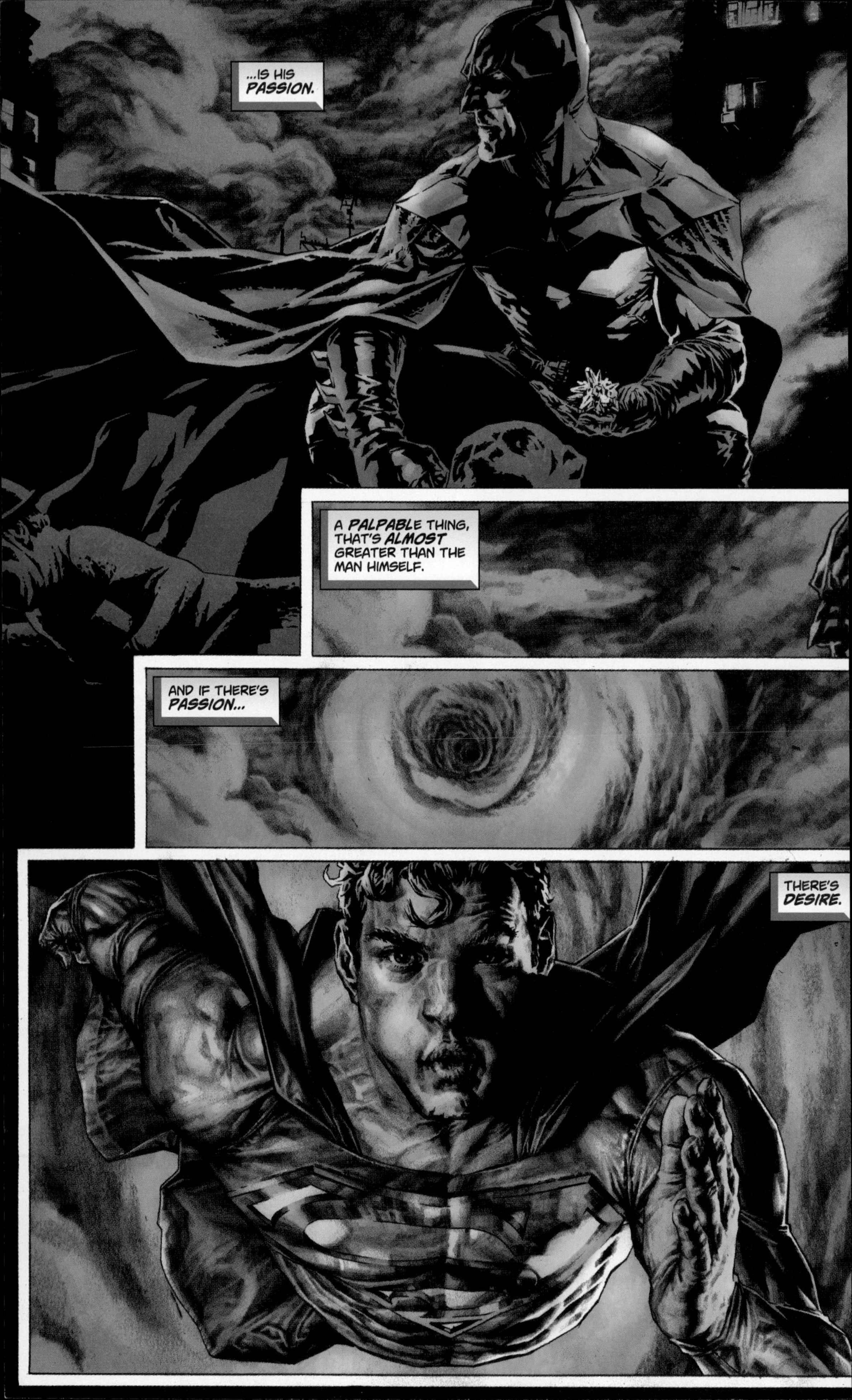
...IS HIS PASSION.
A PALPABLE THING, THAT'S ALMOST GREATER THAN THE MAN HIMSELF.
AND IF THERE'S PASSION...
THERE'S DESIRE.

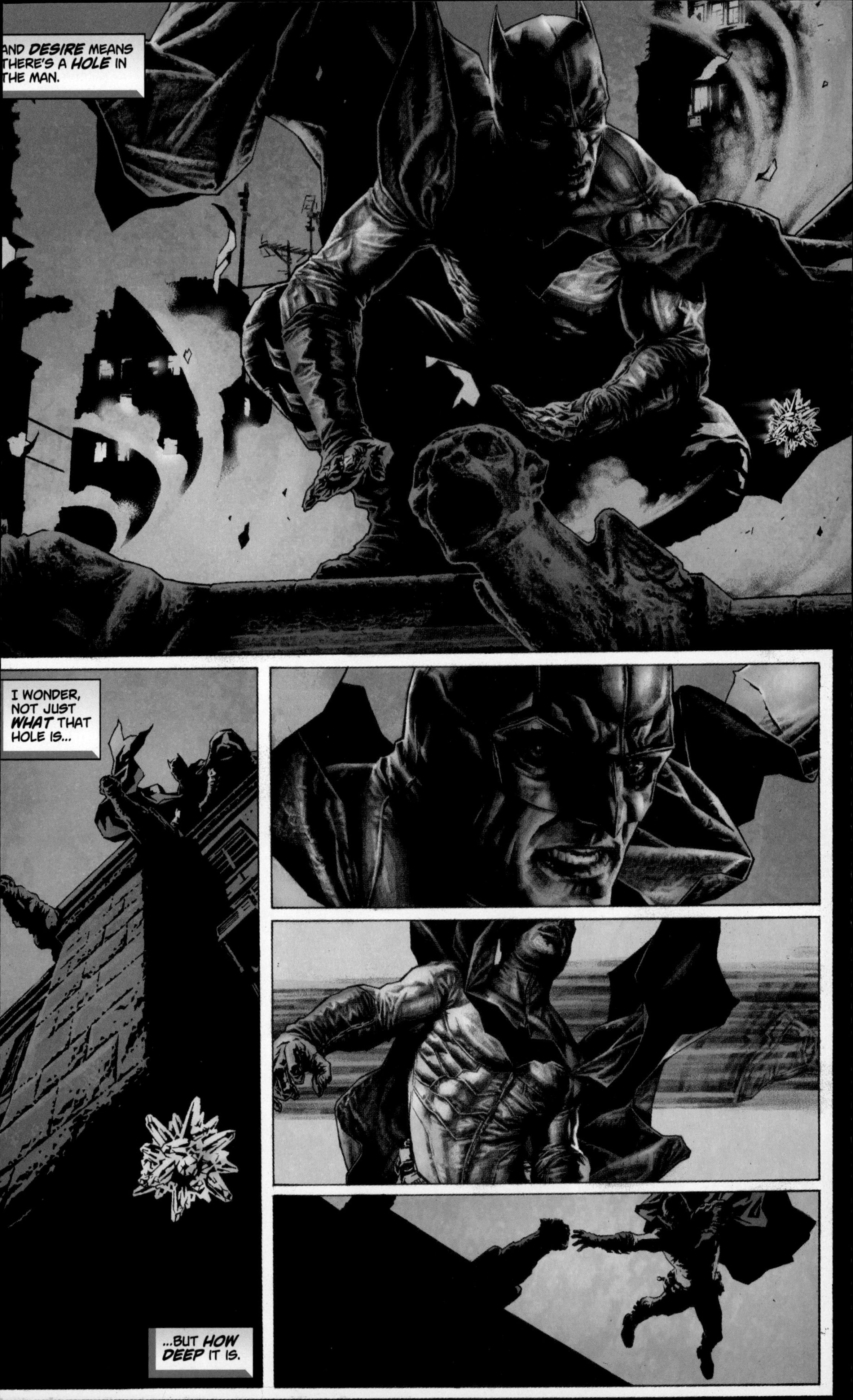

AND DESIRE MEANS THERE'S A HOLE IN THE MAN.
I WONDER, NOT JUST WHAT THAT HOLE IS...
...BUT HOW DEEP IT IS.

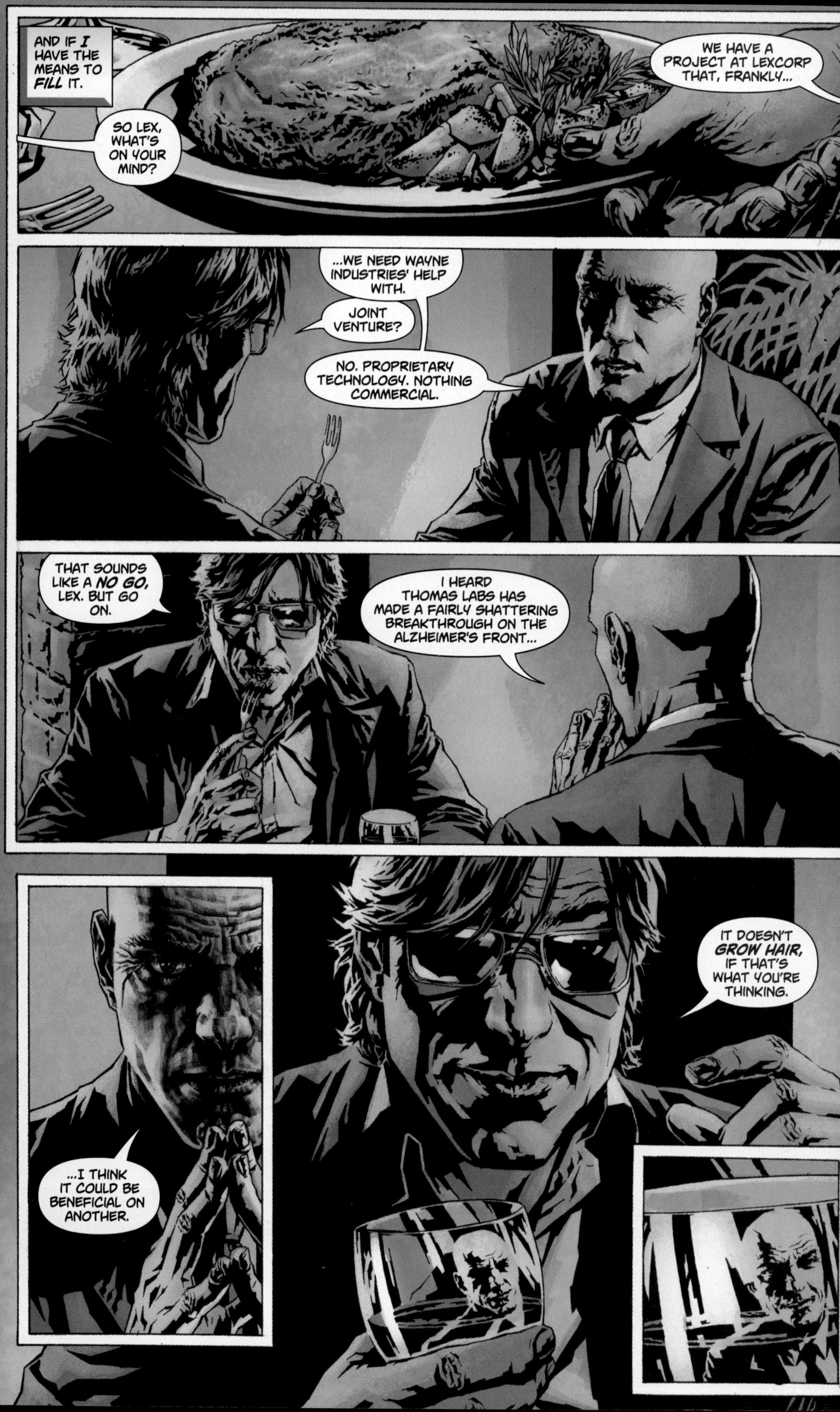
AND IF *I* HAVE THE MEANS TO *FILL* IT.
SO LEX, WHAT'S ON YOUR MIND?
WE HAVE A PROJECT AT LEXCORP THAT, FRANKLY...
...WE NEED WAYNE INDUSTRIES' HELP WITH.
JOINT VENTURE?
NO. PROPRIETARY TECHNOLOGY. NOTHING COMMERCIAL.
THAT SOUNDS LIKE A *NO GO,* LEX. BUT GO ON.
I HEARD THOMAS LABS HAS MADE A FAIRLY SHATTERING BREAKTHROUGH ON THE ALZHEIMER'S FRONT...
IT DOESN'T *GROW HAIR,* IF THAT'S WHAT YOU'RE THINKING.
...I THINK IT COULD BE BENEFICIAL ON ANOTHER.

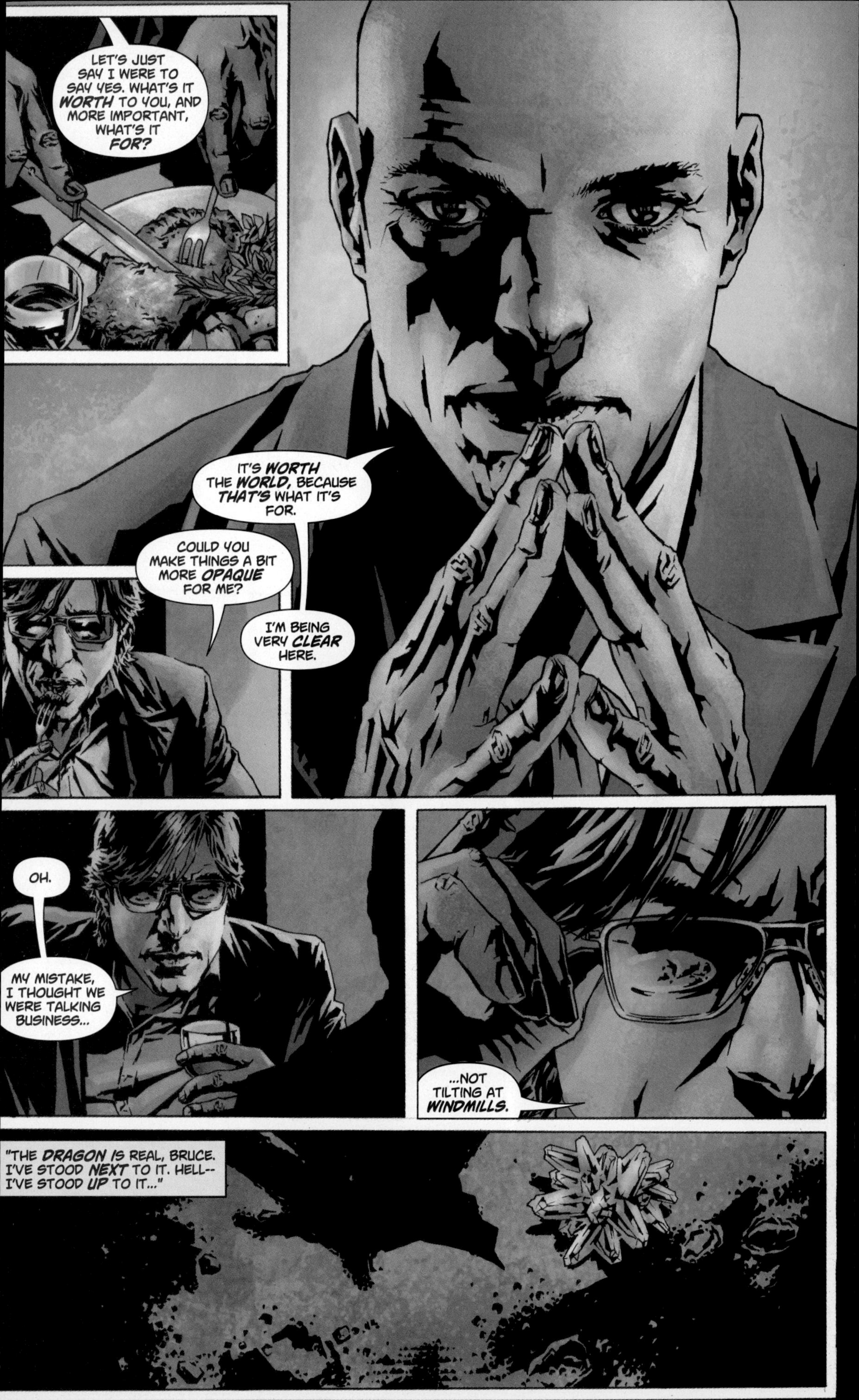
LET'S JUST SAY I WERE TO SAY YES. WHAT'S IT WORTH TO YOU, AND MORE IMPORTANT, WHAT'S IT FOR?
IT'S WORTH THE WORLD, BECAUSE THAT'S WHAT IT'S FOR.
COULD YOU MAKE THINGS A BIT MORE OPAQUE FOR ME?
I'M BEING VERY CLEAR HERE.
OH.
MY MISTAKE, I THOUGHT WE WERE TALKING BUSINESS...
...NOT TILTING AT WINDMILLS.
"THE DRAGON IS REAL, BRUCE. I'VE STOOD NEXT TO IT. HELL-- I'VE STOOD UP TO IT..."

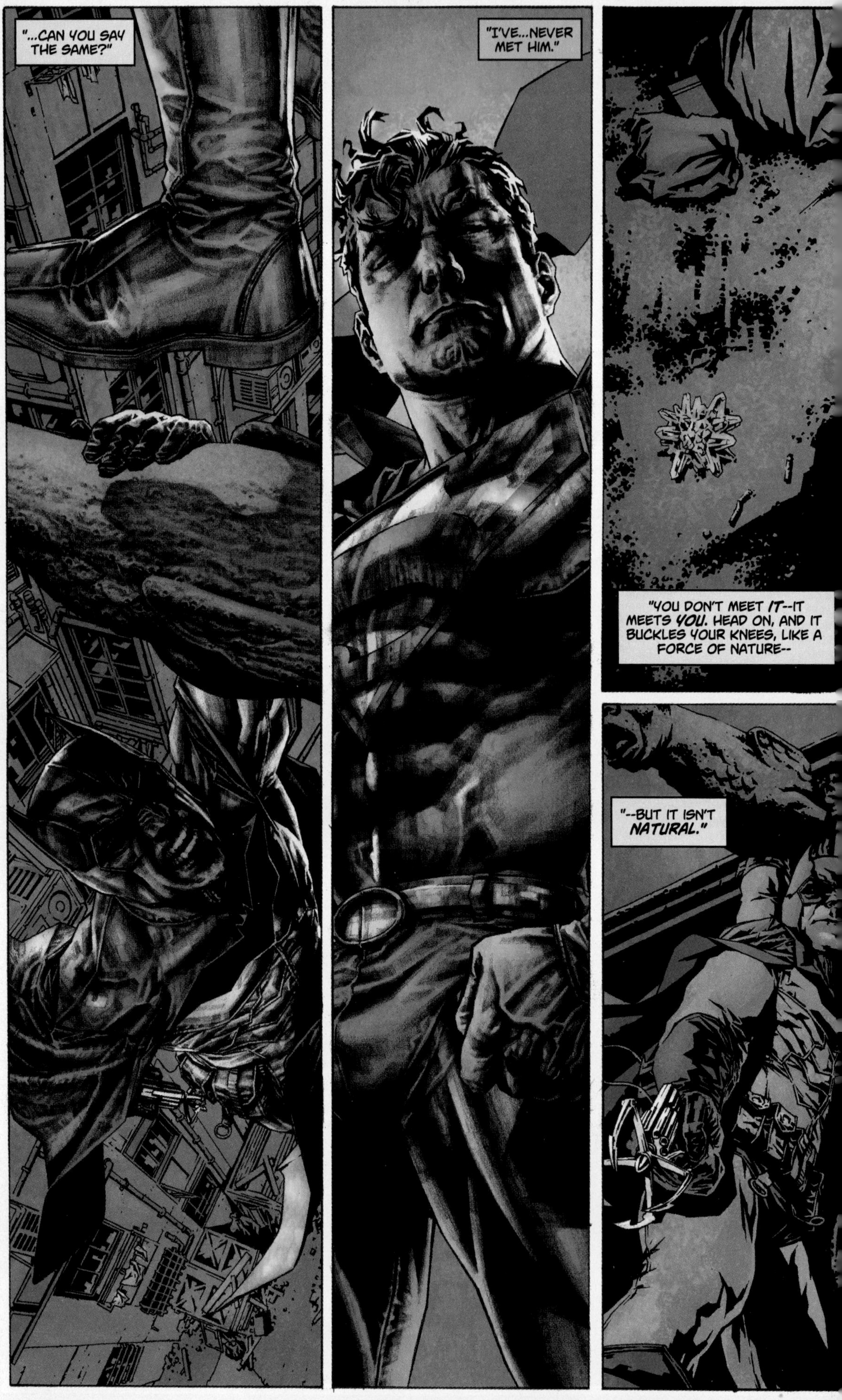
"...CAN YOU SAY THE SAME?"
"I'VE...NEVER MET HIM."
"YOU DON'T MEET *IT*--IT MEETS *YOU*. HEAD ON, AND IT BUCKLES YOUR KNEES, LIKE A FORCE OF NATURE--
"--BUT IT ISN'T *NATURAL*."

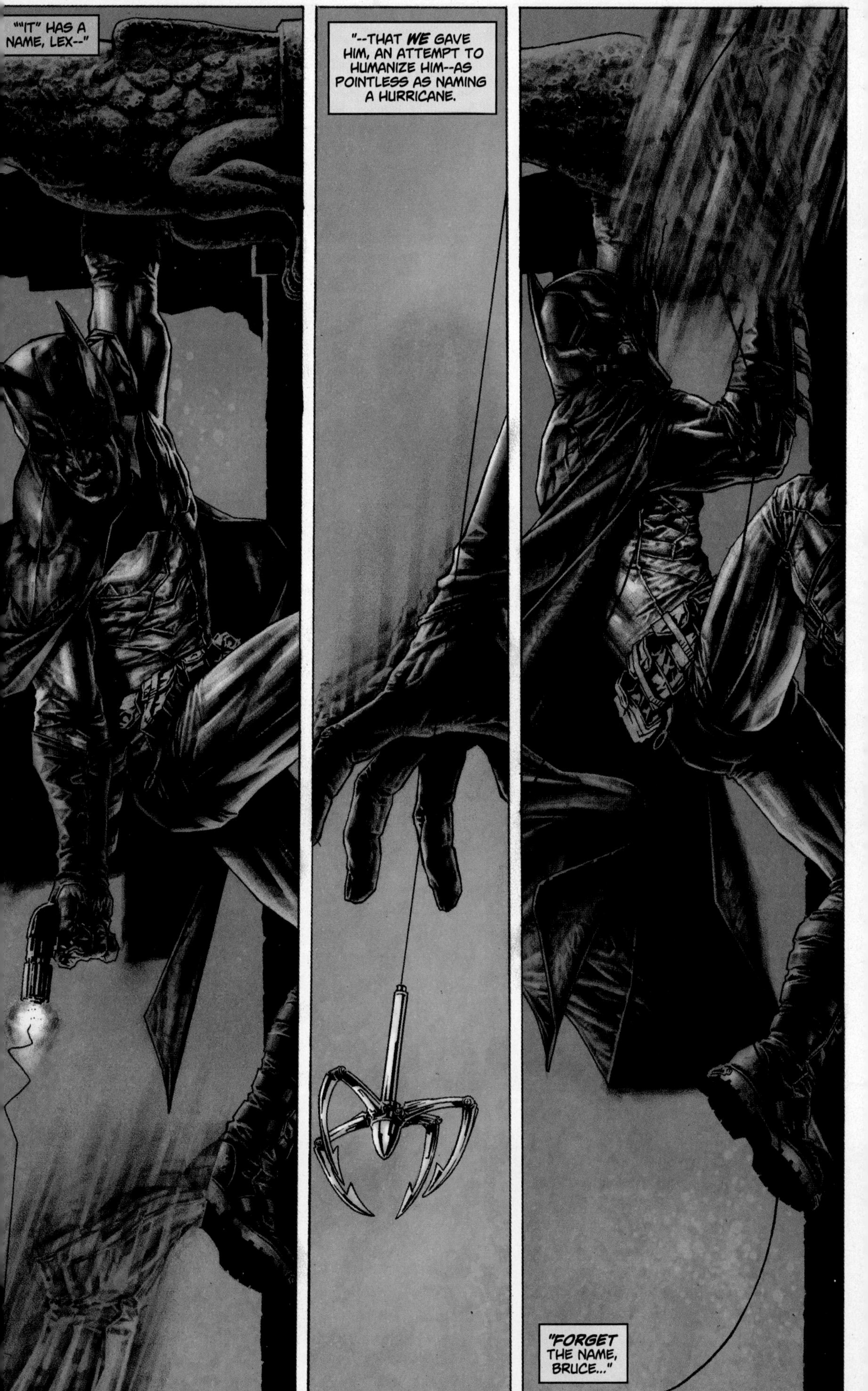
""IT" HAS A NAME, LEX--"
"--THAT *WE* GAVE HIM, AN ATTEMPT TO HUMANIZE HIM--AS POINTLESS AS NAMING A HURRICANE.
"FORGET THE NAME, BRUCE..."

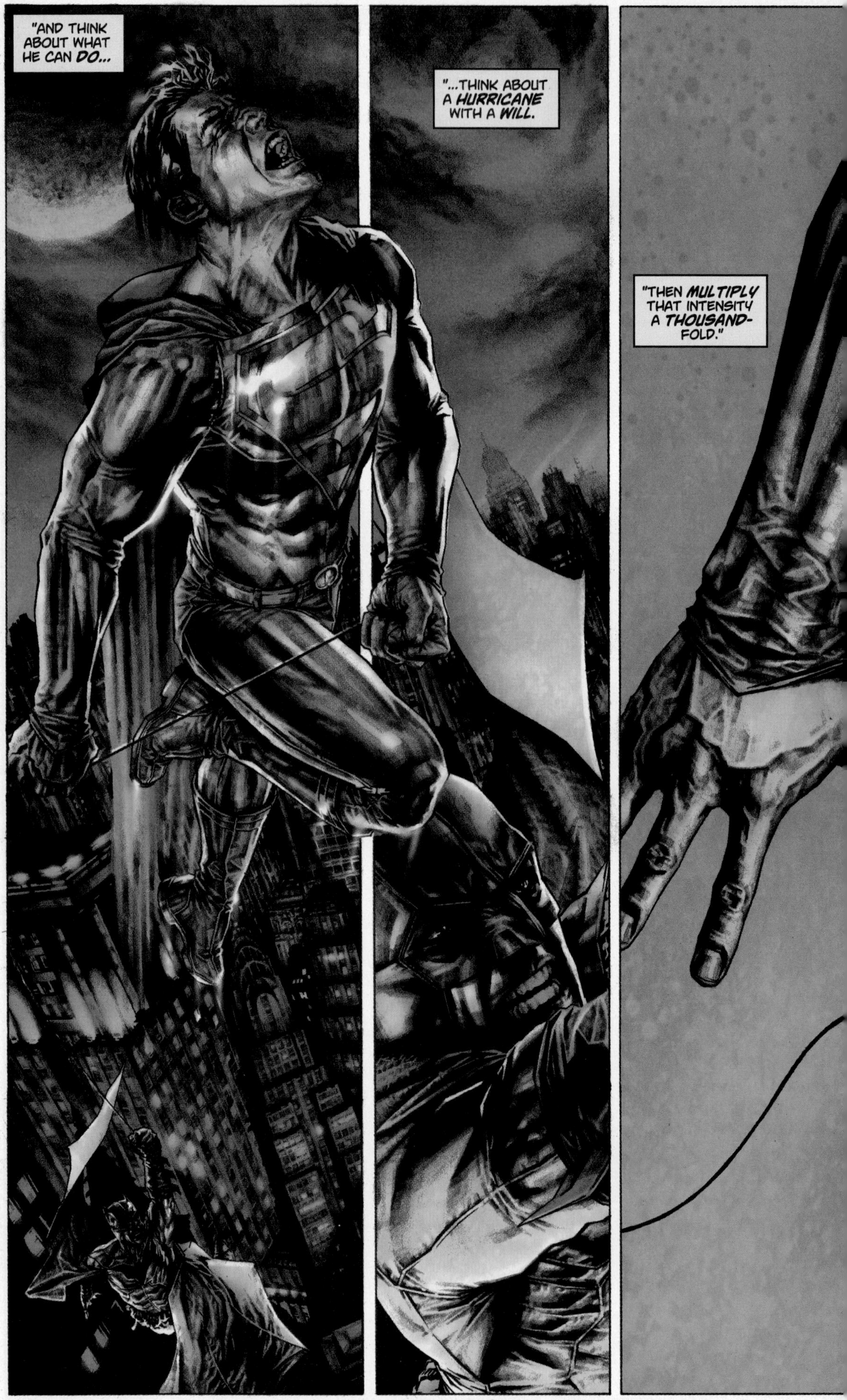
"AND THINK ABOUT WHAT HE CAN DO...
"...THINK ABOUT A HURRICANE WITH A WILL.
"THEN MULTIPLY THAT INTENSITY A THOUSAND-FOLD."

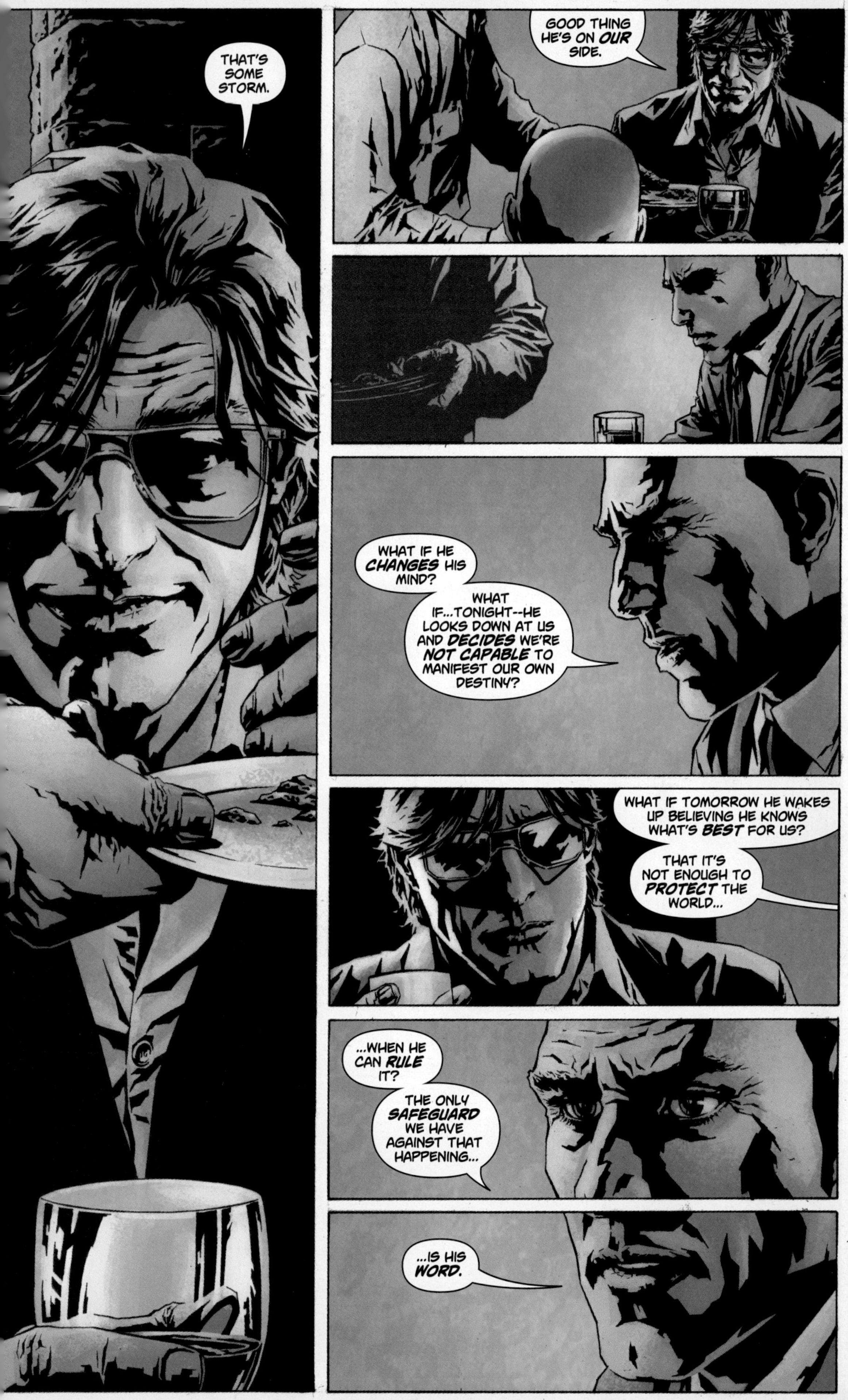
THAT'S SOME STORM.
GOOD THING HE'S ON *OUR* SIDE.
WHAT IF HE *CHANGES* HIS MIND?
WHAT IF...TONIGHT--HE LOOKS DOWN AT US AND *DECIDES* WE'RE *NOT CAPABLE* TO MANIFEST OUR OWN DESTINY?
WHAT IF TOMORROW HE WAKES UP BELIEVING HE KNOWS WHAT'S *BEST* FOR US?
THAT IT'S NOT ENOUGH TO *PROTECT* THE WORLD...
...WHEN HE CAN *RULE* IT?
THE ONLY *SAFEGUARD* WE HAVE AGAINST THAT HAPPENING...
...IS HIS *WORD*.

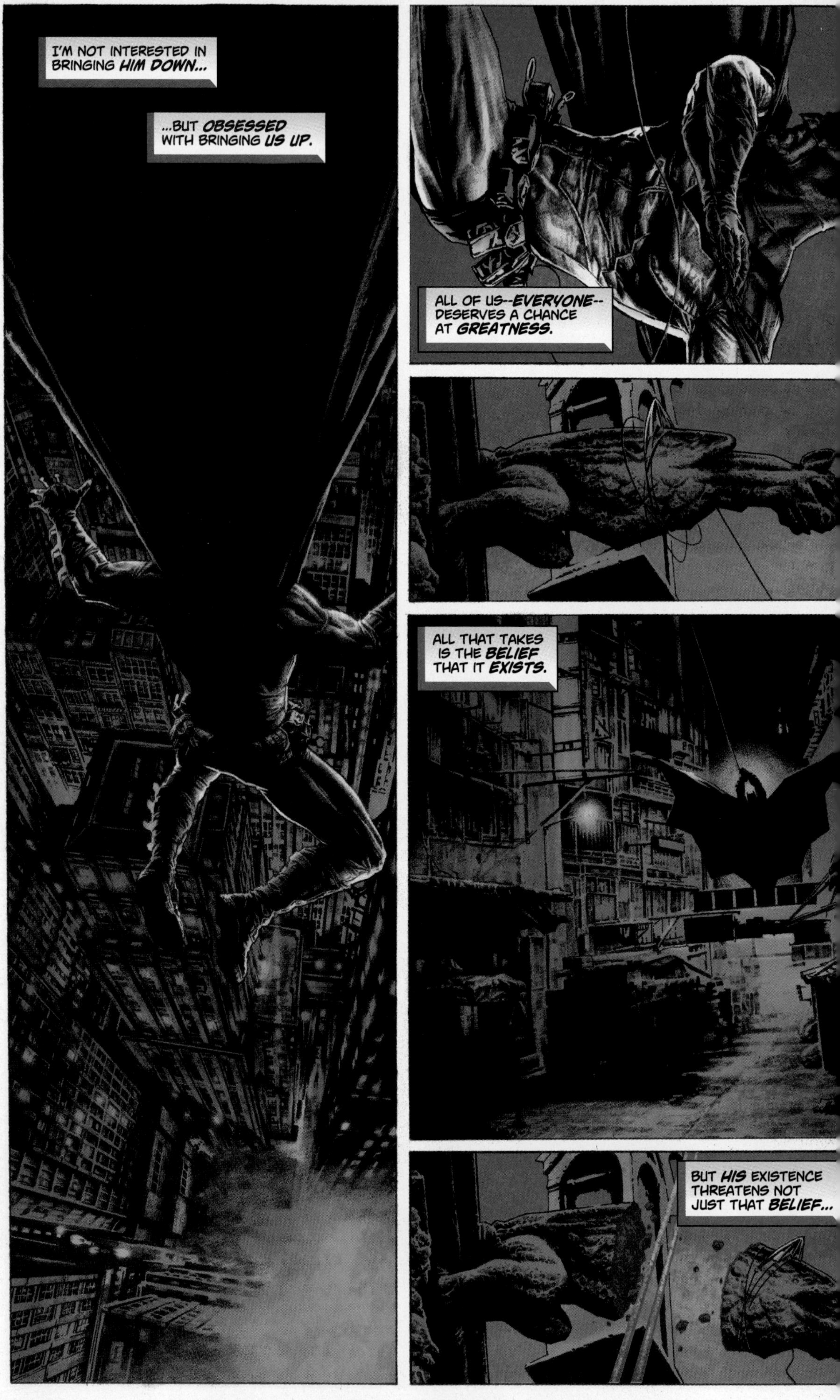
I'M NOT INTERESTED IN BRINGING HIM DOWN...
...BUT OBSESSED WITH BRINGING US UP.
ALL OF US--EVERYONE--DESERVES A CHANCE AT GREATNESS.
ALL THAT TAKES IS THE BELIEF THAT IT EXISTS.
BUT HIS EXISTENCE THREATENS NOT JUST THAT BELIEF...

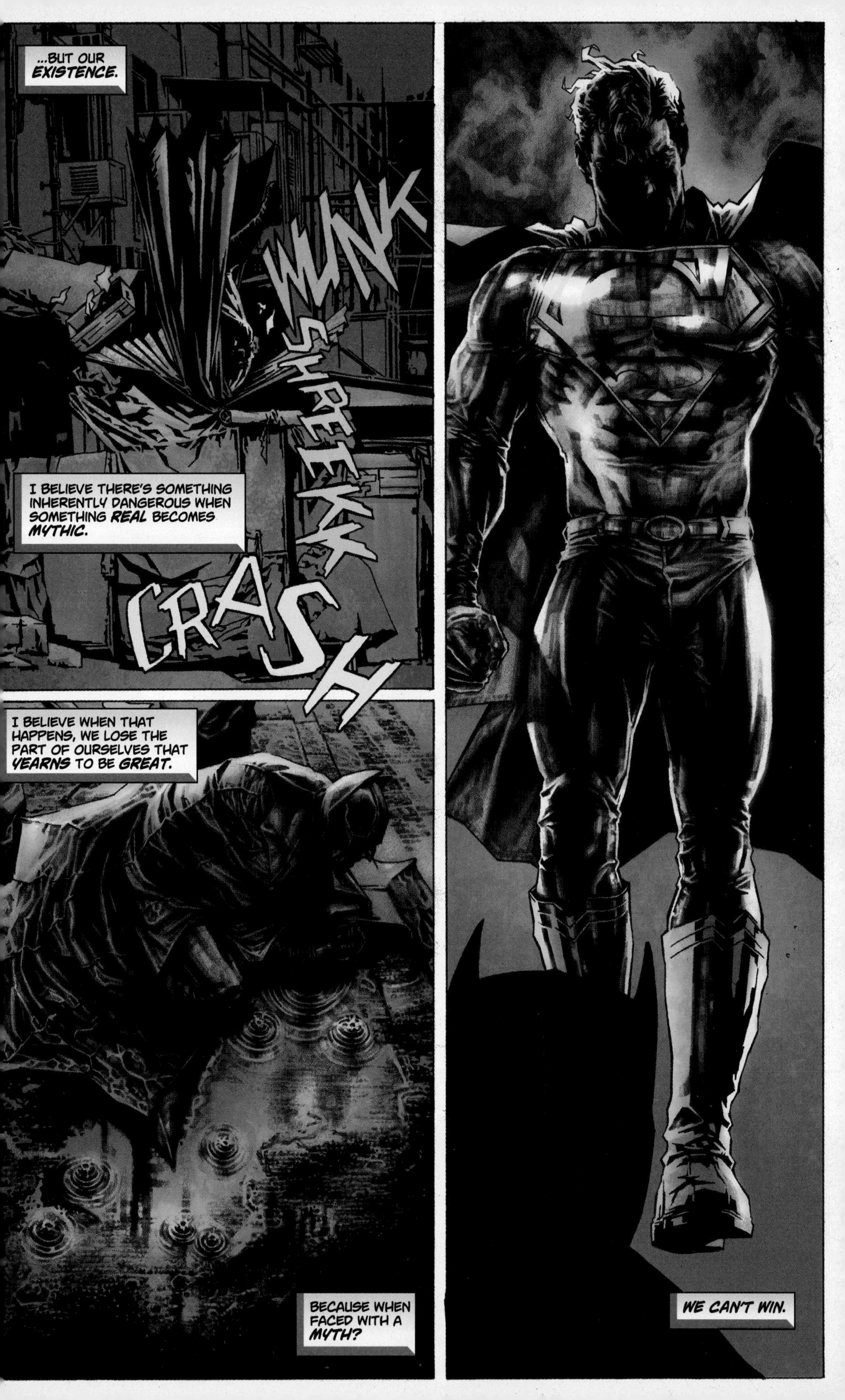
...BUT OUR EXISTENCE.
WUNK
SHREEKK
I BELIEVE THERE'S SOMETHING INHERENTLY DANGEROUS WHEN SOMETHING REAL BECOMES MYTHIC.
CRASH
I BELIEVE WHEN THAT HAPPENS, WE LOSE THE PART OF OURSELVES THAT YEARNS TO BE GREAT.
BECAUSE WHEN FACED WITH A MYTH?
WE CAN'T WIN.

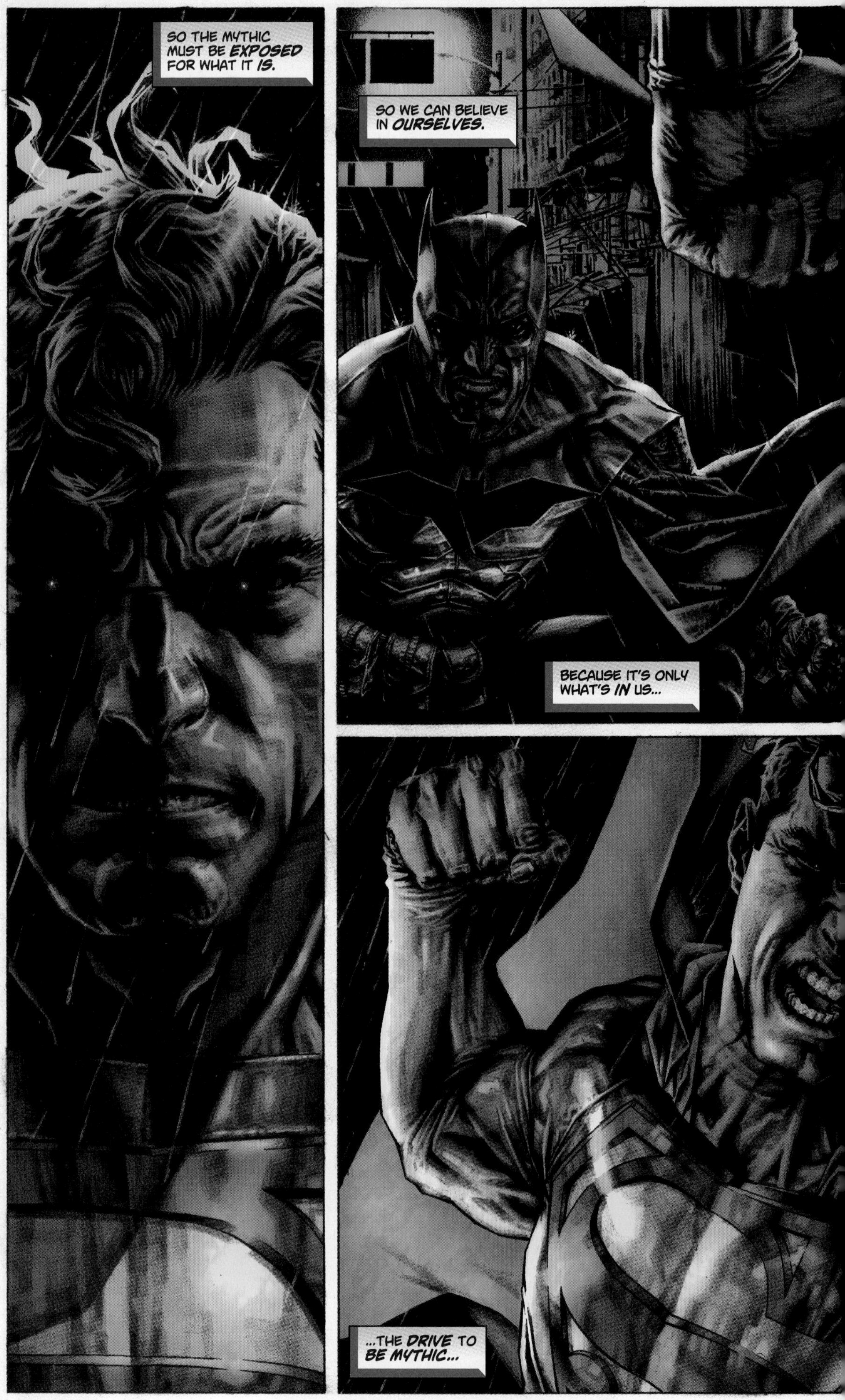
SO THE MYTHIC MUST BE EXPOSED FOR WHAT IT IS.
SO WE CAN BELIEVE IN OURSELVES.
BECAUSE IT'S ONLY WHAT'S IN US...
...THE DRIVE TO BE MYTHIC...

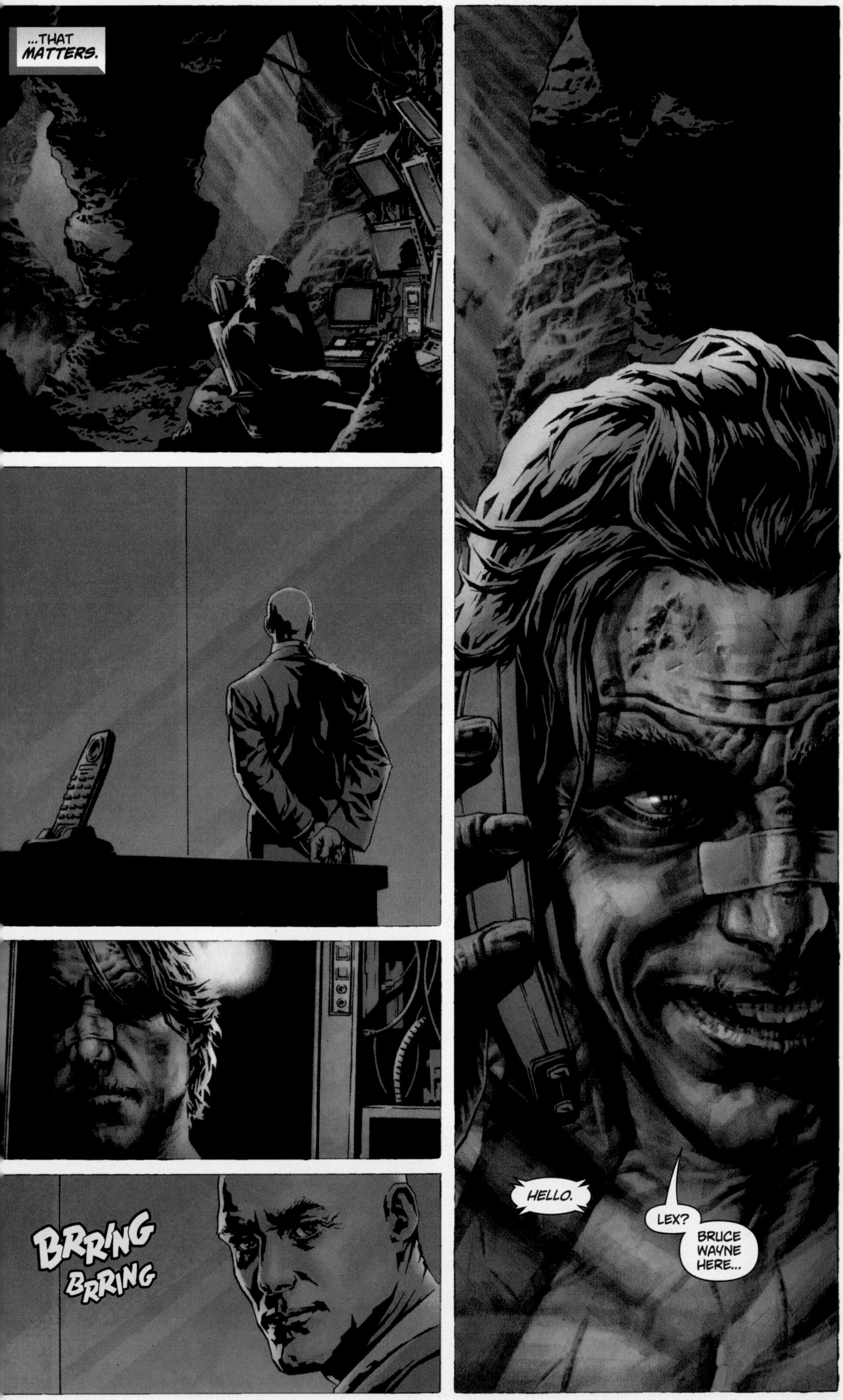
...THAT MATTERS.
BRRING
BRRING
HELLO.
LEX? BRUCE WAYNE HERE...

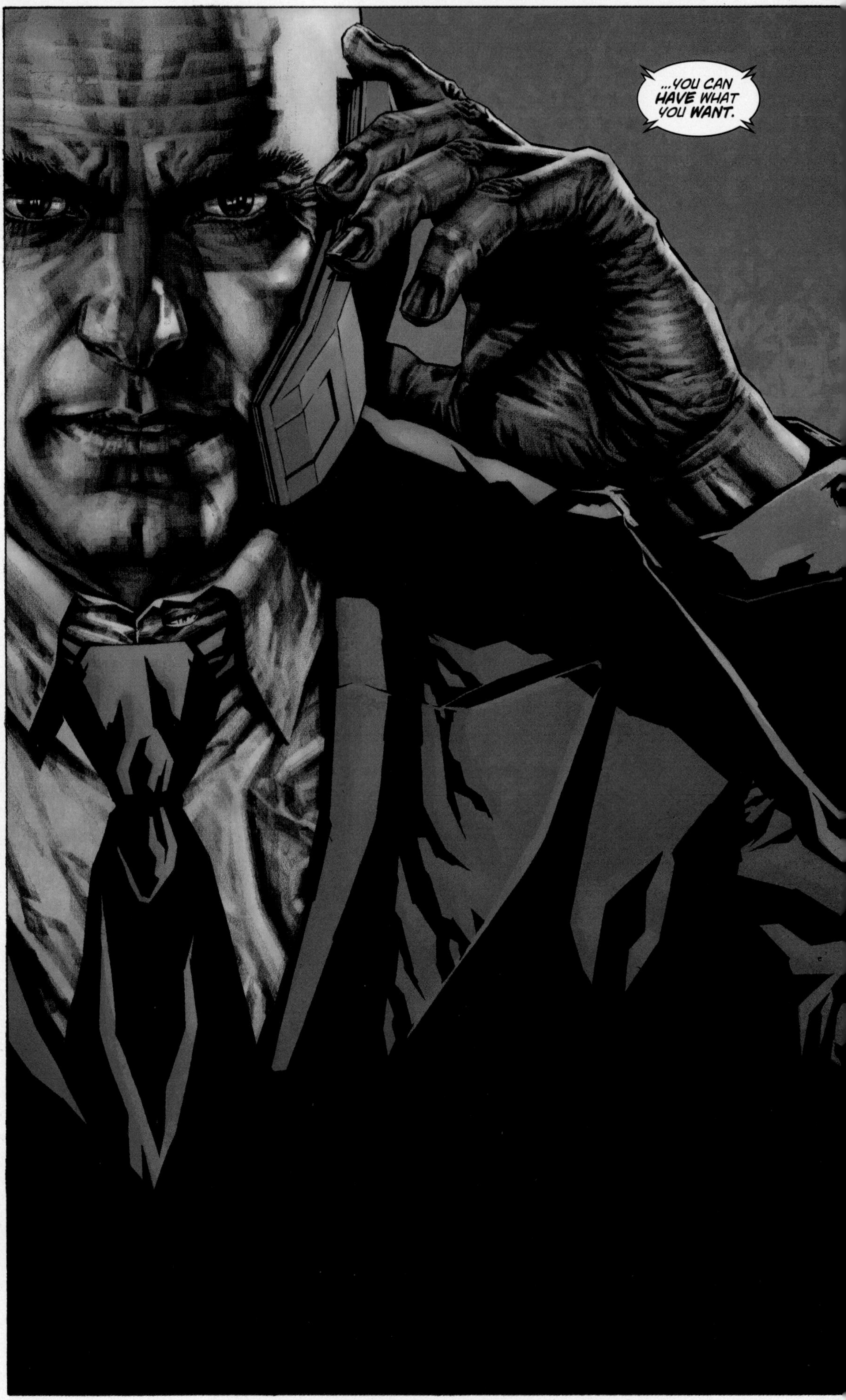
...YOU CAN HAVE WHAT YOU WANT.

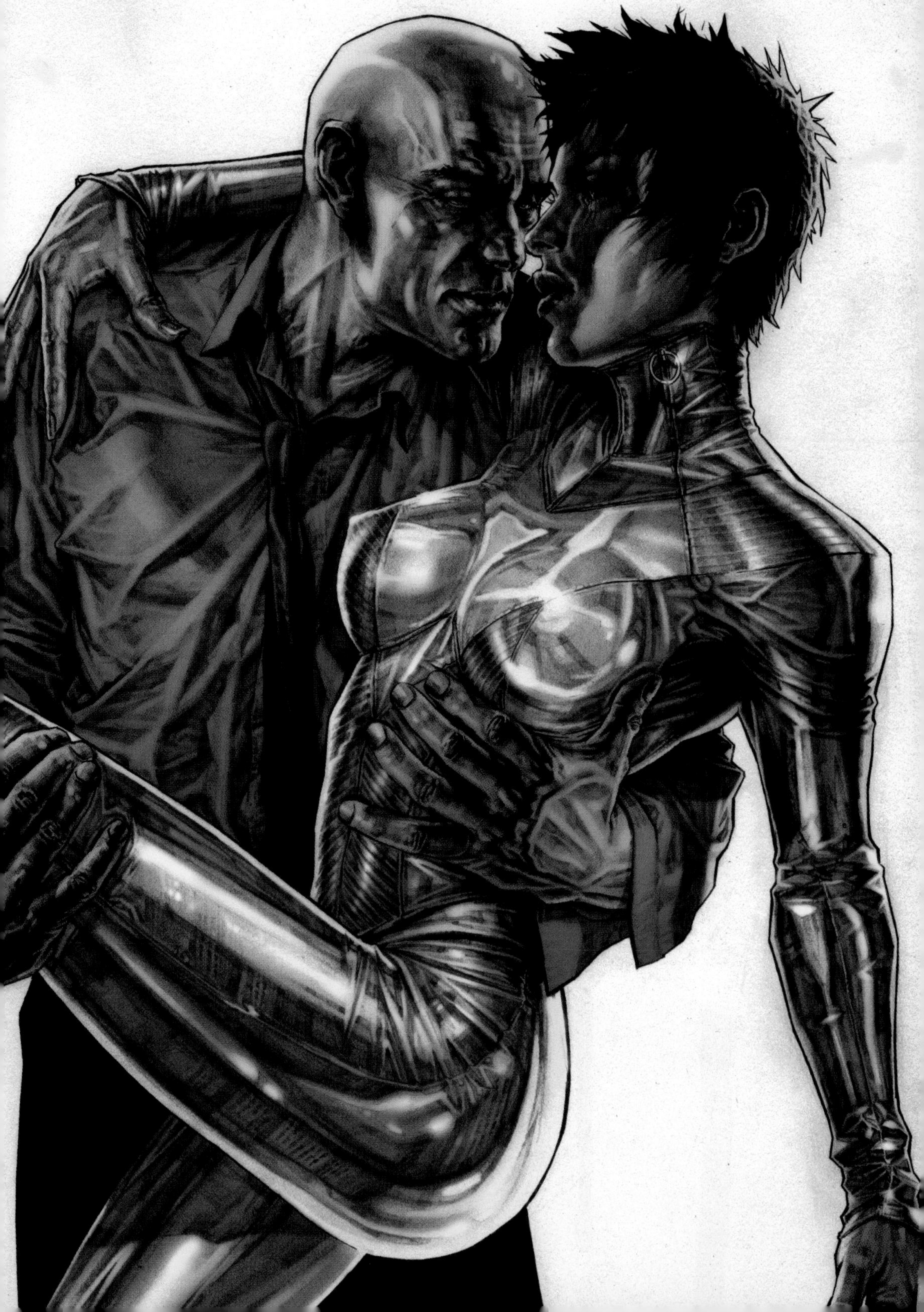

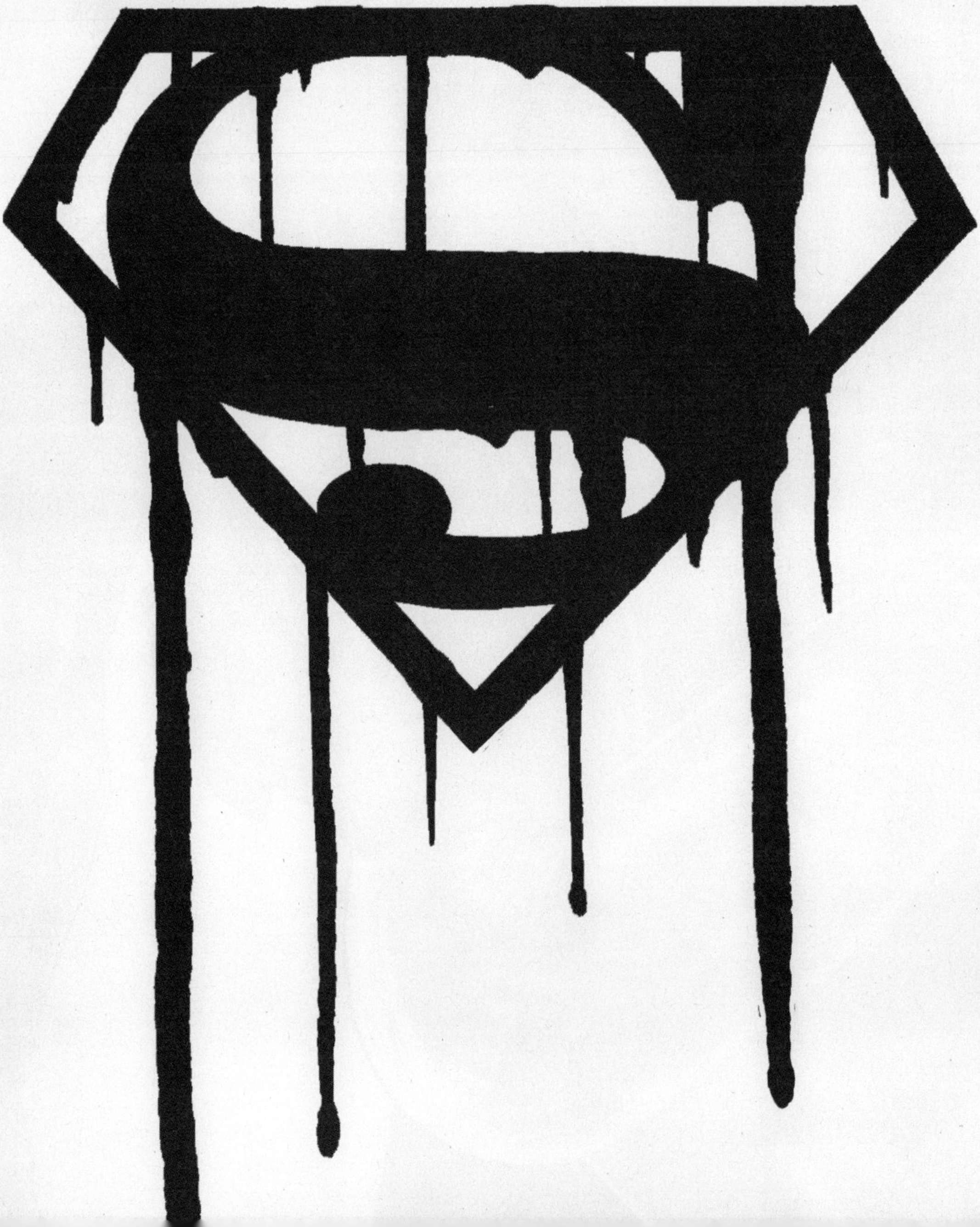

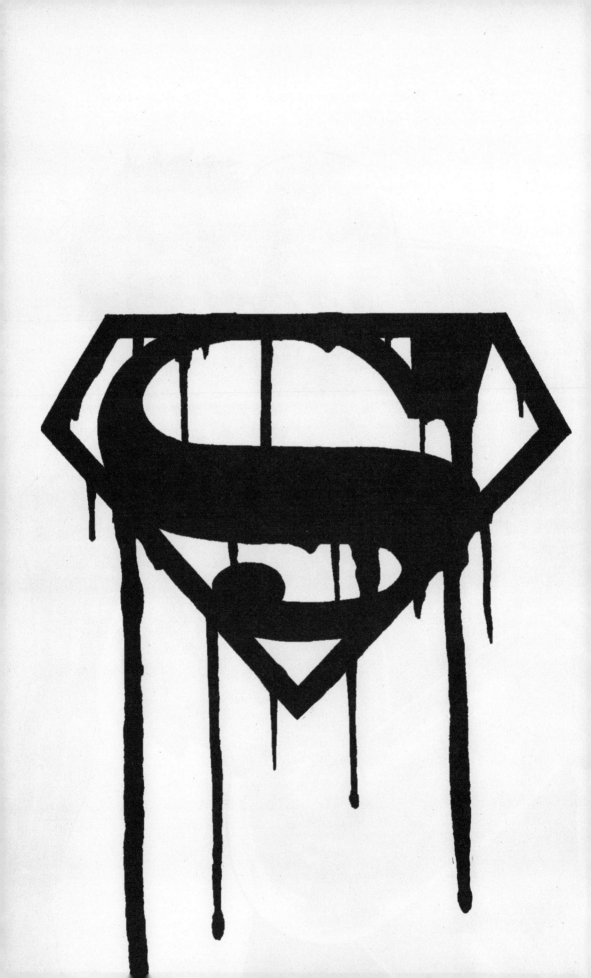

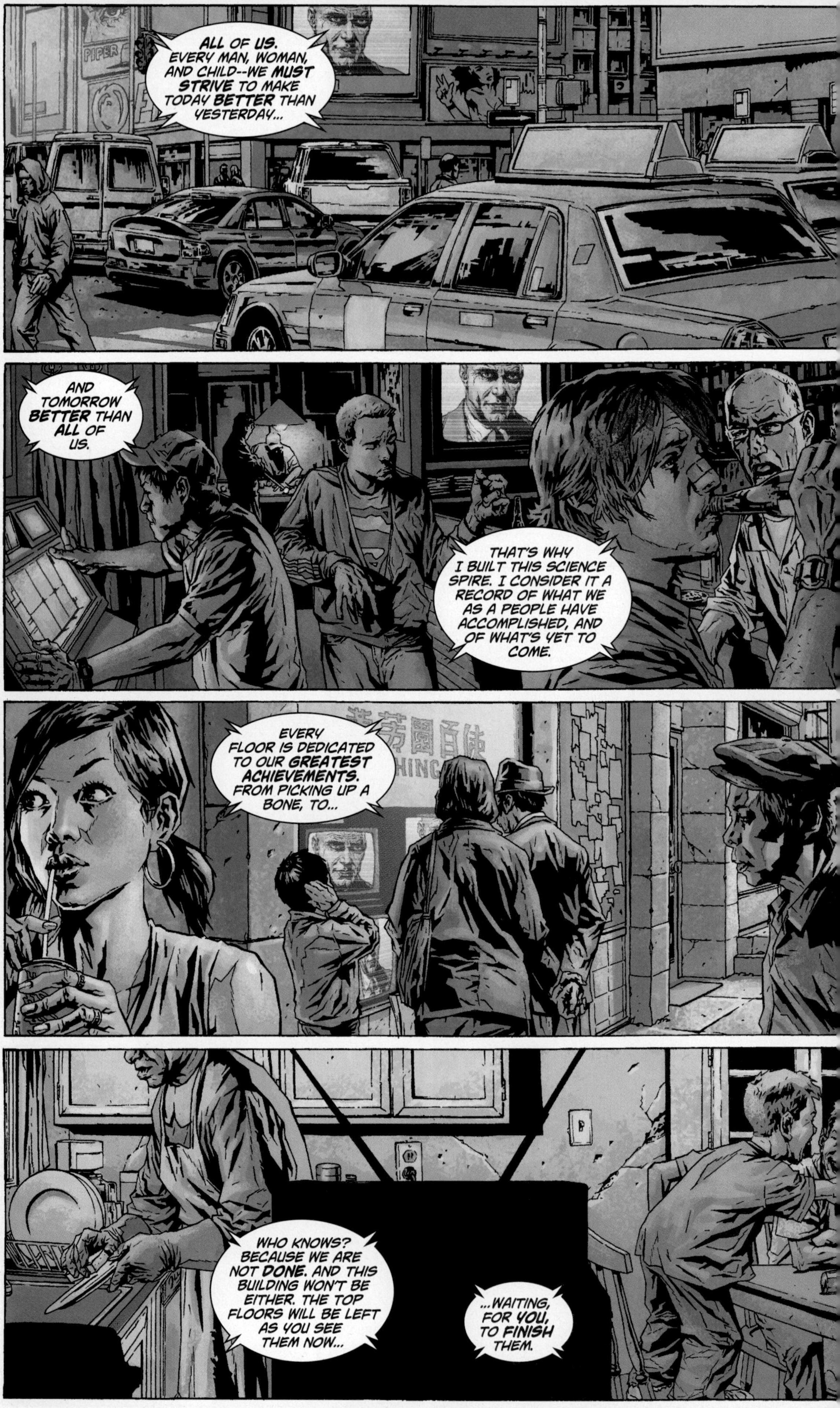
PIPER
ALL OF US. EVERY MAN, WOMAN, AND CHILD--WE MUST STRIVE TO MAKE TODAY BETTER THAN YESTERDAY...
AND TOMORROW BETTER THAN ALL OF US.
THAT'S WHY I BUILT THIS SCIENCE SPIRE. I CONSIDER IT A RECORD OF WHAT WE AS A PEOPLE HAVE ACCOMPLISHED, AND OF WHAT'S YET TO COME.
EVERY FLOOR IS DEDICATED TO OUR GREATEST ACHIEVEMENTS. FROM PICKING UP A BONE, TO...
WHO KNOWS? BECAUSE WE ARE NOT DONE. AND THIS BUILDING WON'T BE EITHER. THE TOP FLOORS WILL BE LEFT AS YOU SEE THEM NOW...
...WAITING, FOR YOU, TO FINISH THEM.

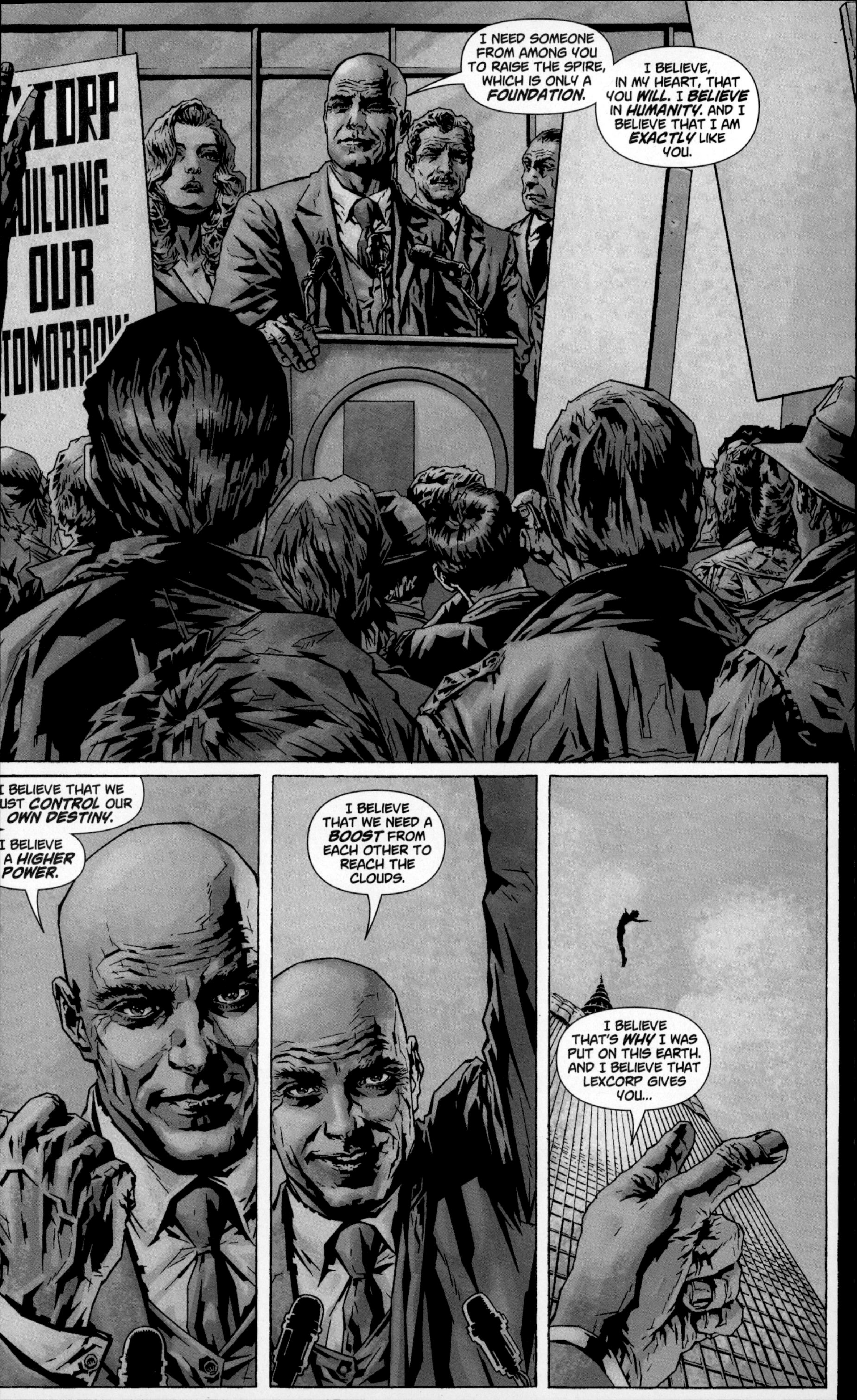

OUR
I NEED SOMEONE FROM AMONG YOU TO RAISE THE SPIRE, WHICH IS ONLY A FOUNDATION.
I BELIEVE, IN MY HEART, THAT YOU WILL. I BELIEVE IN HUMANITY. AND I BELIEVE THAT I AM EXACTLY LIKE YOU.
I BELIEVE THAT WE UST CONTROL OUR OWN DESTINY.
I BELIEVE A HIGHER POWER.
I BELIEVE THAT WE NEED A BOOST FROM EACH OTHER TO REACH THE CLOUDS.
I BELIEVE THAT'S WHY I WAS PUT ON THIS EARTH. AND I BELIEVE THAT LEXCORP GIVES YOU...

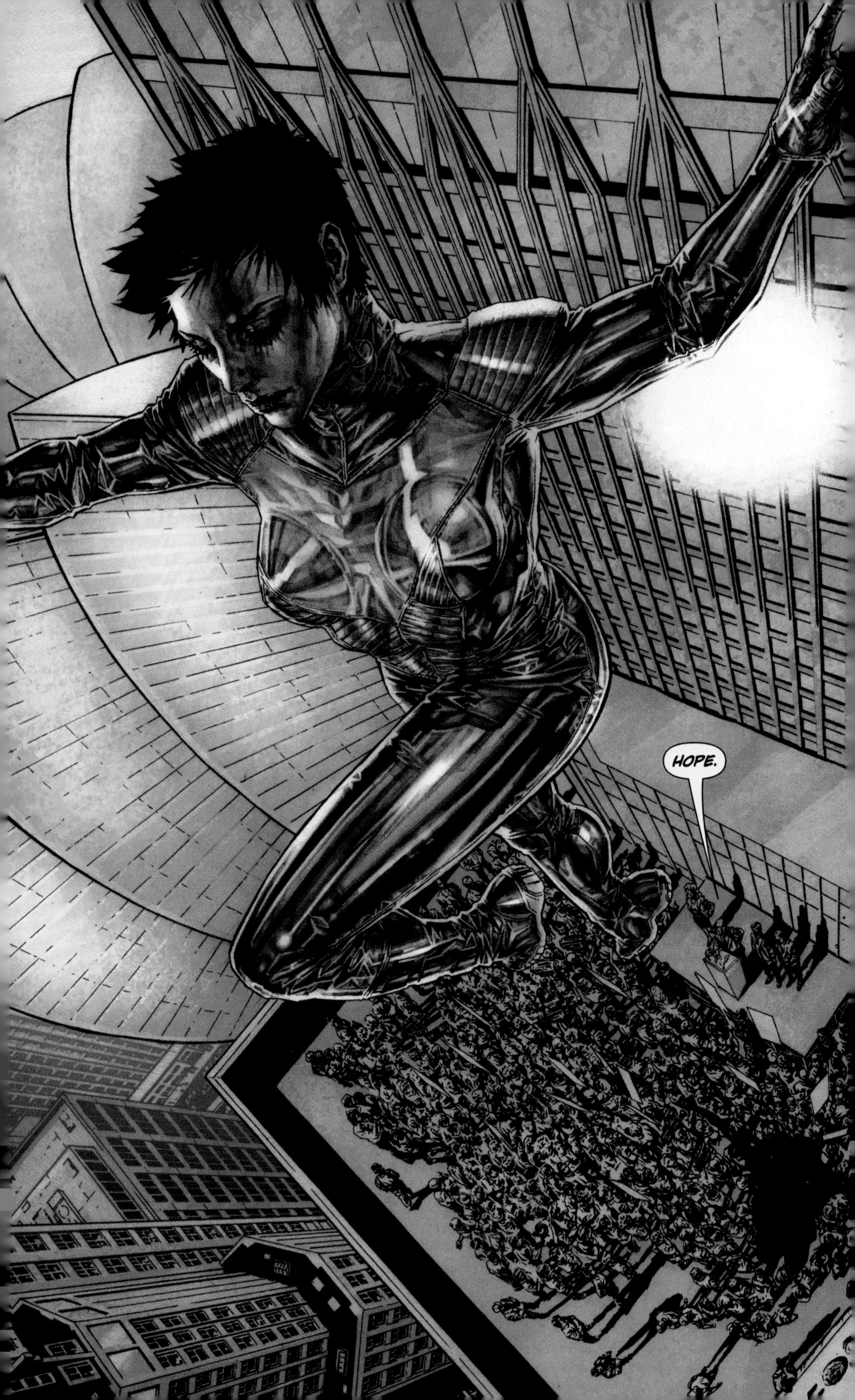
HOPE.

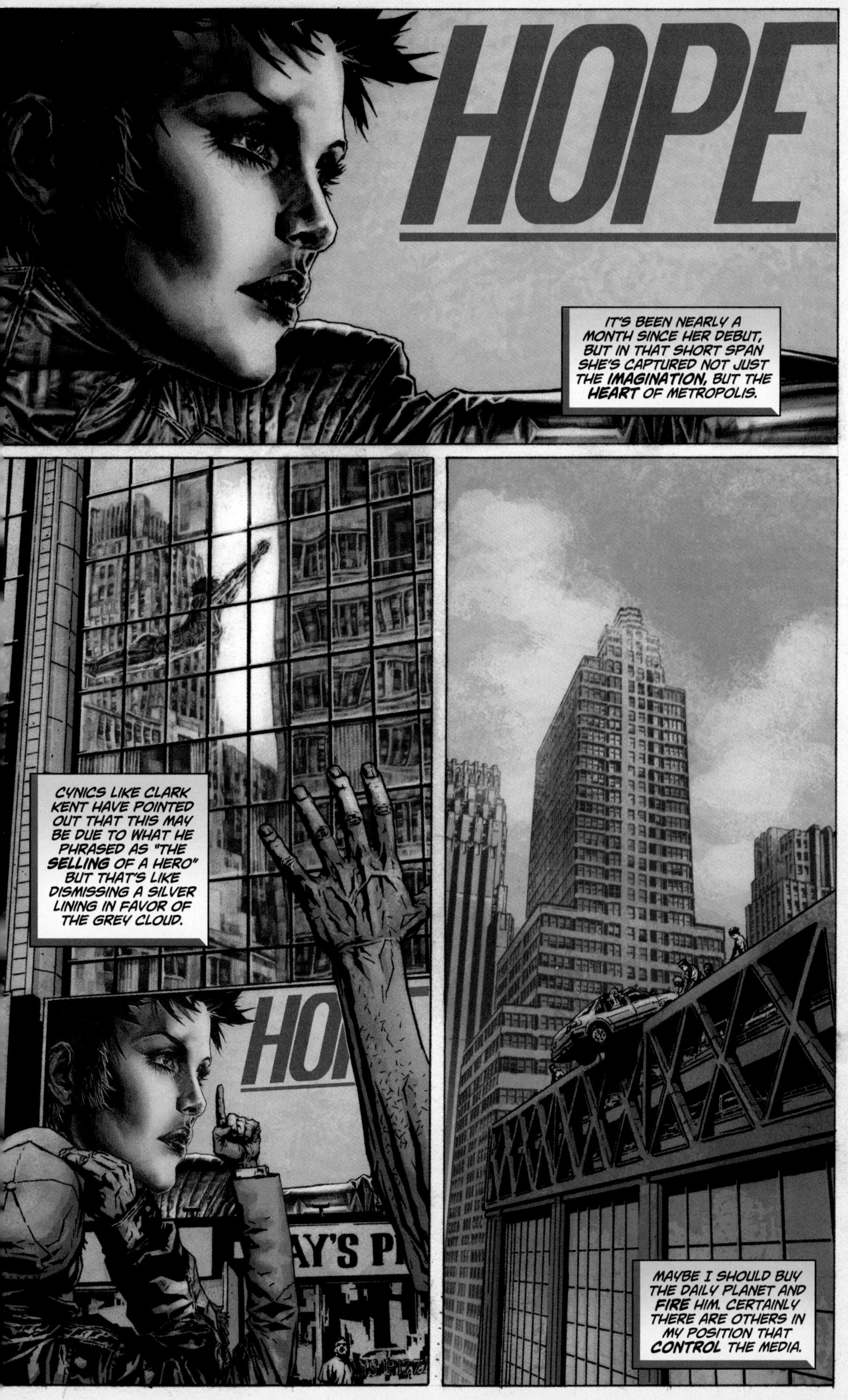
HOPE
IT'S BEEN NEARLY A MONTH SINCE HER DEBUT, BUT IN THAT SHORT SPAN SHE'S CAPTURED NOT JUST THE IMAGINATION, BUT THE HEART OF METROPOLIS.
CYNICS LIKE CLARK KENT HAVE POINTED OUT THAT THIS MAY BE DUE TO WHAT HE PHRASED AS "THE SELLING OF A HERO" BUT THAT'S LIKE DISMISSING A SILVER LINING IN FAVOR OF THE GREY CLOUD.
HOP
AY'S P
MAYBE I SHOULD BUY THE DAILY PLANET AND FIRE HIM. CERTAINLY THERE ARE OTHERS IN MY POSITION THAT CONTROL THE MEDIA.

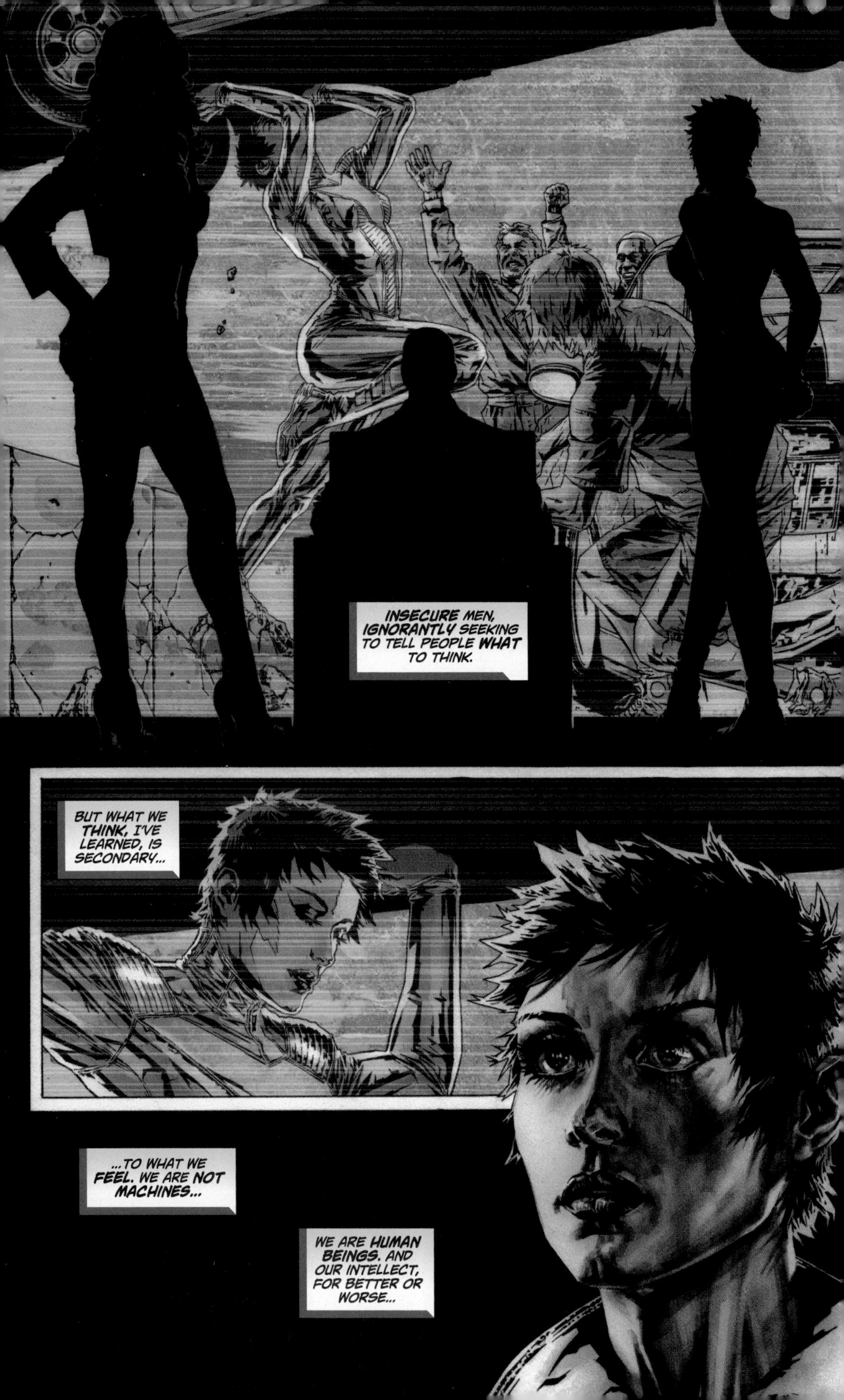
INSECURE MEN, IGNORANTLY SEEKING TO TELL PEOPLE WHAT TO THINK.
BUT WHAT WE THINK, I'VE LEARNED, IS SECONDARY...
...TO WHAT WE FEEL. WE ARE NOT MACHINES...
WE ARE HUMAN BEINGS. AND OUR INTELLECT, FOR BETTER OR WORSE...

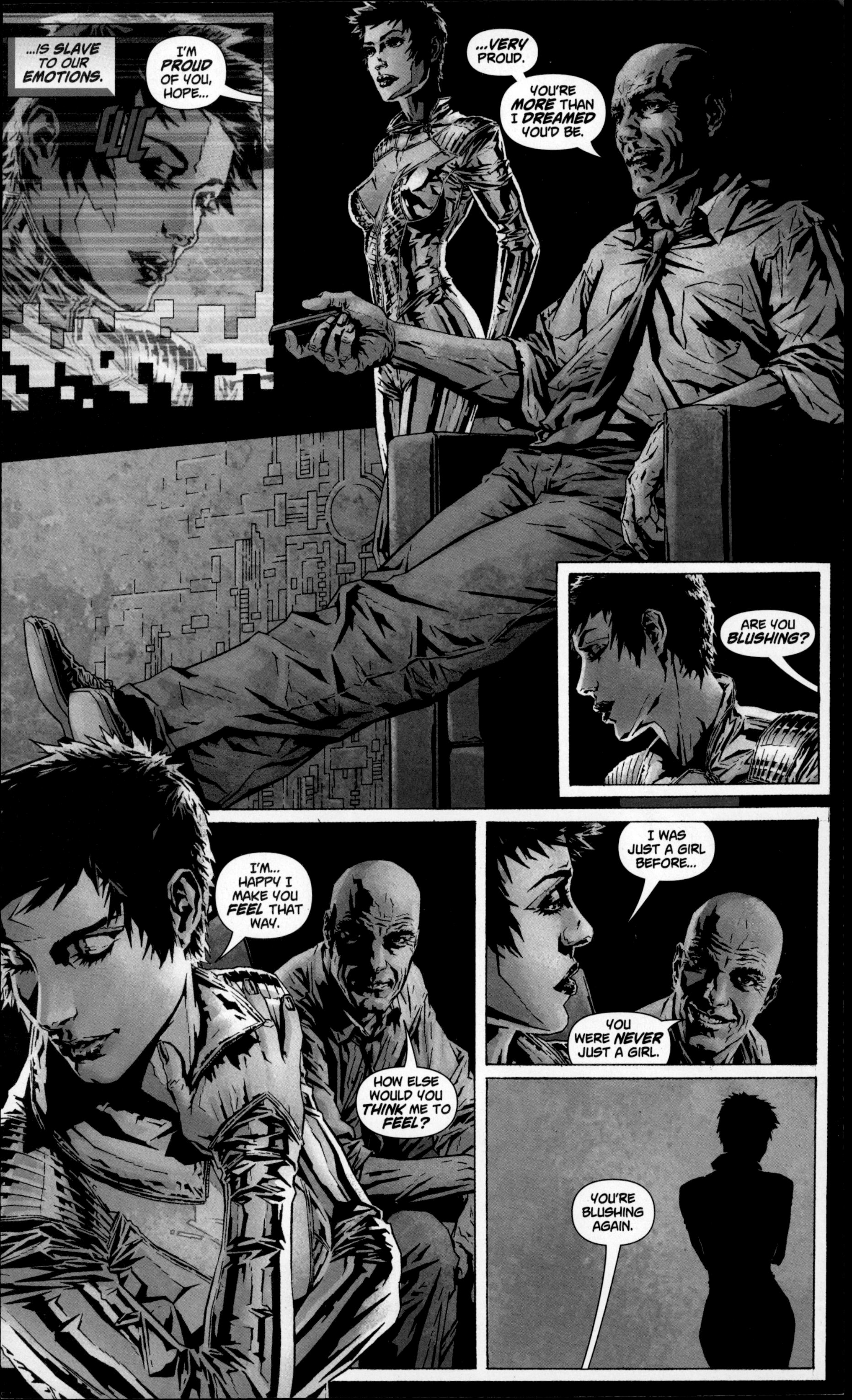
...IS SLAVE TO OUR EMOTIONS.
I'M PROUD OF YOU, HOPE...
...VERY PROUD.
YOU'RE MORE THAN I DREAMED YOU'D BE.
ARE YOU BLUSHING?
I'M... HAPPY I MAKE YOU FEEL THAT WAY.
HOW ELSE WOULD YOU THINK ME TO FEEL?
I WAS JUST A GIRL BEFORE...
YOU WERE NEVER JUST A GIRL.
YOU'RE BLUSHING AGAIN.

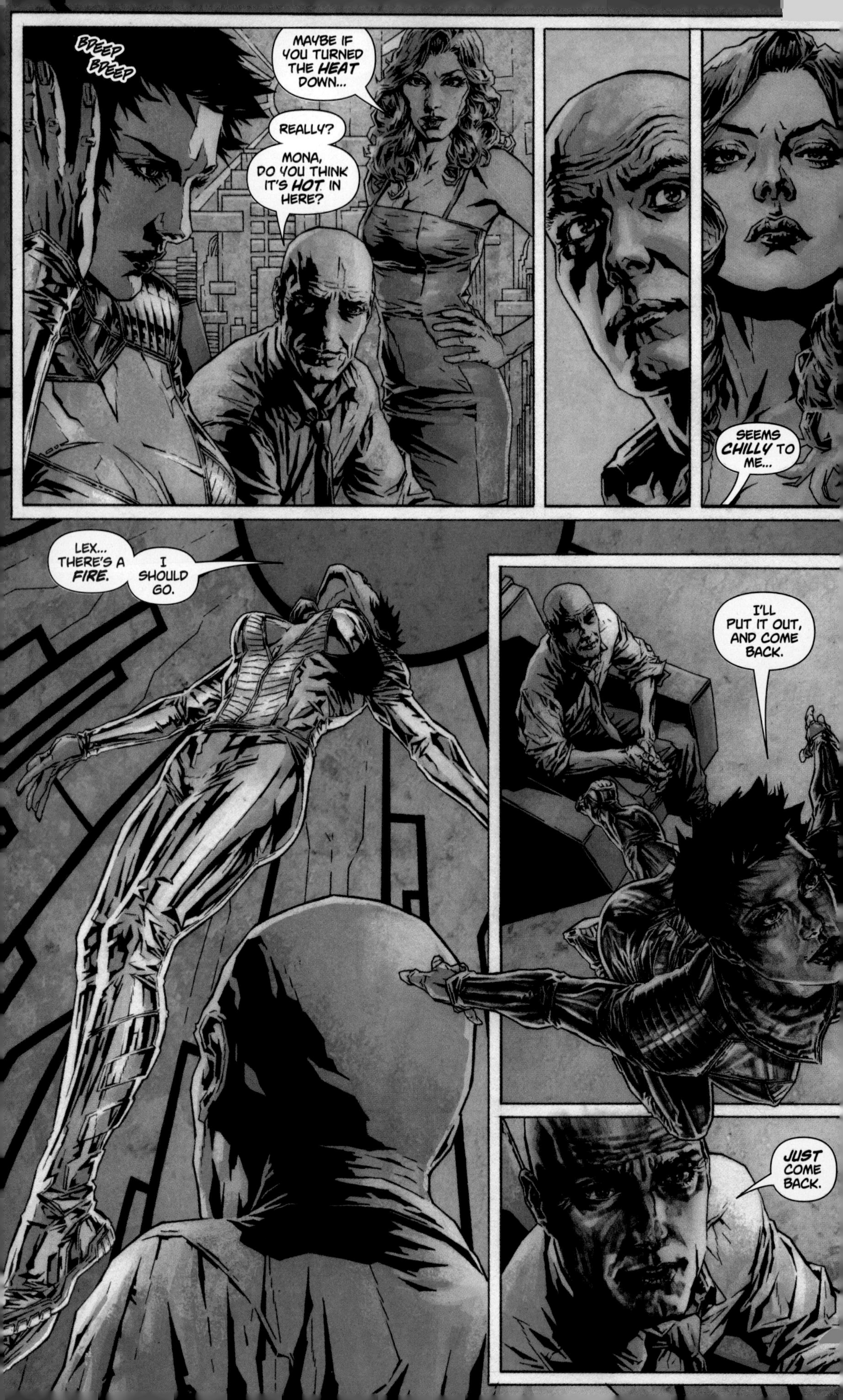
BDEEP BDEEP
MAYBE IF YOU TURNED THE HEAT DOWN...
REALLY?
MONA, DO YOU THINK IT'S HOT IN HERE?
SEEMS CHILLY TO ME...
LEX... THERE'S A FIRE.
I SHOULD GO.
I'LL PUT IT OUT, AND COME BACK.
JUST COME BACK.

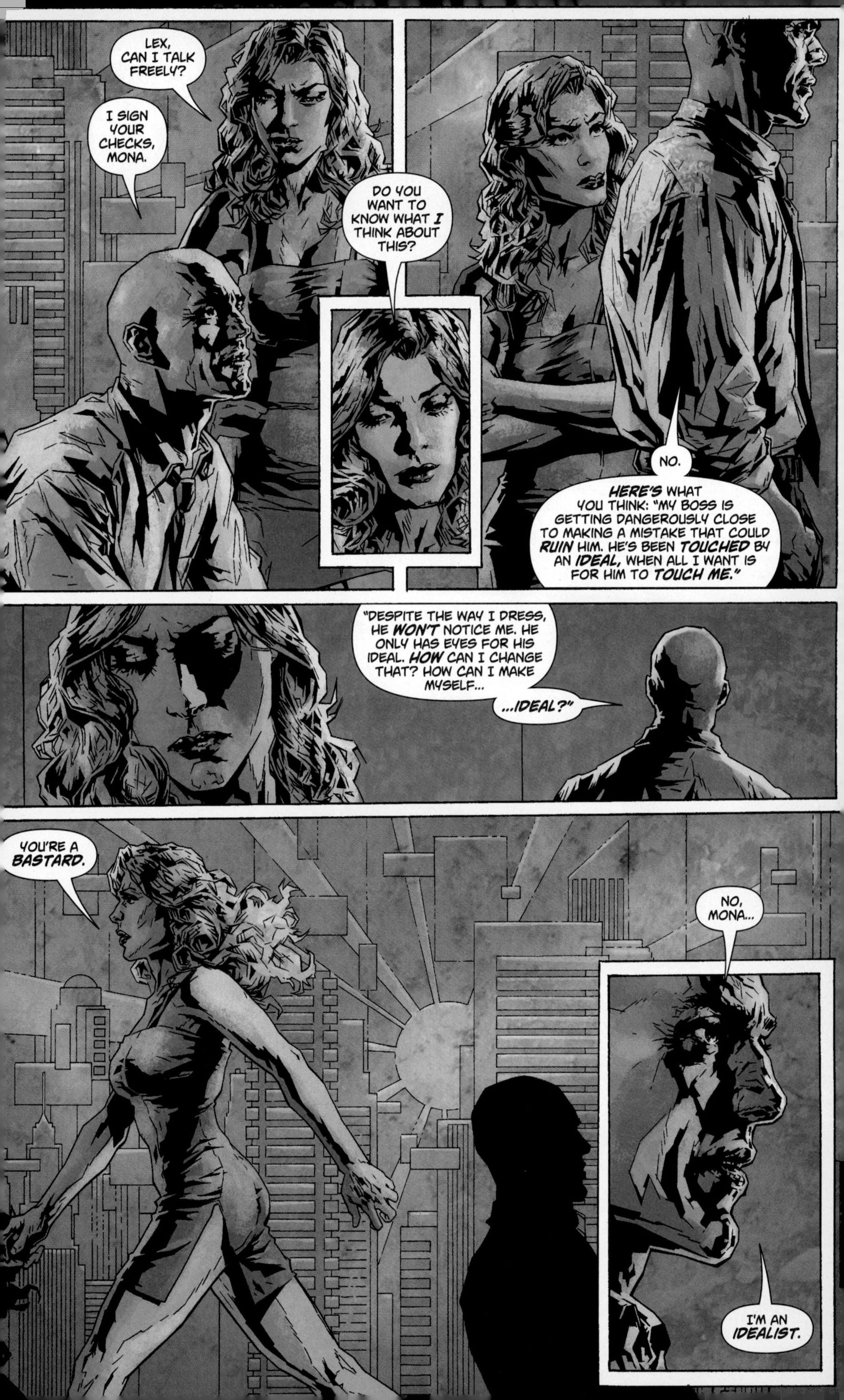
LEX, CAN I TALK FREELY?
I SIGN YOUR CHECKS, MONA.
DO YOU WANT TO KNOW WHAT I THINK ABOUT THIS?
NO.
HERE'S WHAT YOU THINK: "MY BOSS IS GETTING DANGEROUSLY CLOSE TO MAKING A MISTAKE THAT COULD RUIN HIM. HE'S BEEN TOUCHED BY AN IDEAL, WHEN ALL I WANT IS FOR HIM TO TOUCH ME."
"DESPITE THE WAY I DRESS, HE WON'T NOTICE ME. HE ONLY HAS EYES FOR HIS IDEAL. HOW CAN I CHANGE THAT? HOW CAN I MAKE MYSELF...
...IDEAL?"
YOU'RE A BASTARD.
NO, MONA...
I'M AN IDEALIST.

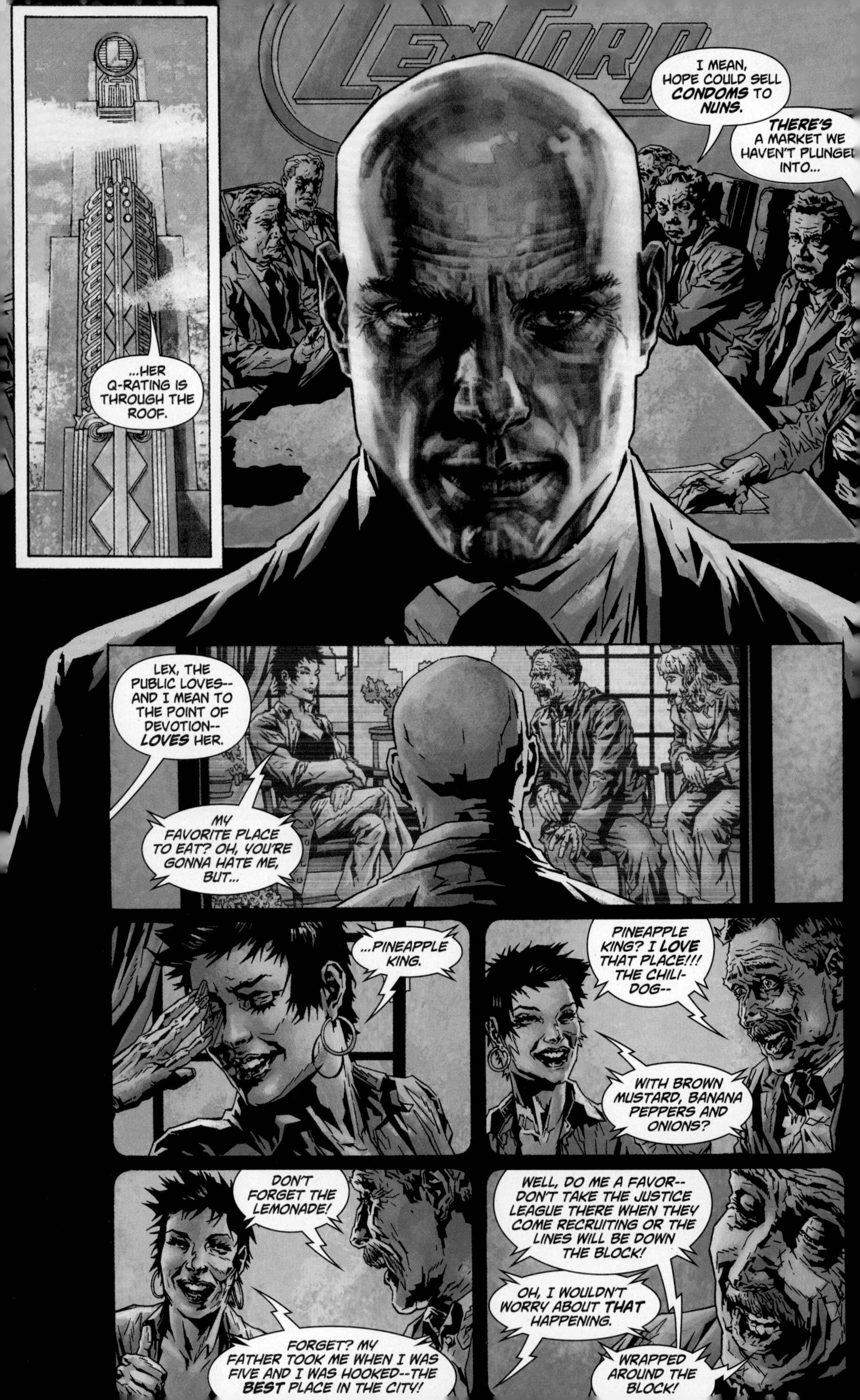

LEXCORP
...HER Q-RATING IS THROUGH THE ROOF.
I MEAN, HOPE COULD SELL CONDOMS TO NUNS.
THERE'S A MARKET WE HAVEN'T PLUNGED INTO...
LEX, THE PUBLIC LOVES-- AND I MEAN TO THE POINT OF DEVOTION-- LOVES HER.
MY FAVORITE PLACE TO EAT? OH, YOU'RE GONNA HATE ME, BUT...
...PINEAPPLE KING.
PINEAPPLE KING? I LOVE THAT PLACE!!! THE CHILI-DOG--
WITH BROWN MUSTARD, BANANA PEPPERS AND ONIONS?
DON'T FORGET THE LEMONADE!
FORGET? MY FATHER TOOK ME WHEN I WAS FIVE AND I WAS HOOKED--THE BEST PLACE IN THE CITY!
WELL, DO ME A FAVOR-- DON'T TAKE THE JUSTICE LEAGUE THERE WHEN THEY COME RECRUITING OR THE LINES WILL BE DOWN THE BLOCK!
OH, I WOULDN'T WORRY ABOUT THAT HAPPENING.
WRAPPED AROUND THE BLOCK!

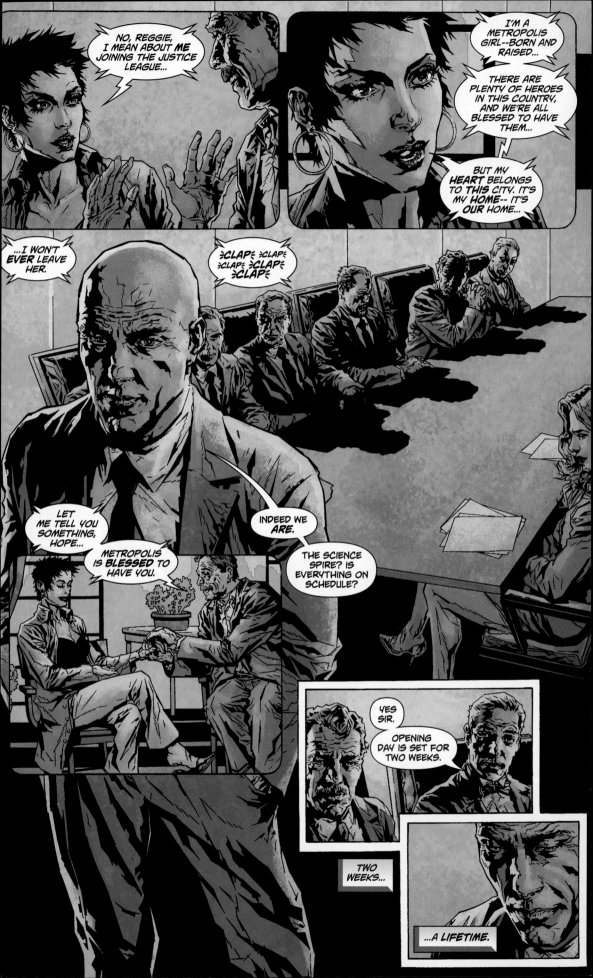

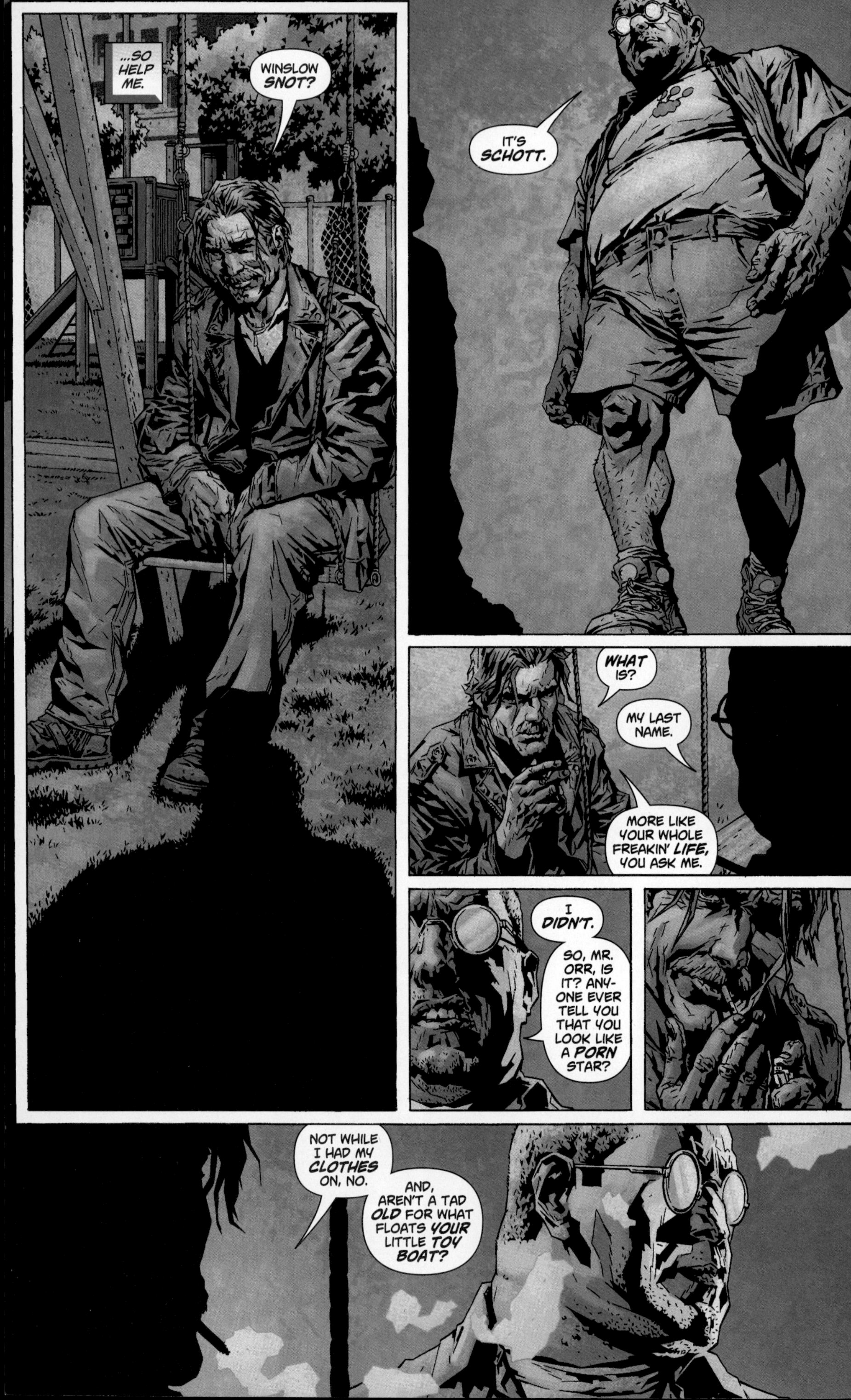
...SO HELP ME.
WINSLOW SNOT?
IT'S SCHOTT.
WHAT IS?
MY LAST NAME.
MORE LIKE YOUR WHOLE FREAKIN' LIFE, YOU ASK ME.
I DIDN'T.
SO, MR. ORR, IS IT? ANY-ONE EVER TELL YOU THAT YOU LOOK LIKE A PORN STAR?
NOT WHILE I HAD MY CLOTHES ON, NO.
AND, AREN'T A TAD OLD FOR WHAT FLOATS YOUR LITTLE TOY BOAT?

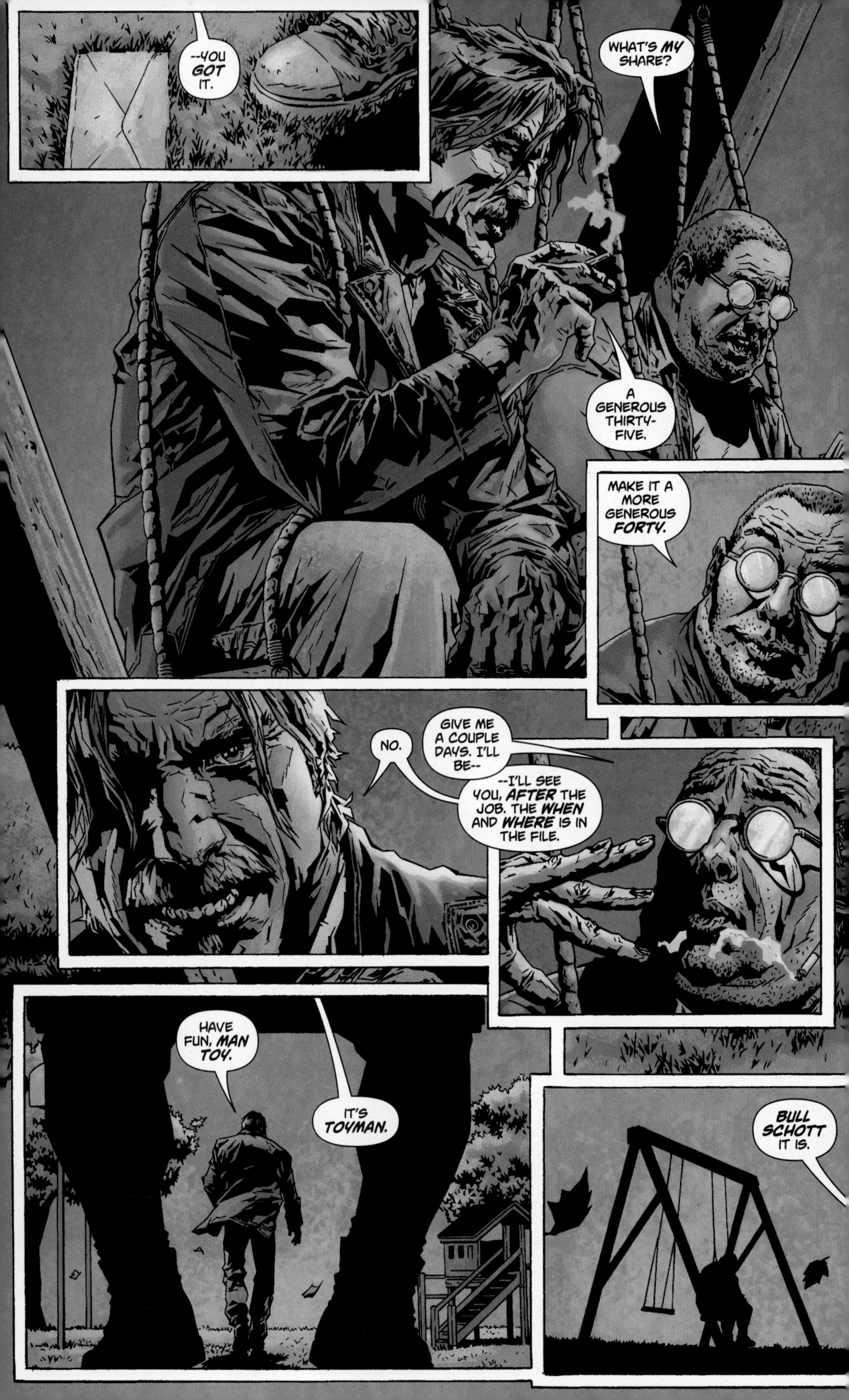
--YOU GOT IT.
WHAT'S MY SHARE?
A GENEROUS THIRTY-FIVE.
MAKE IT A MORE GENEROUS FORTY.
NO.
GIVE ME A COUPLE DAYS. I'LL BE--
--I'LL SEE YOU, AFTER THE JOB. THE WHEN AND WHERE IS IN THE FILE.
HAVE FUN, MAN TOY.
IT'S TOYMAN.
BULL SCHOTT IT IS.

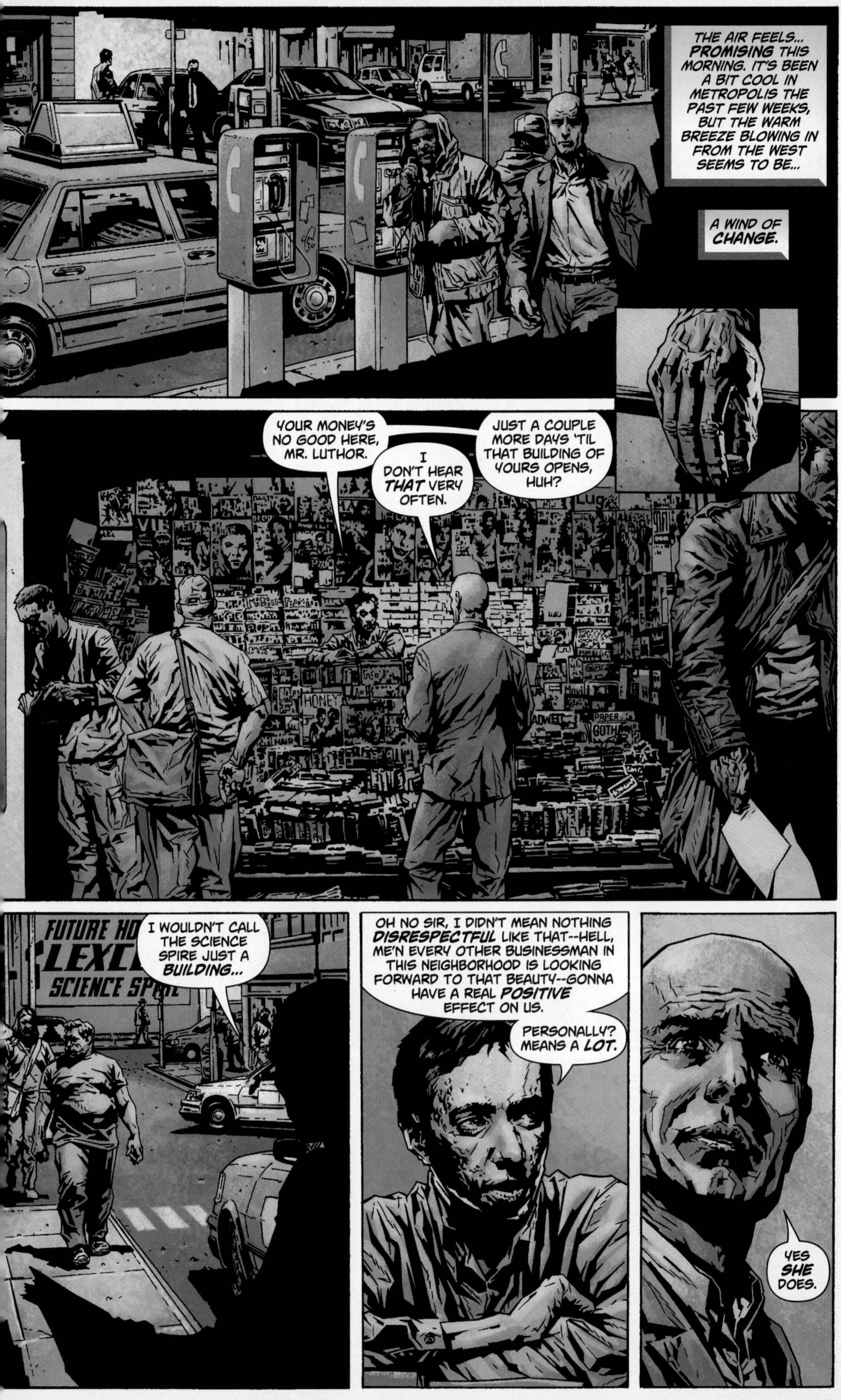
THE AIR FEELS... PROMISING THIS MORNING. IT'S BEEN A BIT COOL IN METROPOLIS THE PAST FEW WEEKS, BUT THE WARM BREEZE BLOWING IN FROM THE WEST SEEMS TO BE...
A WIND OF CHANGE.
YOUR MONEY'S NO GOOD HERE, MR. LUTHOR.
I DON'T HEAR THAT VERY OFTEN.
JUST A COUPLE MORE DAYS 'TIL THAT BUILDING OF YOURS OPENS, HUH?
FUTURE HO
LEXC
SCIENCE SPI
I WOULDN'T CALL THE SCIENCE SPIRE JUST A BUILDING...
OH NO SIR, I DIDN'T MEAN NOTHING DISRESPECTFUL LIKE THAT--HELL, ME'N EVERY OTHER BUSINESSMAN IN THIS NEIGHBORHOOD IS LOOKING FORWARD TO THAT BEAUTY--GONNA HAVE A REAL POSITIVE EFFECT ON US.
PERSONALLY? MEANS A LOT.
YES SHE DOES.

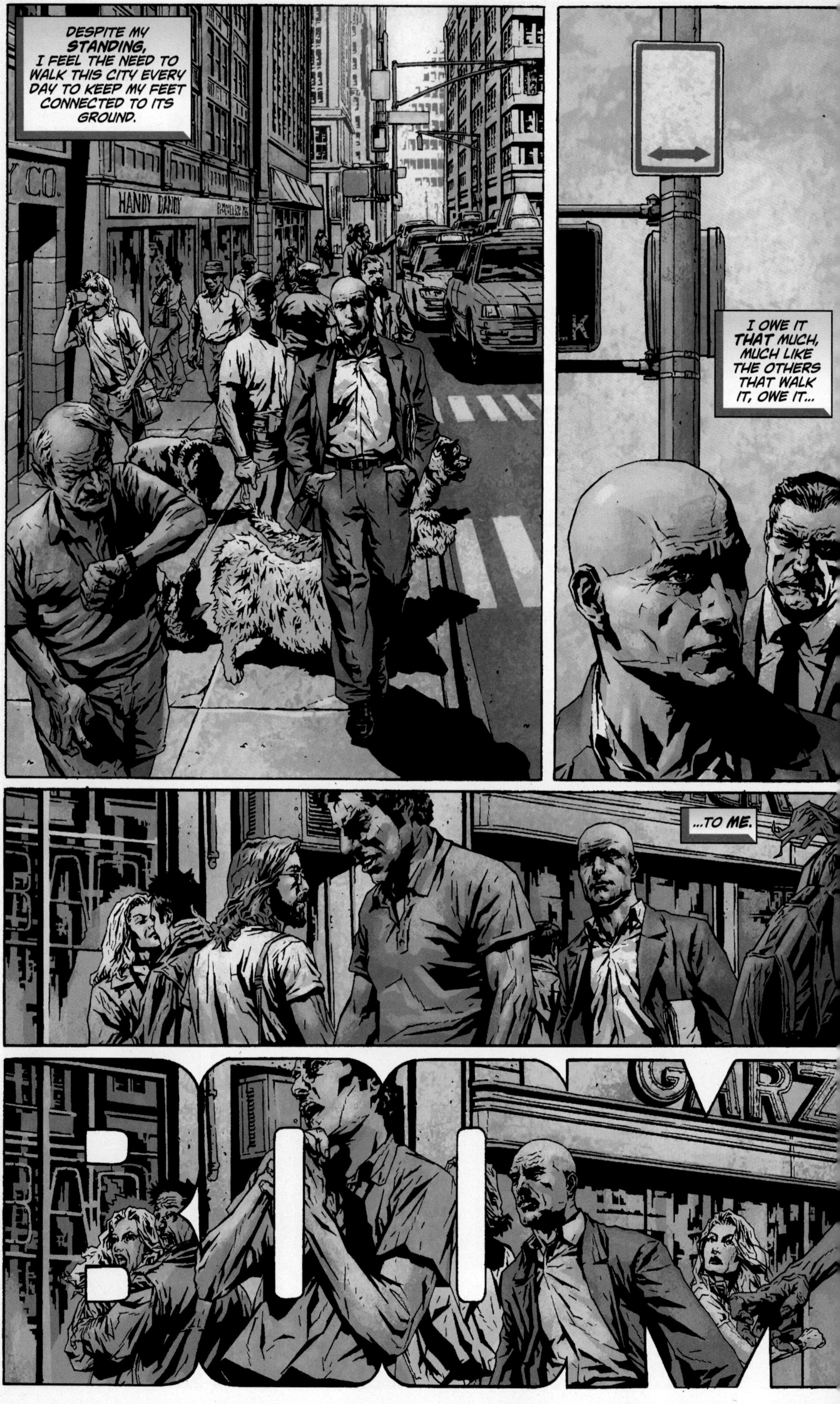
DESPITE MY STANDING, I FEEL THE NEED TO WALK THIS CITY EVERY DAY TO KEEP MY FEET CONNECTED TO ITS GROUND.
HANDY DANDY
I OWE IT THAT MUCH, MUCH LIKE THE OTHERS THAT WALK IT, OWE IT...
...TO ME.
BOOM

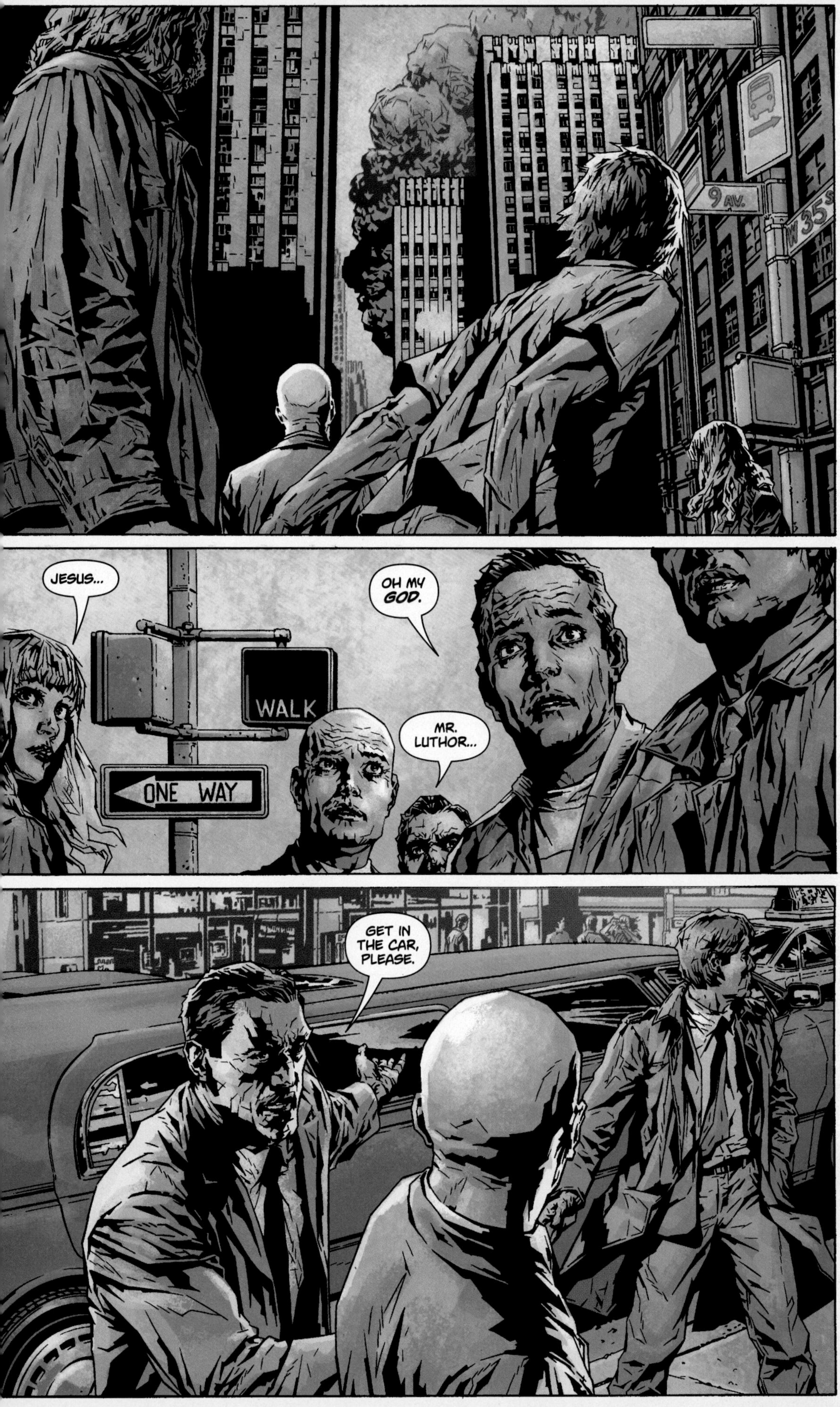
9 AV.
JESUS...
OH MY GOD.
WALK
ONE WAY
MR. LUTHOR...
GET IN THE CAR, PLEASE.

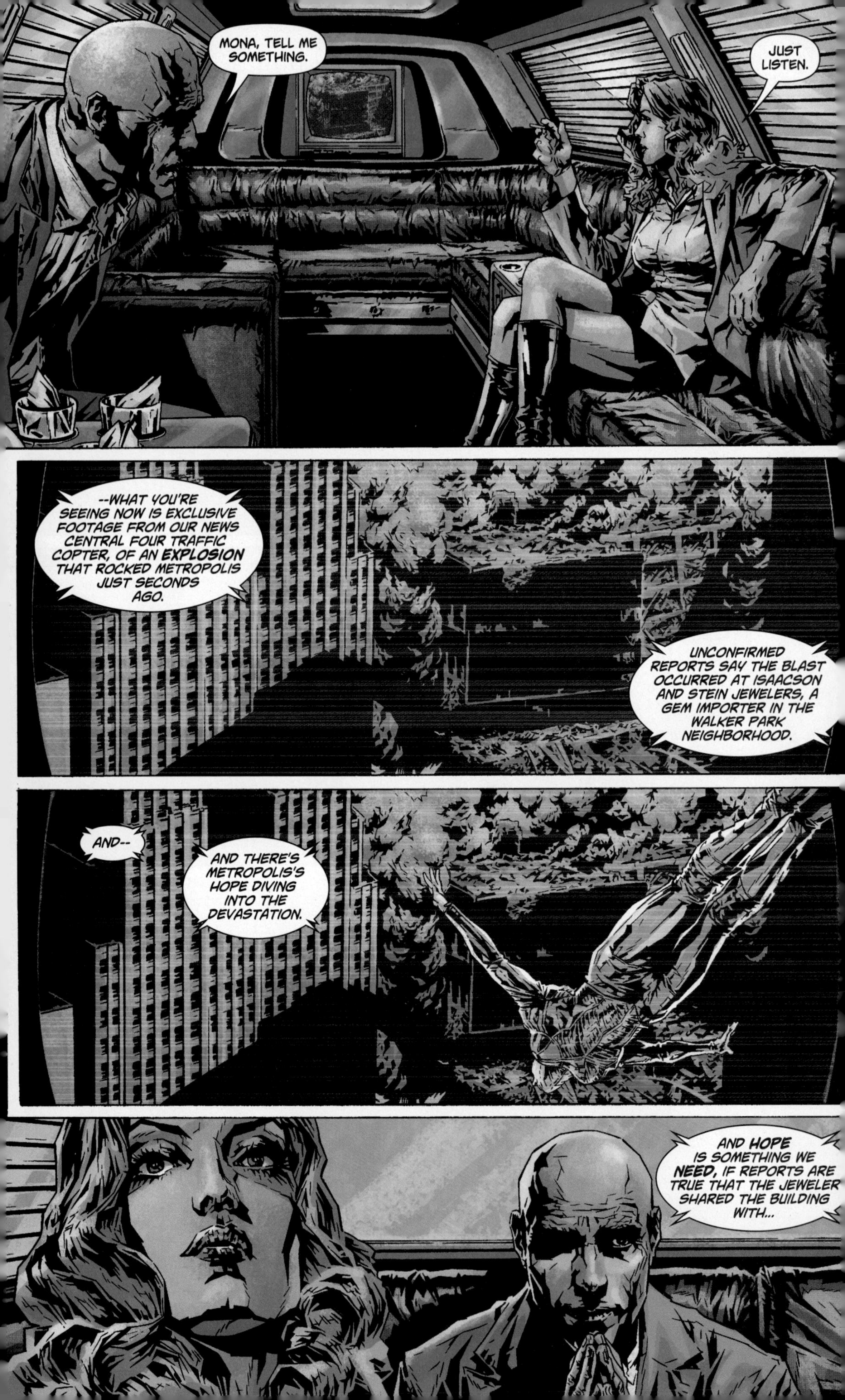
MONA, TELL ME SOMETHING.
JUST LISTEN.
--WHAT YOU'RE SEEING NOW IS EXCLUSIVE FOOTAGE FROM OUR NEWS CENTRAL FOUR TRAFFIC COPTER, OF AN **EXPLOSION** THAT ROCKED METROPOLIS JUST SECONDS AGO.
UNCONFIRMED REPORTS SAY THE BLAST OCCURRED AT ISAACSON AND STEIN JEWELERS, A GEM IMPORTER IN THE WALKER PARK NEIGHBORHOOD.
AND--
AND THERE'S METROPOLIS'S HOPE DIVING INTO THE DEVASTATION.
AND **HOPE** IS SOMETHING WE **NEED**, IF REPORTS ARE TRUE THAT THE JEWELER SHARED THE BUILDING WITH...

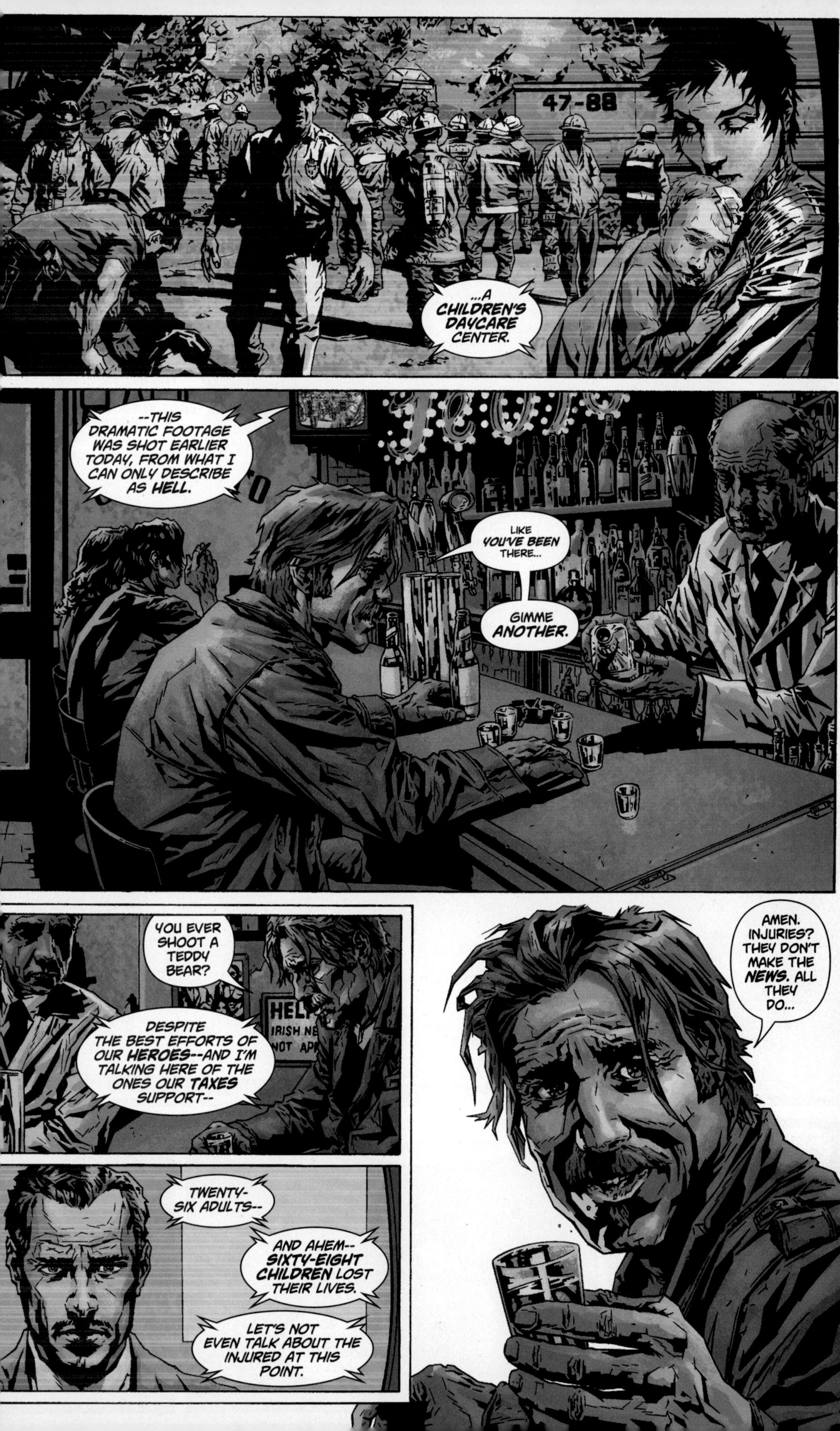
...A CHILDREN'S DAYCARE CENTER.
--THIS DRAMATIC FOOTAGE WAS SHOT EARLIER TODAY, FROM WHAT I CAN ONLY DESCRIBE AS HELL.
LIKE YOU'VE BEEN THERE...
GIMME ANOTHER.
YOU EVER SHOOT A TEDDY BEAR?
DESPITE THE BEST EFFORTS OF OUR HEROES--AND I'M TALKING HERE OF THE ONES OUR TAXES SUPPORT--
TWENTY-SIX ADULTS--
AND AHEM--SIXTY-EIGHT CHILDREN LOST THEIR LIVES.
LET'S NOT EVEN TALK ABOUT THE INJURED AT THIS POINT.
AMEN. INJURIES? THEY DON'T MAKE THE NEWS. ALL THEY DO...

...AND I'M LEFT WITH A **LIFETIME** IN MY HANDS, **UNFULFILLED.**

...MORE LIKELY, THE "SELLING-**OUT**" OF ONE.

THE "SELLING OF A HERO," MR. KENT?...

SASHA FEDEROV AND HIS WIFE WERE DROPPING THEIR CHILDREN AT DAYCARE THIS MORNING WHEN THE EXPLOSION OCCURRED...

THE **ENTIRE** FAMILY IS **DEAD.**

MONA, PLEASE MAKE THE ARRANGEMENTS.

I'LL GET ON IT--

--NOW.

I **HAVE** TO FIND THE TOYMAN...

YES, YOU **WILL.**

BUT THAT HAS TO **WAIT.**

WHAT MONA WAS SAYING...

HOW DOES THAT MAKE YOU **FEEL?**

LIKE BECAUSE OF MY ABILITIES, I'M **LESS** THAN A **WOMAN.**

HOPE...

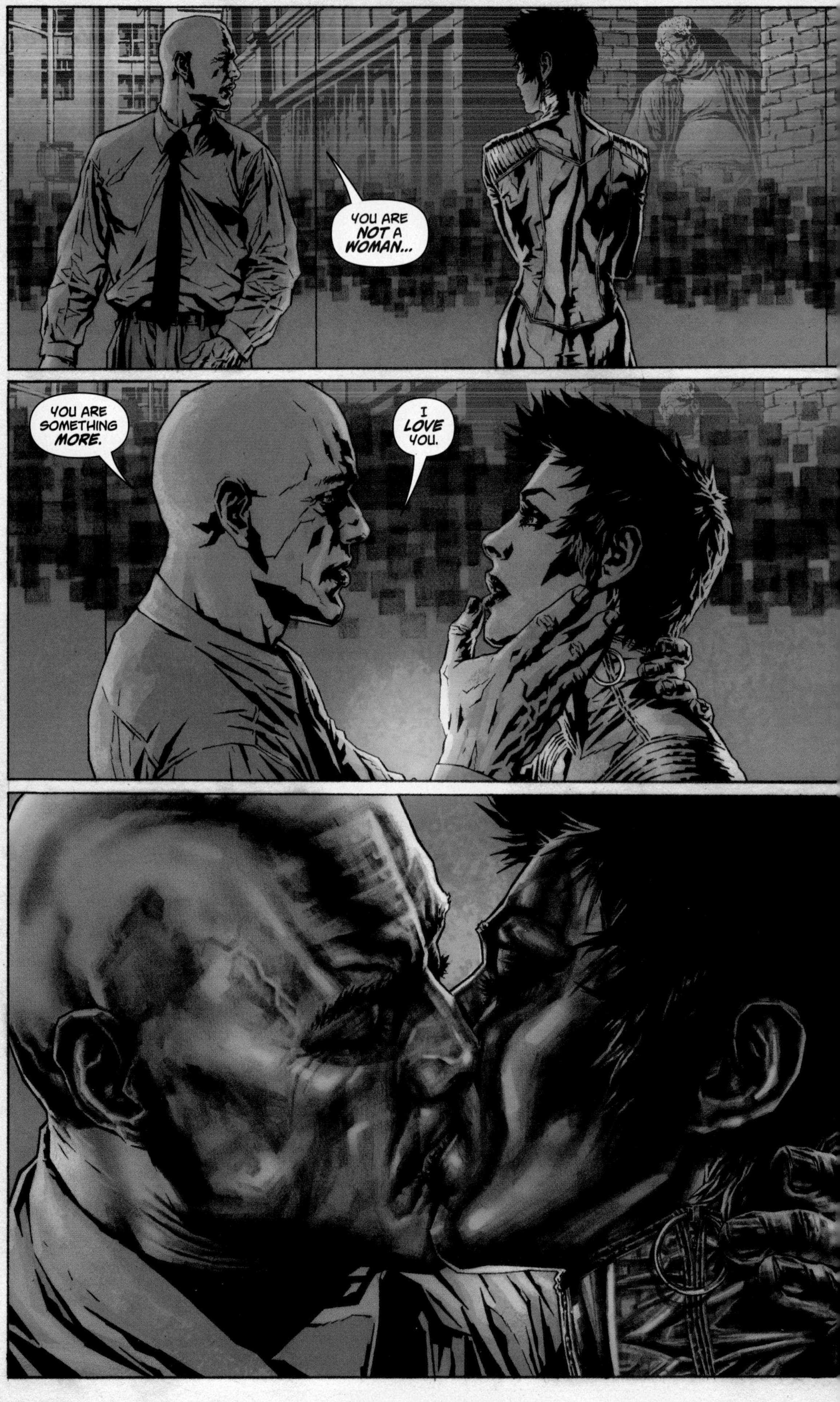
YOU ARE NOT A WOMAN...
YOU ARE SOMETHING MORE.
I LOVE YOU.

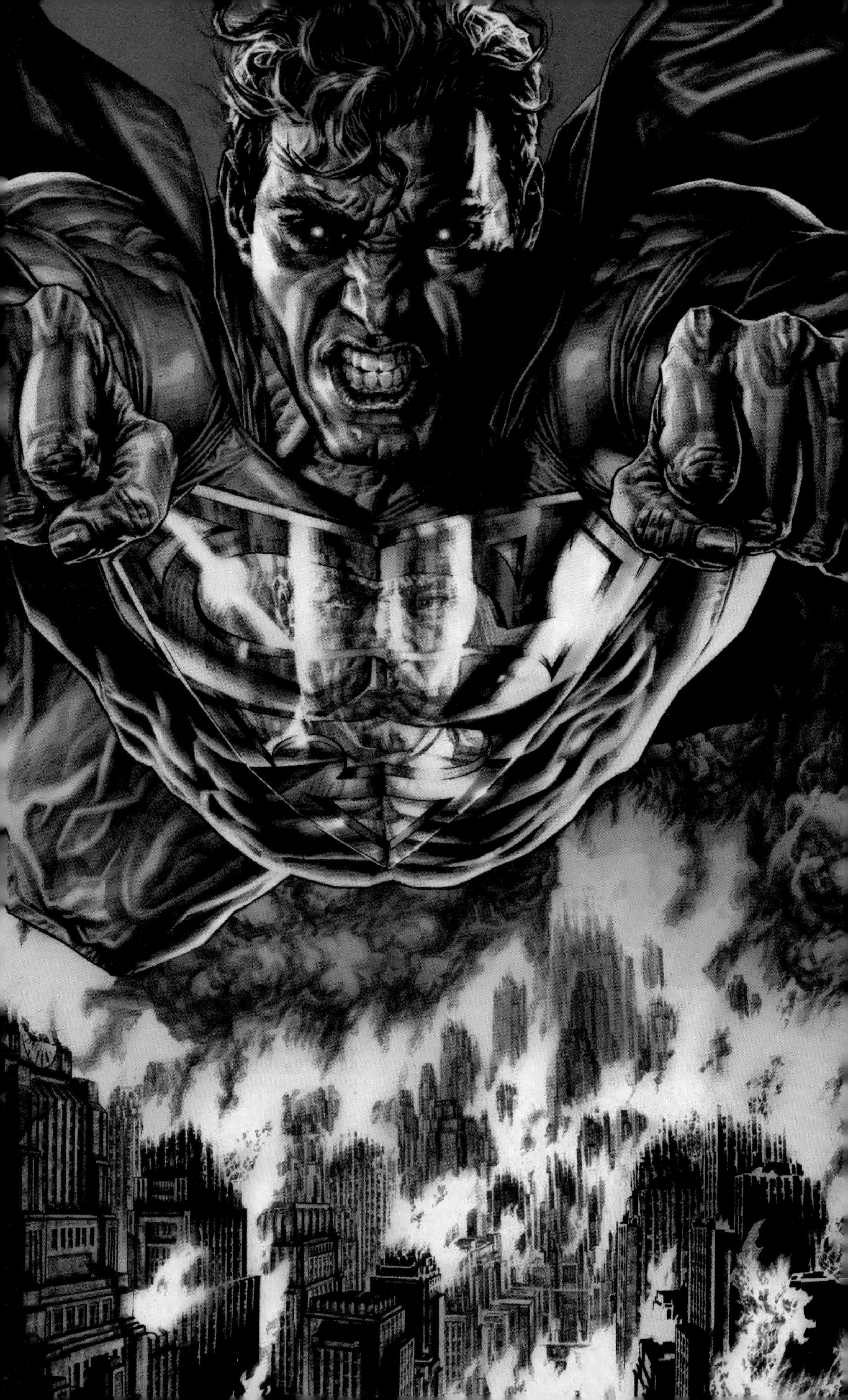

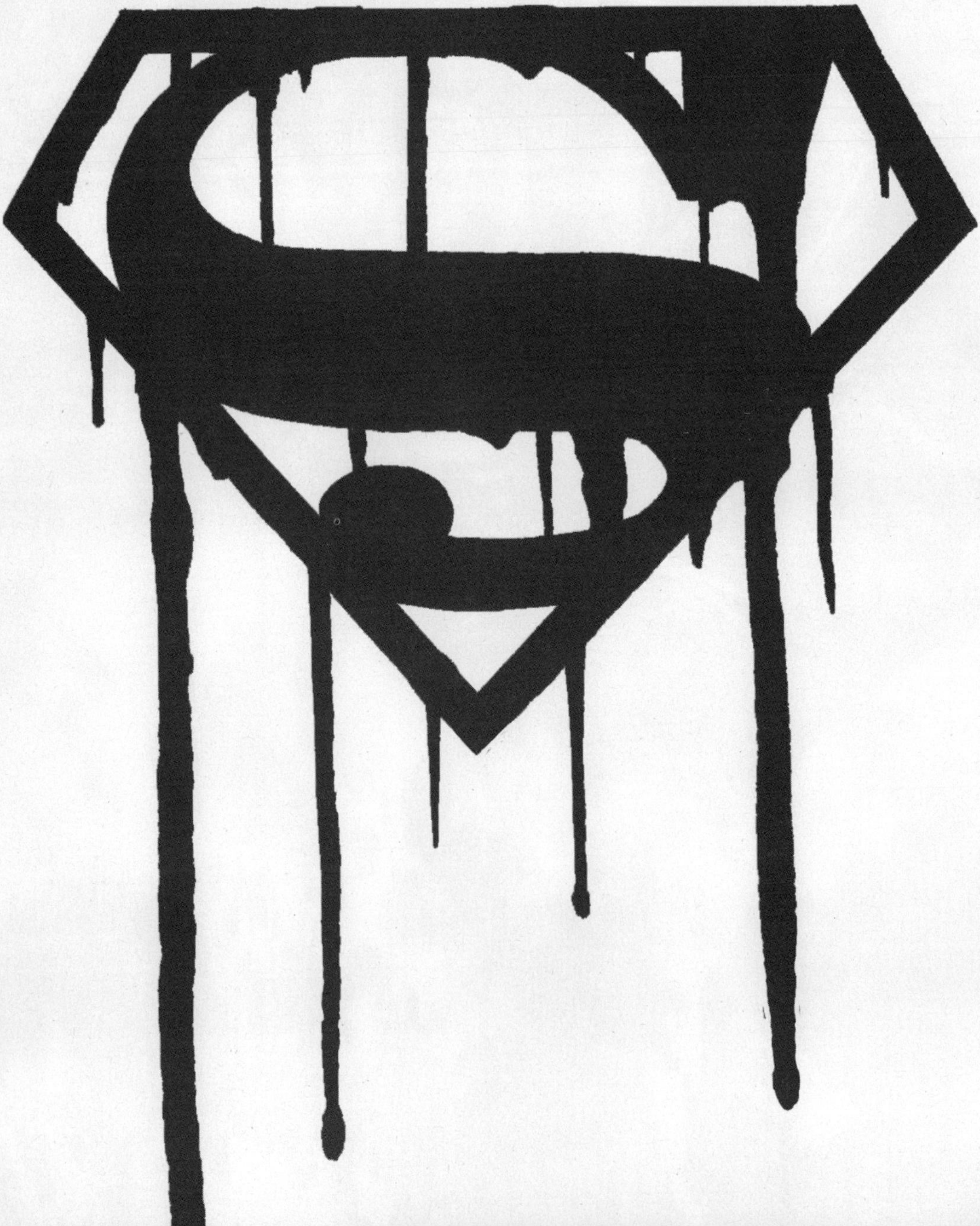

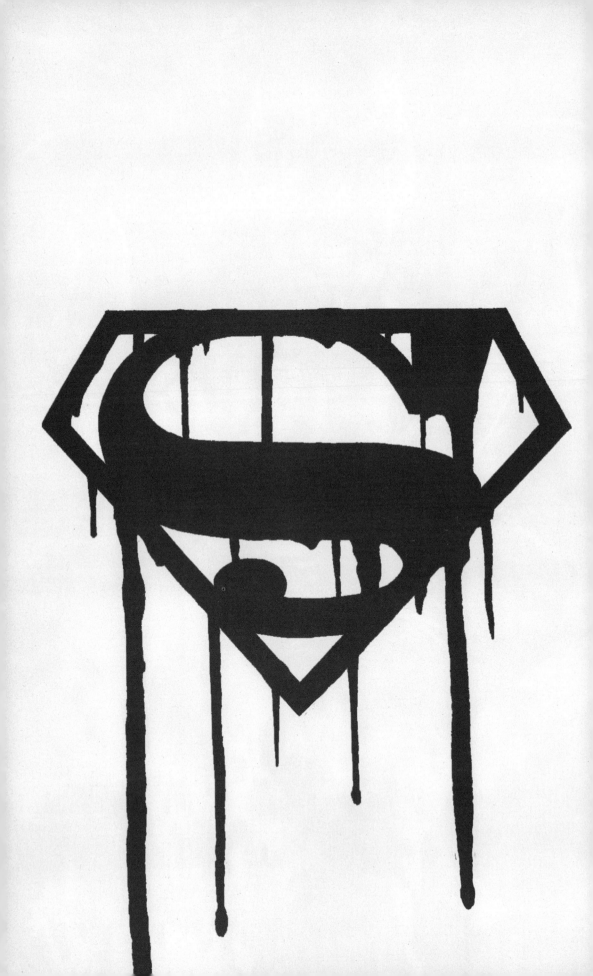

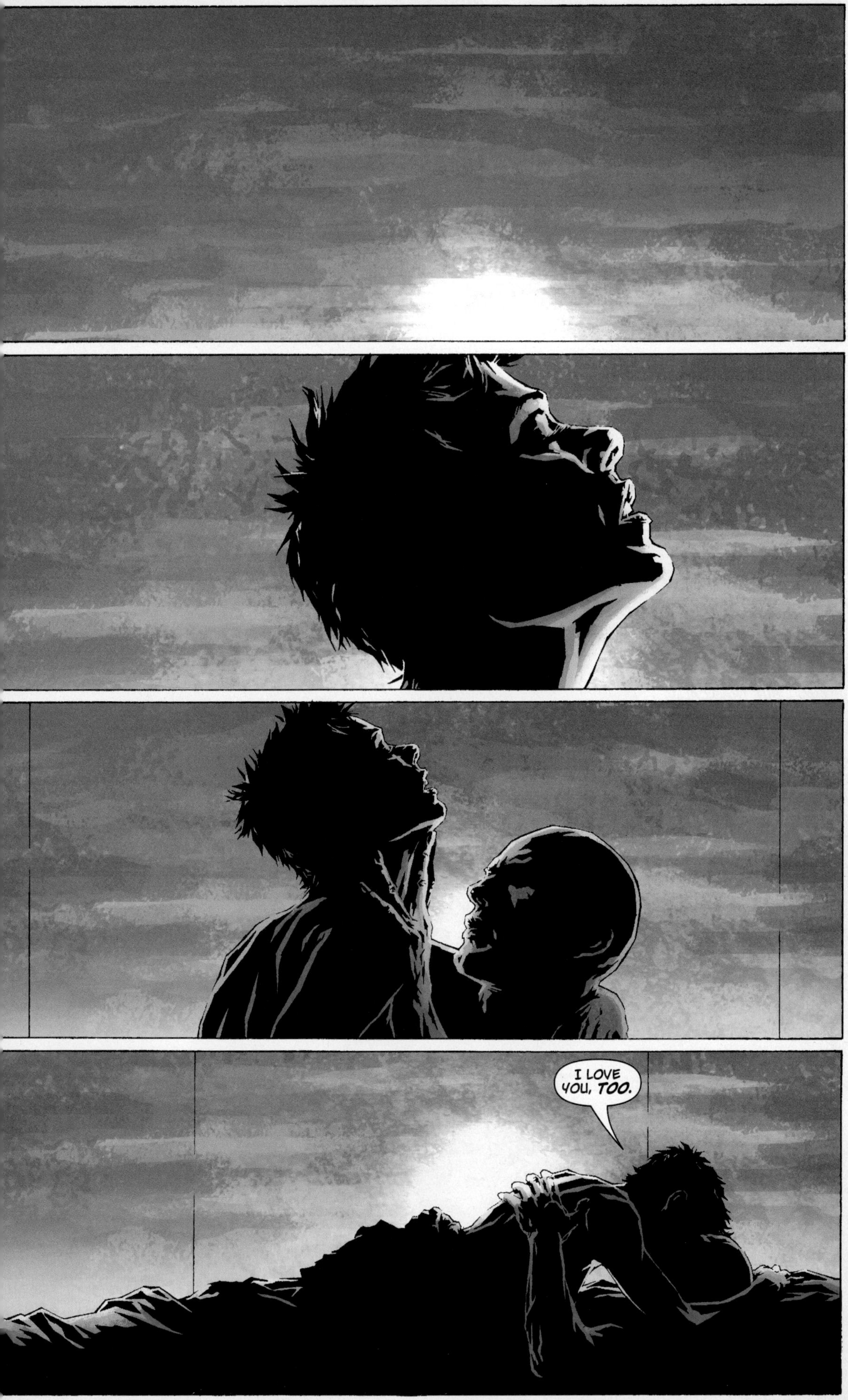
I LOVE YOU, TOO.

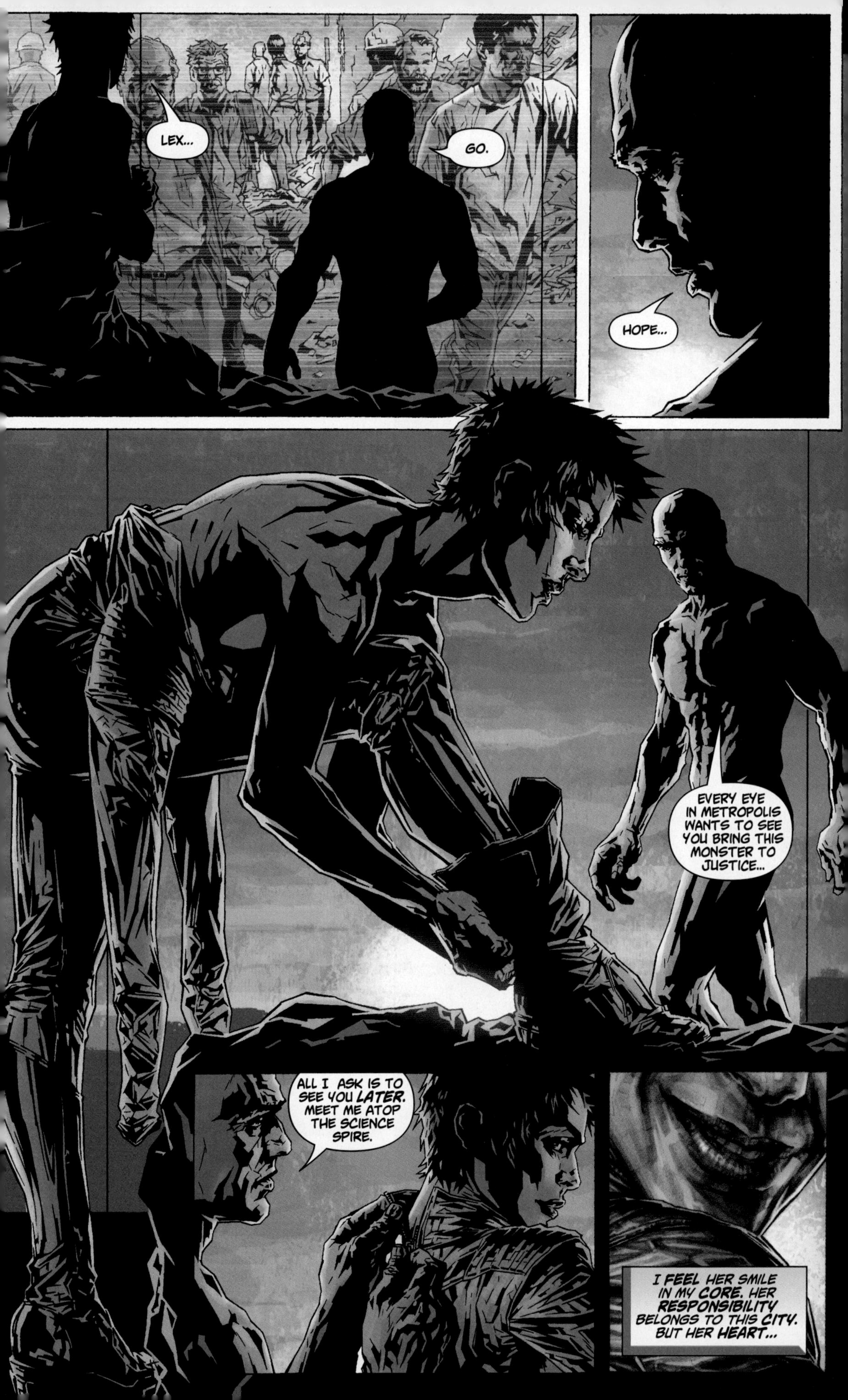
LEX...
GO.
HOPE...
EVERY EYE IN METROPOLIS WANTS TO SEE YOU BRING THIS MONSTER TO JUSTICE...
ALL I ASK IS TO SEE YOU LATER. MEET ME ATOP THE SCIENCE SPIRE.
I FEEL HER SMILE IN MY CORE. HER RESPONSIBILITY BELONGS TO THIS CITY. BUT HER HEART...

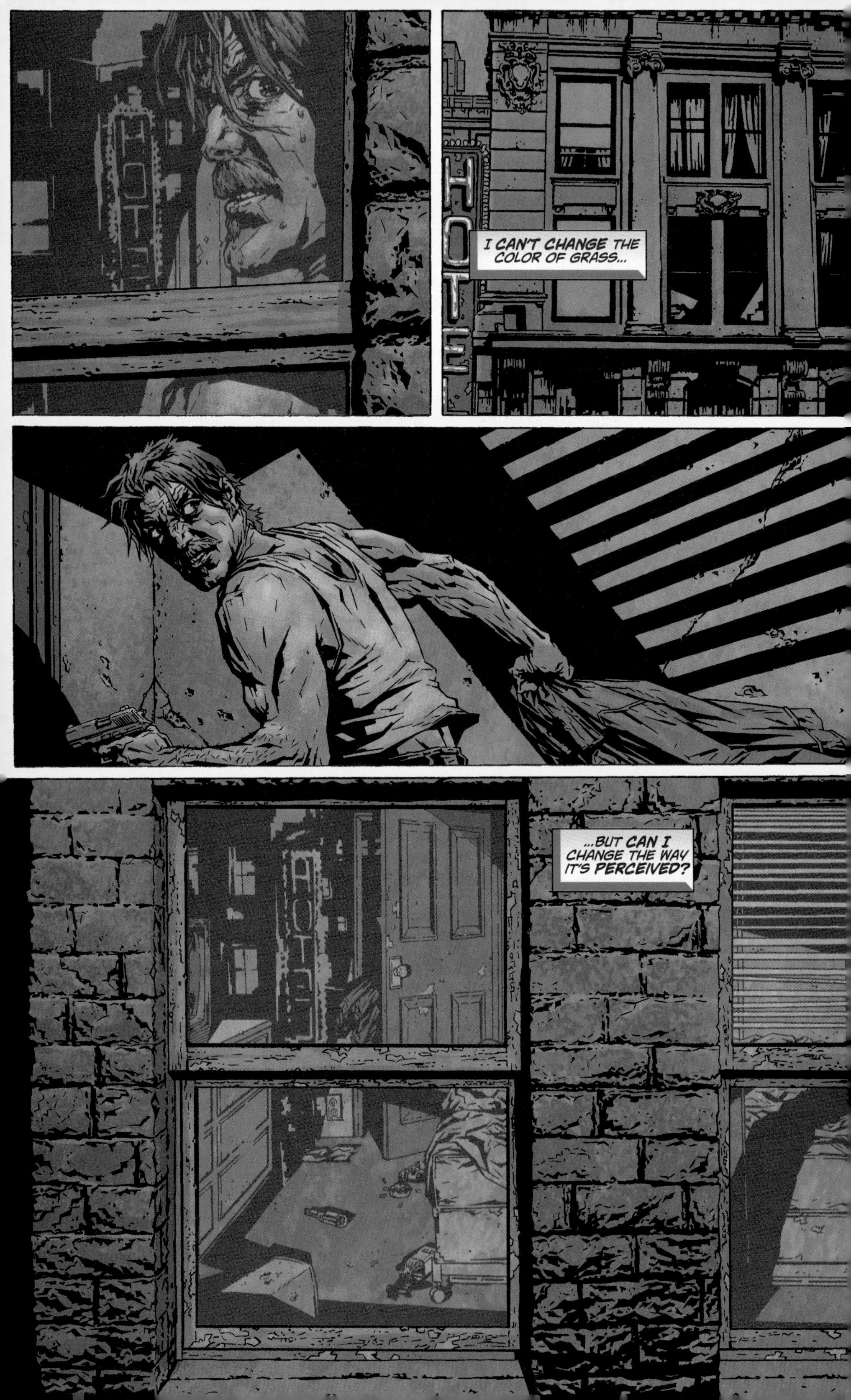
HOTE
I CAN'T CHANGE THE COLOR OF GRASS...
...BUT CAN I CHANGE THE WAY IT'S PERCEIVED?

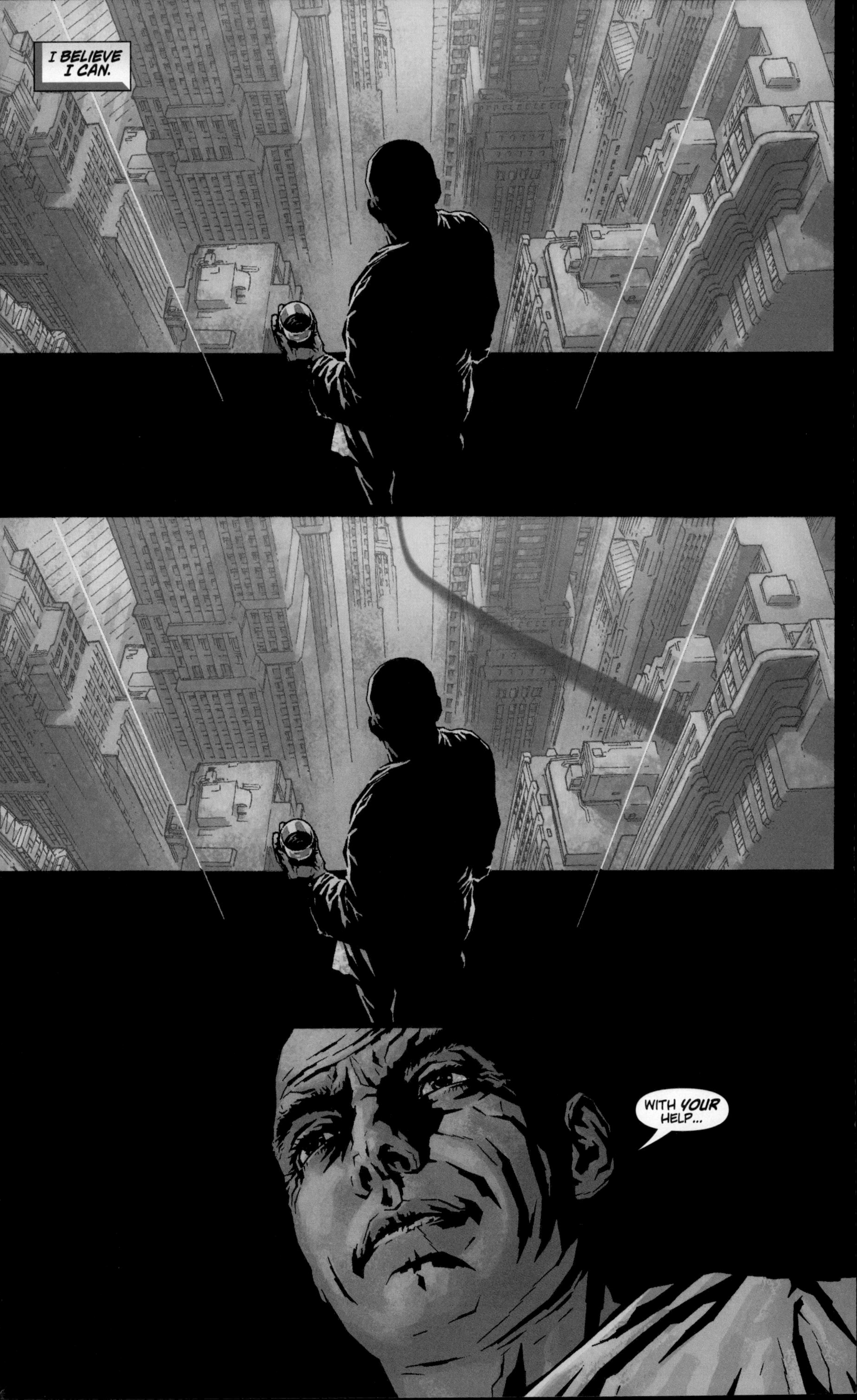
I BELIEVE I CAN.
WITH YOUR HELP...

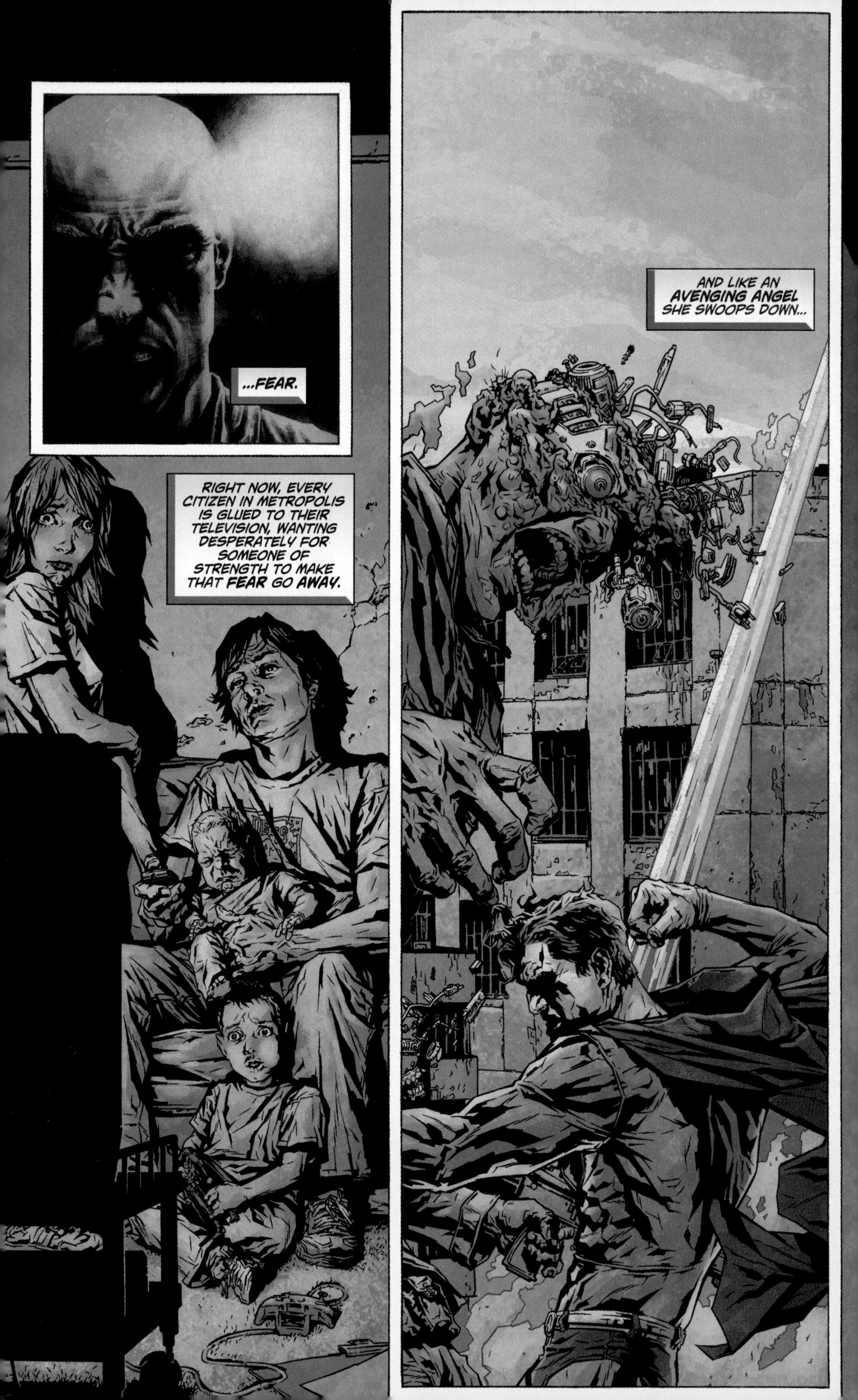
...FEAR.
RIGHT NOW, EVERY CITIZEN IN METROPOLIS IS GLUED TO THEIR TELEVISION, WANTING DESPERATELY FOR SOMEONE OF STRENGTH TO MAKE THAT FEAR GO AWAY.
AND LIKE AN AVENGING ANGEL SHE SWOOPS DOWN...

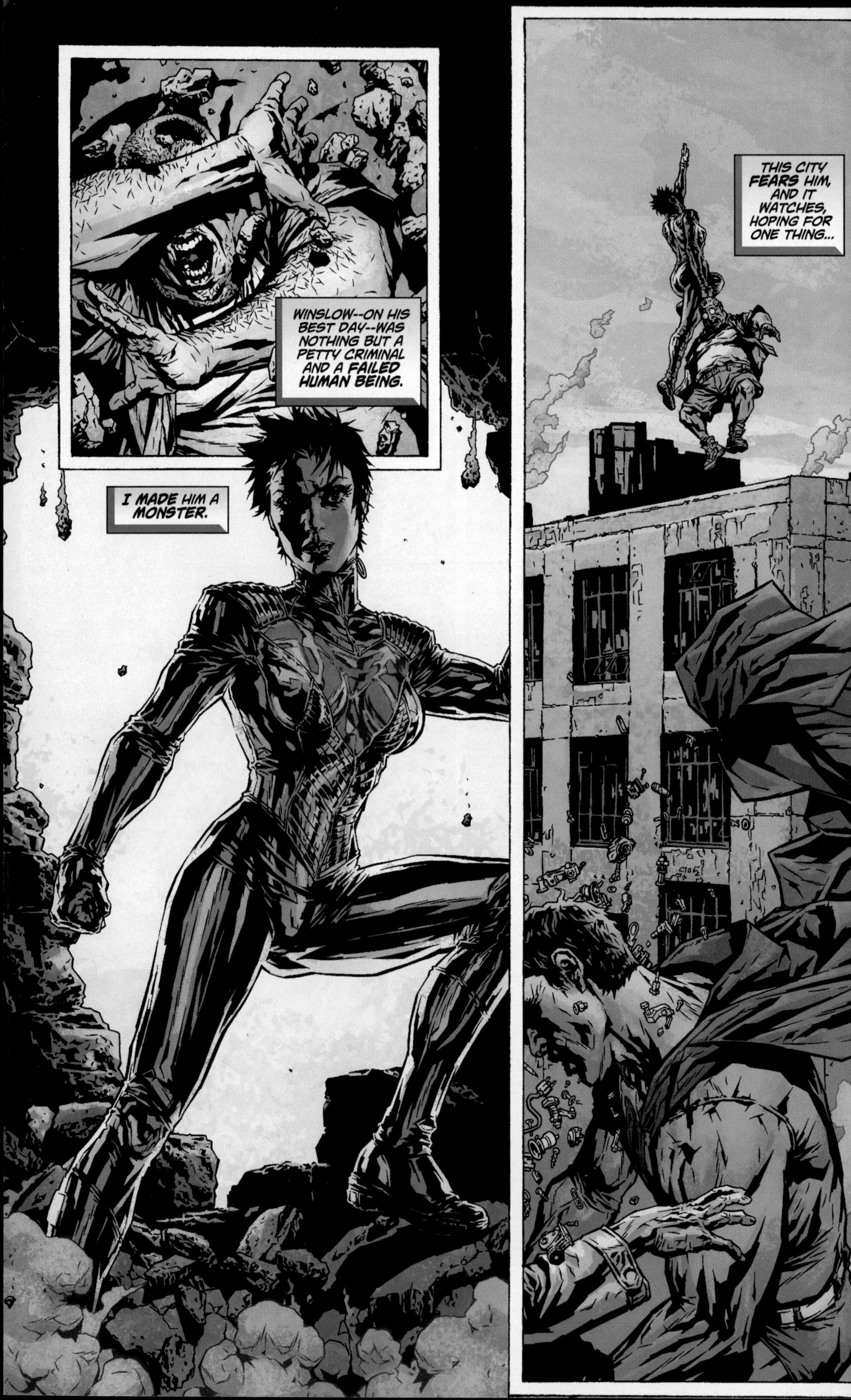
WINSLOW--ON HIS BEST DAY--WAS NOTHING BUT A PETTY CRIMINAL AND A FAILED HUMAN BEING.
I MADE HIM A MONSTER.
THIS CITY FEARS HIM, AND IT WATCHES, HOPING FOR ONE THING...

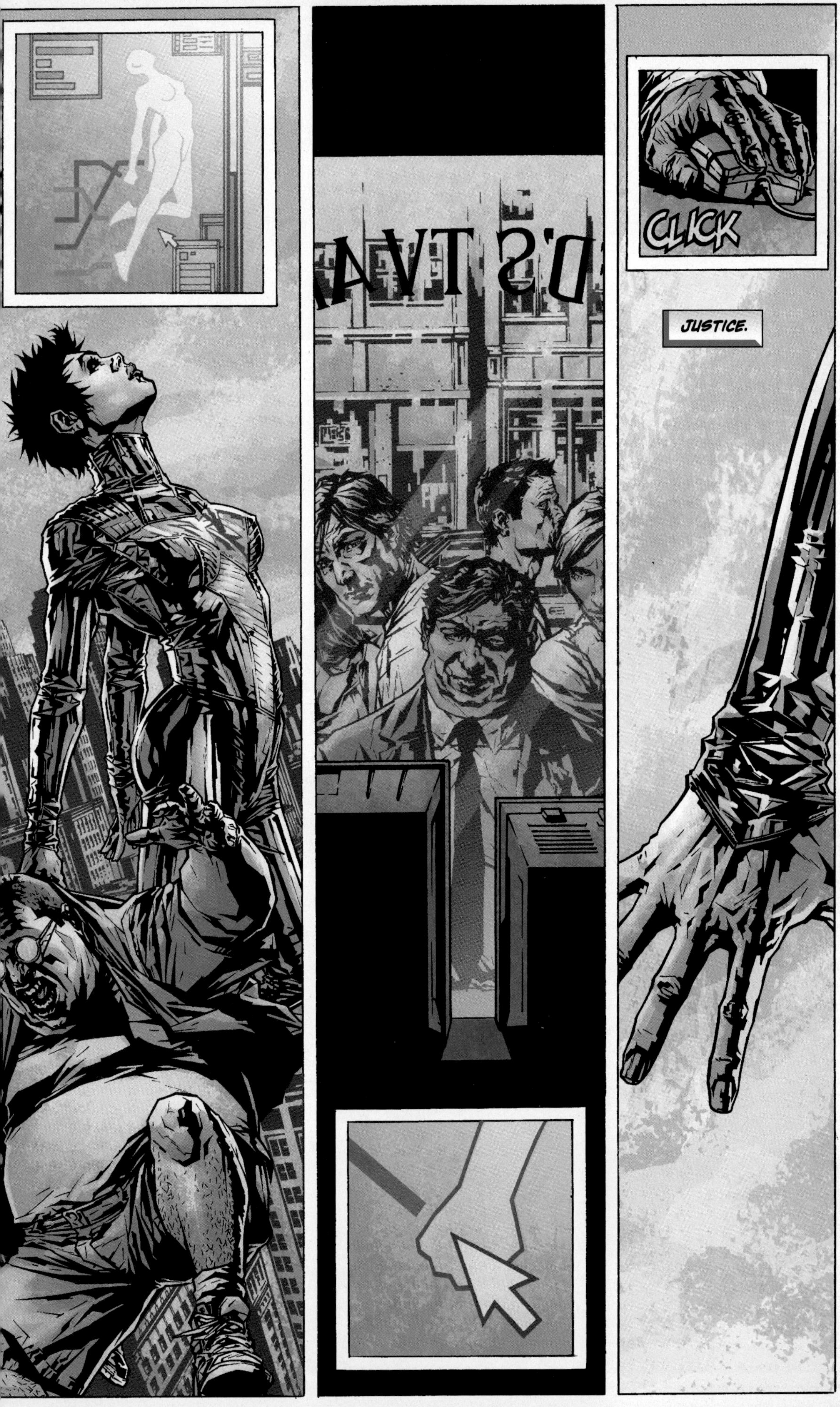
CLICK
JUSTICE.

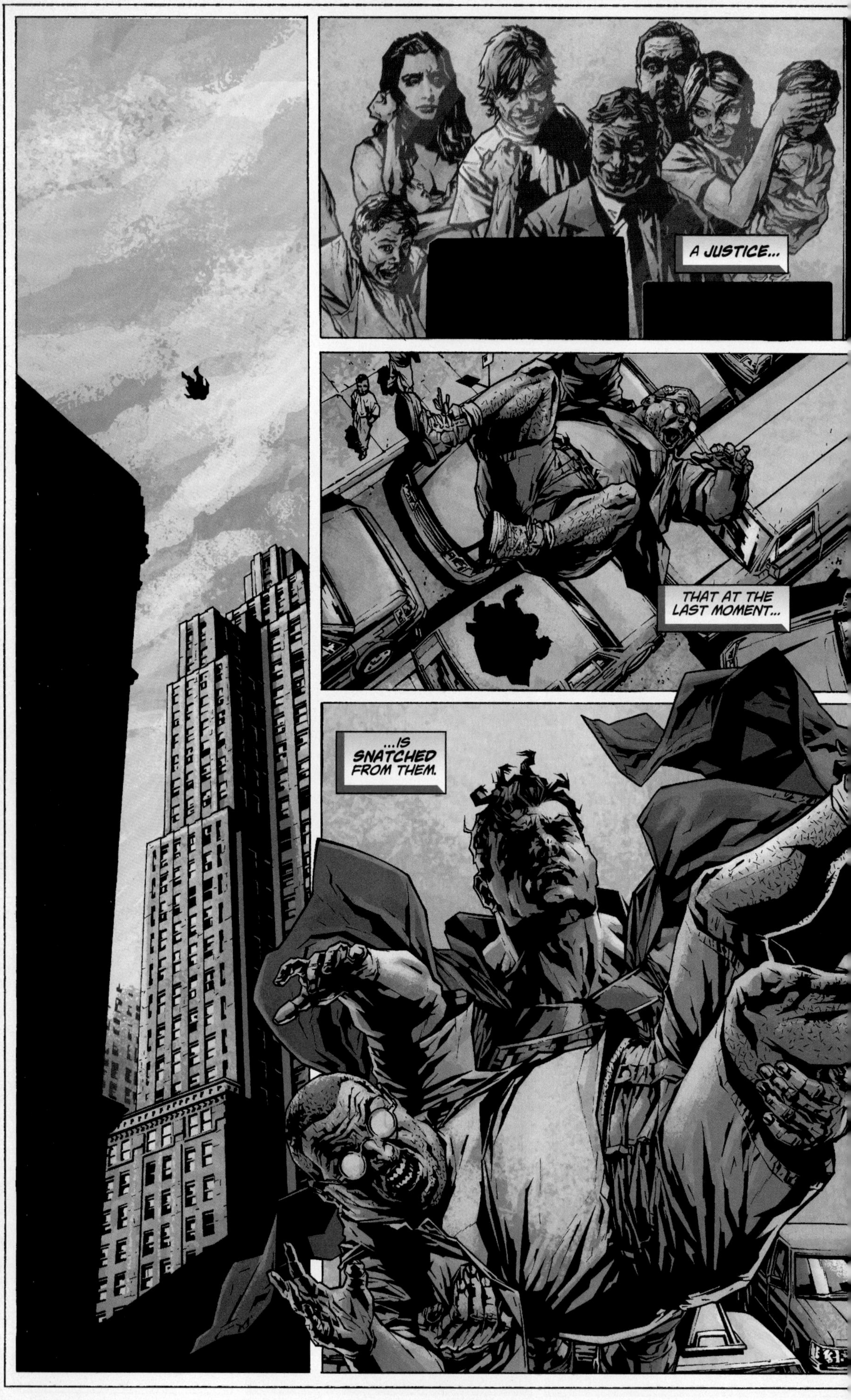
[redacted]
A JUSTICE...
[redacted]
THAT AT THE LAST MOMENT...
...IS SNATCHED FROM THEM.

BUT THEN, HOPE IS AN ASPIRATION.

A BEACON THAT SHINES BRIGHTER THAN ANY STAR, LIGHTING THE WAY FOR ALL MANKIND.

OQ111DHH_JUFJJNWMNDM093762_0001000100110110000100...JWY 0001111KSDHH1KSDHH_JUFJJNWM 762_0001000100110110000100

AUTO-
DESTRUCT_

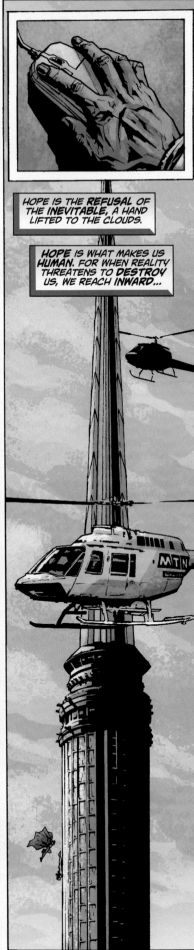

HOPE IS THE REFUSAL OF THE INEVITABLE, A HAND LIFTED TO THE CLOUDS.

HOPE IS WHAT MAKES US HUMAN. FOR WHEN REALITY THREATENS TO DESTROY US, WE REACH INWARD...

...AND WE CREATE HOPE.

IT'S THE GREATEST GIFT WE CAN GIVE EACH OTHER.

THOUGH, IT JUST MAY BE THE FOUNDATION....

OQ111DHH_JUFJJNWMNDM093767 0001001101100001000...JW KSDHH1KSDHH_JUFJJNW 10110000100

DETONATE_

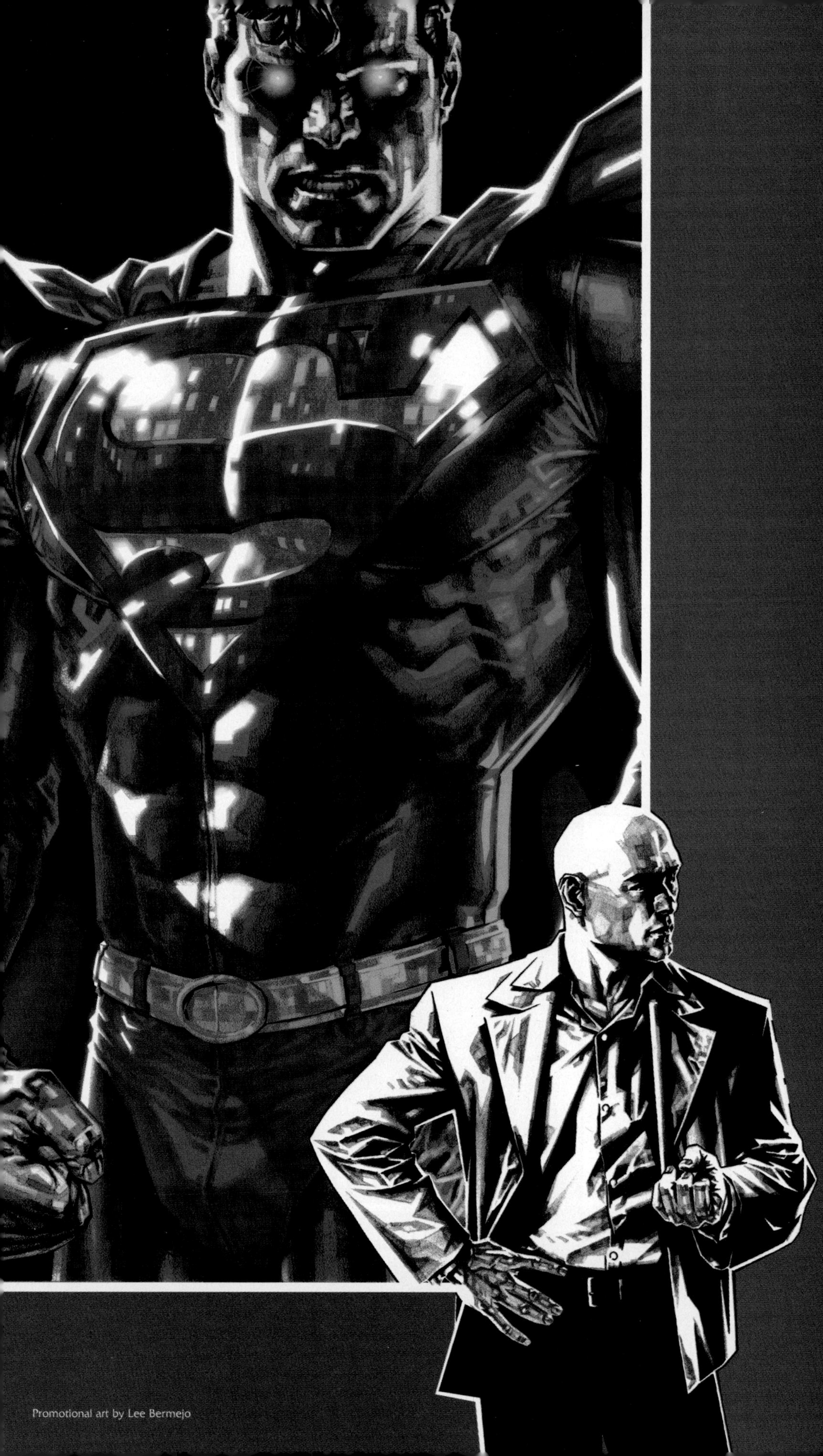

Promotional art by Lee Bermejo

SUPERMAN

SUPERMAN FOR ALL SEASONS

A tale of Superman's earliest adventures told on a mythic scale by the award-winning creative team of **Jeph Loeb** and **Tim Sale**, with spectacular colors by **Bjarne Hansen**.